TESTICLES

BALLS IN COOKING AND CULTURE

TO THOSE WHOM I HAVE IN ALL WAYS SEEN AS UNIQUE

'Testicles are one of the rarest morsels of human flesh, and deserve to be eaten.'

Philip José Farmer,
quoted by Dominique Noguez
in *Dandys de l'an 2000*
(Sixth Canto: 'Simple anthropometrics', 2002)

TESTICLES

BALLS IN COOKING AND CULTURE

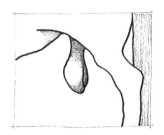

Blandine Vié

TRANSLATED FROM THE FRENCH BY
GILES MACDONOGH

PROSPECT BOOKS

2011

First published in 2011 by Prospect Books,
Allaleigh House, Blackawton, Totnes, Devon TQ9 7DL.

Testicles is a translation of the book *Testicules* by Blandine Vié, published in Paris by Les Éditions de l'Épure in 2005.

BRITISH LIBRARY CATALOGUING IN PUBLICATION DATA:
A catalogue entry of this book is available from the British Library.

Typeset and designed by Sue Snell and Tom Jaine.

The decorations are the work of Andras Kaldor.

ISBN 978-1-903018-83-5

Printed and bound by the Gutenberg Press, Malta.

BUYING BALLS IN BRITAIN

It must be admitted that the subject of this book is not the easiest thing to source in the butchers' shops of Britain. However, I have taken advice from my butcher, Christopher McCabe of Totnes, and other informants, and thought it wise to include a short note.

Most ram lambs are castrated in the first weeks of life, using rubber rings to constrict the blood-supply to the testes which then atrophy. This is painless and usually trouble-free. Some breeds, of hill lamb for example, do not respond well to this method of treatment and are castrated somewhat later in life using the Burdizzo clamp (for which, see page 75 below). This is not a surgical procedure and the testes remain in place. It is merely the spermatic cord that has been interrupted. This results in the number of testicles available to butchers being vastly reduced at a stroke, or a squeeze. However, not all lamb is castrated and it should be remembered that according to the rules of *halal* or *kosher*, castrated animals are not desirable. Therefore, the most likely place to find a ready supply of lamb's fry is a *halal* butcher. Just as the most likely place to find them on a menu is a Middle Eastern restaurant. However if you ask any butcher nicely he should be able to supply you.

The story with pigs was once broadly similar, as most male piglets were surgically castrated by the farmer or breeder quite early in life. The tiny testes might be thrown to the farmyard cat but were rarely saved for human consumption. They were castrated to avoid 'boar taint' and for the usual reason that a castrated animal puts on weight more quickly. However, there have been many surveys which deny that boar taint is a problem, certainly in young stock, and the butchers' preference now is for a lean carcase – which is promoted by the possession of testicles (as is unwanted muscularity). This change in practice means that many male pigs are now slaughtered entire. The abattoirs do not package the testicles for retail sale but if you ask your butcher politely he should be able to secure you a supply.

Bull's testicles are more problematic. I am informed that some supermarkets sell bull beef so that if you are able to find an abattoir that is part of the supermarket supply chain then you could order up the surplus offal. But in general it is not easy to find them in a British butcher's. You should go to Spain instead.

Cock's stones are no longer available. It's a fact of life.

The Publisher

A *TESTICLE* TO SERVE AS INTRODUCTION

It was François Vatable Brouard (1556–1626) who, writing under the pseudonym of François Béroalde de Verville at the dawn of the seventeenth century, came up with the delicious lines, 'we have no greater regard for the poor than we do for our balls, we leave them outside, they are never allowed in.'

And so it is with cookery books: balls hardly figure, despite the fact that they were considered one of the choicest of all morsels at the court of Louis XV, were a much-esteemed hors d'oeuvre in the classic and bourgeois cooking of the nineteenth century and the preferred offal of the butchers of La Villette during the great era of the abattoirs. It therefore seemed to me that I owed a duty to their memory to pay them homage by gathering up the recipes and casting new light on them. And then, finally, to quite simply pay them their due – both those that we prepare for the table and those which we taste unseasoned.

My book is therefore presented as a collection of scrumptious things in the widest sense: where one might just as well dig out a dish to feed the stomach as another to fuel the brain. In its way, it is a contribution to our knowledge of 'little things'.

The French words *saveur* (taste) and *savoir* (to know) share a common etymological root – as *saveur* ('quality perceived by the sense of taste') comes from the Latin verb *sapere* which initially meant 'having taste, exhaling a smell, feeling in the sense of taste', before signifying, in a more figurative way, 'having intelligence, judgment, to know, understand and have knowledge.' It is a common ancestry that seems obvious to me: just another way of killing two birds with one stone… Or, if you prefer, of making two balls a pair.

Blandine Vié
Paris, 2005

AUTHOR'S ACKNOWLEDGEMENTS

I would like to thank especially: Henri Ballester, the commercial representative in the Ile de France of SA Languedoc Lozére Viande; Michel Baubois, president of Interbev-Équins and president of the Fédération Bouchère Hippophagique de France; Gilles Brochard, for his wise counsel and testicular friendship; Isabel Calvache Gisbert, for information and recipes from Spain; Gérard Cathelin, Cabadis SA at Rungis, for having received me in the middle of the night at the tripe pavilion at Rungis; Dominique Couvreur, whose shared passion for dictionaries meant him lending me books I did not have; Marie-France Dayot, Éditions Fleuve Noir, for her assistance and her offer of a large box of books by San-Antonio; Jean-Marc Delcourt, vice-president of the Fédération National du Cheval; Perrine Dequecker, for her unconditional support; Coralie Marcadé for help with the lexicon and research on the Internet; Yves Mousset, for having put me in touch with livestock breeders; Dr Bernard Poulain, veterinary surgeon; Marc Vanhellemont, for not having (figuratively) bust my nuts when I addled his brain with questions about *choesels* and *couques*; Pascal Vié, for a myriad of facts of all sorts; Colette Ranson, for her contributions to the lexicon.

Blandine Vié

TRANSLATOR'S NOTE: OF SCROTUM AND SCROTUMS

It might be a fanciful to compare the household of my childhood to the court of the long-absent Odysseus on Ithaca, but it had something of that. There were certainly plenty of unsuitable suitors. Possibly the worst of them was a small, pale, wimpy man with long black hair and a droopy moustache. His repellent aspect was compounded by his even more rebarbative speech, which was peppered with inappropriate archaisms such as 'I must ablute' or 'I shall avaunt.' We children called him 'Scrotum' and 'avaunt' he did, as quickly as we could bundle him out of the door.

The only other man who I can recall meriting the epithet 'Scrotum' was a well-known food writer. Once, when there was a good crowd of us around the dinner table, the late Jennifer Paterson, a self-confessed virgin and sometime cook who ended her days 'big' on television, asked, 'what does a scrotum look like? I don't think I have ever seen one.' Without reflection, I named the food writer. The comparison was apposite: with his fat, flabby wrinkled cheeks sprouting here and there the little wisps of an inadequate beard (not to mention the tight curls on his head), he looked every inch a scrotum. The nickname didn't stick, however: there was only room for one scrotum in our world.

I mention these examples because in English at least, everything that concerns scrotums and the testicles they carry within them is considered either stupid or disgusting (possibly both). In short: Britons are embarrassed by their balls.

If Blandine Vié is anything to go by, the French do not share our discomfort. They and other Latins have an heroic attitude to sex and sexual organs; they are curious about them, talk about them, praise them and – when they get the chance – eat them. They eat those of our four-legged friends – living and dead – and metaphorically at least, they eat those of one another. If proof is required of this consuming passion by the Mediterranean shore, you need only go to the third section of this book, the lexicon of testicular terms. Where the English language can match like with like in the multitudinous metaphors it has to describe testicles, there are no convincing ones (in British English at least) comparing them to food.

French, on the other hand, provides the entire menu, from sucking sweets to cakes and buns, to meat, fruit and vegetables. There is an obvious conclusion to be drawn here: the French have been indulging in oral sex for centuries, and these gourmand terms are more than adequate proof. In Britain, the practice of oral sex is not more than a generation old, for all but a few daring libertines, dating from the 'swinging' sixties. There are probably large numbers of Britons who still consider it disgusting, and who also dislike earthy food, and references to sex in food. Needless to say, this book is not for them.

A Briton reading this book will also be struck by the sheer creativity of French popular language, and not just when it comes to food and sex. This might come as a surprise, but it shouldn't. There used to be plenty of Francophiles and francophones here, but more than two decades of poor language-teaching in schools has taken its toll. Not more than a fortnight ago I was looking for a restaurant in a London guide and I came across the line 'the French have never really grasped puns'. The writer was attesting to an ignorance that fairly takes your breath away: in French you can scarcely move for puns, and it is the imagery, wealth and nimble wit of the language that makes it a challenge to confine it to what are often the narrower purlieus of English.

We have become so used to a self-congratulatory tone when we speak of the success of the English language we have begun to believe in our own propaganda: we have the greatest language, it is concise, expressive and 'cuts the crap' that pads out the idioms of our neighbours. As for the French, they have (as we all apparently know) the Académie Française sitting up there like some prim governess, confiscating any amusing neologism they find and sporting the oak when it comes to the wonderful English language that is banging on the door just longing to come in and sort them out.

Now, it is quite true that the Académie Française is there to vet the language, which might be one reason that the French tongue is so concise – possibly more concise than our own; but it is to some extent as a result of that strait-laced Académie that French slang (and many of the expressions used in this book come from argot) is so fecund. For there is nothing moribund about French, it is in a constant flux. In some respects argot is another French, and there is not just one argot: there is Parisian slang and the slang of the meat market; there are regional slangs, and regional languages such as Provençal and Breton; and there is Madame Vié's favourite writer, Frédéric Dard (alias San-Antonio), who makes his slang up as he goes along.

Madame Vié's book is divided into three sections: a first part is a learned disquisition on the history and 'mythology' of testicles, while a second tells us how to cook them. As she herself admits, this isn't easy, largely because they are hard to obtain. However, when I asked two butchers local to me in north London, one promised me pork testicles, while the second could order me lamb. What are harder to obtain are cocks' testes, which used to figure in the preparation of some of the great set-pieces of French gastronomy, like *bouchées à la reine*. This would now would be particularly difficult in Britain, as well as in other countries in Europe, where it is illegal to caponize cocks.

The final panel of the triptique is a glossary of testicular terms, again figuring Madame Vié's insights into language and etymology. The author aimed the book at a French readership and sometimes that means that some of her more sparkling observations are dimmed in translation. By agreement with the publisher, I have had to make some small changes to have a wider appeal. We have dropped a short section on testicular *contrepèteries* (*intentional* Spoonerisms of the 'Friar Tuck' – 'Try a fuck' sort) because no matter how much you juggle them they cannot be made to say the same thing in translation. It has also been necessary to re-jig the lexicon of testicular terms so that a reader who is unversed in French can look first to the idea in English before he or she discovers the wealth of imagery in other languages. I have also taken the liberty to add more English terms to alter the balance in favour of the target readership.

I know that I learned much from this book, and I hope that others appreciate it too. It is to be hoped that it will go a little way to change how we look at testicles in English-speaking countries, both our own much-maligned gonads and those of the animals we eat.

Giles MacDonogh
London
Feast of the Epiphany, 2011

MYTHOLOGY

Having a Ball: A Little Mythology of Testicles

At the same time she placed her hand at the base of his penis which had risen in celebration, and started to feel the two little balls which formed its appendages and which we call testicles. Not, as is commonly held, because they serve as witnesses to the consummation of the act of love, but rather because they are the little heads that conceal the cervical matter which spurts from the mentula* or little intelligence, in the same way as the head contains the brain that is the home of all mental functions.

Guillaume Apollinaire, Les Onze Mille Verges *ou* Les Amours d'un Hospodar

---

* *Mentula* in Latin itself derives from the word *mens* meaning 'wit' or 'intelligence' (from which we have the English 'mental'). It was used to designate the flaccid virile member as opposed to *fascinus*, which means the erect male penis, and from which comes the word 'fascinate' (see Mythology).

Fitz Stephen [recounts] a singular act of cruelty perpetrated on the clergy by Geoffrey [Count of Anjou], the father of Henry II. 'When he was master of Normandy, the chapter of Séez presumed, without his consent, to proceed to the elction of a bishop; upon which, he ordered all of them, with the bishop elect, to be castrated, and made all their testicles be brought him in a platter.' Of the pain and danger they might justly complain; yet, since they had vowed chastity, he deprived them of a superfluous treasure.

Edward Gibbon, The Decline and Fall of the Roman Empire, *vol. VII.*

ADMISSABLE EVIDENCE

A little anatomy

Testicles are the twin glands that constitute the genital organs of male mammals – and therefore of men. They are also called 'gonads'. Testicles perform two functions: on the one hand they produce spermatozoa, and on the other, they secrete the male hormone known as testosterone, which particularly affects hairiness, the chest and the voice.

Testicles are conceived first in the foetal abdomen before descending into the scrotum by way of the inguinal canal. In this bag of natural skin, which is also called a pouch, the temperature is lower than the body's in order to ensure spermatogenesis (the production of spermatozoa). The function of the pouch is, really, to regulate temperature: when it is cold, it contracts in order to push the glands into the body and keep them in the warmth; on the other hand, when it is hot, the scrotum relaxes, making the testicles migrate outside the body and its 37.2º Celsius. Gonads also retract in reaction to powerful emotions such as arguments and worry.

Testicles do not generally fall to the same height. The reason for this slight lack of equilibrium is that, on the left hand side, the spermatic veins are connected to the left renal vein, whereas on the right hand side, they connect to the veins of the lower cavity. In adulthood, each testicle weighs roughly 20 grams and is about five centimetres in length. It is surrounded by a fibrous albuginean membrane. On the surface, the thin fold of skin that forms a vertical separation along the pouch is called the raphe.

TESTICULTURAL FOREPLAY

At the risk of upsetting Descartes, who left us his famous postulation: 'I think therefore I am', or Shakespeare, who, upon the lips of his hero Hamlet, bequeathed the no less celebrated metaphysical question – 'to be or not to be'; this is not the central issue to our existences. *The question* (because it presupposes one even more fundamental) is – to wit – do we have them or not?

As – there is no doubt about this – to 'be' anything other than a creature – a 'case of flesh and blood' in the seminal sense, and not simply a 'creation' in the semantic sense,* you need to have been created, and that means *pro*created, meaning – you had a progenitor.

---

* Two more words – seminal and semantic – having the same roots, as both derive their marrow from a word that began by meaning 'seed', a word that gave in turn the Greek *sêma* (sign) and the Latin *semen* (seed) in parallel developments.

And, as Dominique Noguez stresses in *Dandys de l'an 2000* (Dandies of the Year 2000, Fourth Canto: 'Le lit de Daniel Rops de Jaques Lacan'): 'If we are thinking about ourselves (in the same way as does Descartes in his *Meditations*), it is never done without revisiting, in mind-boggling detail, the moment when the spermatozoon – the stubborn or terrified thing that we were then – was engulfed by the brobdingnagian ovum; and earlier still when we were present for the coital chafing that expelled us from the purses of our respective fathers.'

It is children who provide the innocent version of the story when they say that the reason babies are born is because daddies plant a little seed in the bellies of mummies... Now, we all know that testicles are the nurseries which nurture these mysterious seeds that are called spermatozoa.

In fact, if this seed has been held sacred since the dawn of time, testicles – which are its natural receptacle – have been blessed too by a metonymic effect which is no more than linguistic artifice: the contents and the container being as precious and revered as one another. It is similar to the case of the Eucharist, where the Host is presaged by the ciborium, or the wine by the chalice. In France, testicles are commonly referred to as 'bourses' or purses – a word that encompasses both the envelope of skin or scrotum and the glands inside – it is enough to say that they witness (*'témoigne'* – this is another word where the etymology is particularly revealing: we will deal with it later) their value.

Myths and legends

If you believe Greco-Roman mythology, the first creatures to whom we granted the appearance of life were the children of Gaia (the earth, or primary material) and Uranus (the original sky). From their union were born the twelve Titans that Uranus entombed in the Tartarus (the depths of the earth, or the subterranean world) because he was frightened they would steal his throne. His youngest son Cronos (Saturn to the Romans), however, revolted. In alliance with his mother he sought to liberate his brothers. To do this, he emasculated Uranus with a blow from his sickle. Gaia was inseminated by the blood from the wound and produced six Olympian giants, among whom figured Zeus (Jupiter) and Aphrodite (Venus). This is Zeus, who would dethrone Cronos when the time came, the greatest of the gods called by Homer the 'the father of gods and men', who is not considered to be a simple creator-god, but rather a 'procreator-god'. And this is Aphrodite, the loveliest of the Olympians, daughter of fertility and fecundity and the goddess of love.

In his book *The Banquet*, the philosopher Plato uses Aristophanes to tell the story of the myth that confirms for us Zeus' role in the creation of mankind and in the way man procreates:

In the beginning there were three sorts of human beings: males, females and a third sort, composed of the other two. This creature no longer exists and only the name has survived. The name is 'androgyne' because it was a blend of male and female. It was spherical in shape... One head bore two faces and had four ears... They had strong bodies and lots of determination, indeed so much that one day, they decided to climb up to heaven to do battle with the gods... Zeus consulted the other gods to decide what action to take. The matter wasn't cut and dried. The gods were in no way in favour of exterminating the people with a thunderbolt, as they had once destroyed the giants, as they would cease to make the offerings and sacrifices due to them. On the other hand, they were not going to put up with such audacity and insolence among the mortals. So, after a period of mature reflection, Zeus addressed his fellow gods; "I believe I have found a way to spare mankind and to punish its arrogance the while. I am going to reduce their power. I will divide them in two, and by doing so, weaken them." [...] The god did just that. He separated mankind in two, just as one does eggs when you want to salt them [...] In their desire to recover their initial unity, the androgynes perished from a mixture of hunger and idleness, one not wanting to do anything without the other. When one half died, the surviving half looked for another to latch on to, half-man or half-woman and thereby the race began to expire. Touched by pity, Zeus dreamed up another solution: he placed the organs of generation at the front, when they had previously been behind. Until then it had been the case that the androgynes had not conceived their young not on top of one another, but by scattering their seed upon the ground like crickets. Zeus placed the organs at the front and from then on conception occurred by a conjunction of male and female. This is naturally the reason for the love that we bear one another. It is the means by which we find our first unity; of reuniting our divided halves and reliving our ancient perfection.

When it comes to Aphrodite, nothing explains her symbolism so well as the painting by Botticelli entitled *The Birth of Venus* where she emerges naked and triumphant from the sea born up by a shell on an explosion of spume, which does in fact represent the spermatozoa of Uranus.

That idea of a fecund spume that was the generator of humanity found its way also into the Koran:

Do not the infidels see that the heavens and earth were both a solid mass, and that we clave them asunder, and by means of water we give life to everything? And we created all living things from the water.

21, 30; trans. J.M. Rodwell

The water would not cease glorifying the Creator by its shaking and agitation. That is why God chose it to be the source for the seed of everything. When, however, on the orders of the Creator, the waters ceased to agitate, it became clear water, without spume, which distinguished it therefore from the primary or seminal water.

Vladimir Grigorieff, Les Mythologies du monde entier *(All the World's Mythologies, 1987)*

A swinging life

Some see the 'The Origin of the World' – in the sense of the human race – as a woman's sexual organs. That is how Courbet represented it in his famous painting of that name. And the metaphor certainly works: woman is a fertile soil for germinating the seed. Is not the coming child the 'fruit' of her womb? But without seed, no harvest, however fertile the garden. Man is certainly born, is born into the world, issuing from the belly of a woman, but it is because a male gardener has put it there in the form of seed; and even today, when it is possible to conceive by artificial insemination, the seed remains that of a man. Therein lies all the mystery of life. We should stress that the word mystery comes from the Greek *mustês*, which means 'initiated'. Understand that as you will.

The real or supposed value of that seed – eminently wished for and a constant of our fantasies – explains its attraction as both a symbol and an everyday reality. It also explains the importance (symbolic and literal) of testicles, the organs which carry the seed: like a strongbox where a man conceals his most precious possession, his 'credit'. The difference here is that the credit has the value of 'being', and of being empowered with the essence of man. And everyone knows that you don't show off your strongbox and you don't expose your lust to just anyone. You keep it under lock and key, you arm it with sophisticated bolts and ratchets, you plate it with steel, you hide it. By a metonymic metaphor, the same is done for testicles: as the Bible demonstrated at the outset. The treasure needs to be protected at any price, and that means preserving the mystery. In any case, to deviate from the rule is an infraction of the laws invoked in the sacred texts.

And so it is in the Old Testament that Noah's son dares to flaunt that ban, and is cursed for his pains:

And the sons of Noah, that went forth of the ark, were Shem, and Ham, and Japheth: and Ham is the father of Canaan.

These are the three sons of Noah: and of them was the whole world overspread.

And Noah began to be an husbandman, and he planted a vineyard:

And he drank of the wine, and was drunken; and he was uncovered within his tent.

And Ham, the father of Canaan, saw the nakedness of his father, and told his two brethren without.

And Shem and Japheth took a garment, and laid it upon both their shoulders, and went backward, and covered the nakedness of their father; and their faces were backward, and they saw not their father's nakedness.

And Noah awoke from his wine, and knew what his younger son had done unto him.

And he said, Cursed be Canaan; a servant of servants shall he be unto his brethren.

And he said, Blessed be the Lord God of Shem; and Canaan shall be his servant.

God shall enlarge Japheth, and he shall dwell in the tents of Shem; and Canaan shall be his servant.

Genesis 9, 18–29 (King James Bible)*

Also in the Bible are those unequivocal instructions on priests' vestments that God handed down to Moses on Mount Sinai:

And for Aaron's sons thou shalt make coats, and thou shalt make for them girdles, and bonnets shalt thou make for them, for glory and for beauty.

And thou shalt put them upon Aaron thy brother, and his sons with him; and shalt anoint them, and consecrate them, and sanctify them, that they may minister unto me in the priest's office.

And thou shalt make them linen breeches to cover their nakedness; from the loins even unto the thighs they shall reach:

And they shall be upon Aaron, and upon his sons, when they come in unto the tabernacle of the congregation, or when they come near unto the altar to minister in the holy place; that they bear not iniquity, and die: it shall be a statute forever unto him and his seed after him.

Exodus, 28, 40–43 (King James Bible)

---

* The author uses the Jerusalem Bible. She points out that 'nakedness' is a euphemism for sexual organs in most religious texts. *Translator.*

Biblical underpants

It is in these episodes of the Bible that first mention is made of underpants, the article of clothing meant to conceal the shameful parts of man. In the West it was after Cicero's initiative that the Romans obliged citizens to wear them under their togas.

And finally, this barbaric and draconian order was addressed to women:

> When men strive together one with another, and the wife of the
> one draweth near for to deliver her husband out of the hand of him
> that smiteth him, and putteth forth her hand, and taketh him by the
> secrets:
>> Then thou shalt cut off her hand, thine eye shall not pity her.
>> Deuteronomy 25, 11–12 (King James Bible)

In the light of these examples, you do not even have to commit adultery to suffer punishment, as touching, or even just seeing, merit divine wrath. It is clear that the symbolic value is just as well applied to the container as the contents.

The sporran: a little Scots purse designed to conceal what you are not supposed to see

They say there is nothing worn under a Scotsman's kilt, but it appears that the sporran, a leather purse attached by little chains that they wear on top of the aforesaid kilt, was specially designed to be positioned at the height of the male bounty in order to hide it. In reality, as the organs swing free you can guess what they look like through the cloth, which renders otiose this prudent and prudish precaution. The sporran is therefore like a pair of pants worn on the outside.

The naming of parts: the great taboo

The laws of God prohibited seeing and touching our private parts and, by extension, their naming became a sacrilege too. The word – the Word of God – is dogma, the orthodoxy or 'correct opinion', in other words: 'speaking properly'. The taboo was borne of this: it was created to preserve the social and moral order.

Coming at it from the opposite direction, to name unmentionable parts is to transgress; it is a form of rebellion in itself, against religious, social or parental authority. So, for example, when a child swears, he or she is challenging the family ban (or a social one at school). Every individual, every microcosm, every entity, every society even, calculates its own scale of values from different parameters: era, culture, religion, age, education, etc. Some will call things quite simply by their proper names, some prefer to soften their impact to a greater or lesser extent, while others will insist on quite the opposite, using crudity to deliberately flaunt the rules or disrupt the social order.

The hidden taste of words

Calling a spade a spade is one thing, but words are just envelopes: caskets filled with hidden drawers. They can contain hidden treasure unimaginable at first sight, shedding layer upon layer of meaning. They are fascinating; and who would not be fascinated if he knew – which is what Pascal Quignard teaches us in *Le Sexe et l'effroi* (Sex and Fright, 1994) – that the word fascinate itself derives from the Latin *fascinus* which means an erect penis (a close relative of the Greek *phallos* which gives us the French [and English] phallus)! And that 'fascination' therefore points ineluctably to castration, as in a game of mirrors. This is how Pascal Quignard explains it:

> The ancients did not believe that castration was about the erect male member, far from it: castrating someone who could see meant putting their eyes out. By extension, the castrated man is blind – like Homer, Tiresias, Oedipus. The person who has been fascinated, who has looked on face to face, loses his sight.
>
> It is obvious that we want to see. Desiring and seeing are the same. That's the dream.

And further on:

> Tertullian says clearly that *voluptas* is a form of prostration of sight because it provokes 'a weakening of vision'. The shot of pleasure itself blots out pleasure by its blinding light. Add that to the original scene, there is no pleasure that may be taken blind. The moment of pleasure tears the scene we have experienced from visibility. The *fascinus* is the greatest drug of all: it blinds.

He continues:

> There is a place known to every man that is at the same time unknown: the maternal belly. All men have known a banned time and place that amounted to absolute desire. That absolute desire is this: the existence of this desire, that wasn't ours but from which our desire was the result. Every man has an utopia and an uchronia or ideal time. There is a time of mystery. The passion the baby feels at feeding is a continuation of the spasm that marked his conception. The discharge of milk from the mother continues the emission of spermatozoa that occurred nine months before. There is a great *Fascinus*: a perpetual erection which governs the cycle of the moon, births, years, couplings and death.
>
> It always contains an object that lives outside place and time and which fascinates children and which is always hidden behind the veils of human language. In this the *fascinus* is always the secret.

In this sense I should like to say that it is a close relation – if not the twin – of the word *apocalypse*, the etymology of which means in the first place (on the surface) 'revelation' in the banal sense of 'discover, unveil.' The original sense, however, is 're-veil', that is 'cover again with a veil', as if there was always another mystery behind the first.

This taste of words, or knowledge of words, is not always stuffed into the shell of academic, dryasdust etymology. It blooms occasionally under the more or less lurid skirts of slang, the language of the streets. It can be like so many masks and disguises. However up-front and literal this sort of language may be, it is often the case that this aspect only adds to the mystery.

As far as testicles are concerned, the gamut of nicknames they possess requires a classification, a taxonomy. We will look therefore at the subtlety of meanings, be they above or below the surface of the words.

The Koran's idea of Heaven

In Islamic symbolism, the connection between a look, sexuality, pleasure, the visible and the invisible are very different to our own. This has been analysed by Abdelwahab Bouhdiba in his pertinent essay La Sexualité d'Islam *(2001). He couldn't put it more clearly:*

'From a Christian point of view, it is unthinkable for flesh and blood, the source of original sin, to find a place in the beyond. Man's redemption can only be obtained at the price of renouncing sexuality, for which the mission is at best worldly. For Islam, on the other hand, Eros contains something essential. The original couple disobeyed [God], but they mostly paid for their mistake with their expulsion from Eden. The test of earthly life is quite enough to buy back God's bounty.

'Getting to paradise is then a personal accomplishment. This accomplishment may not be achieved except by a love conceived in the form of a transfiguration, in the transcendence of self. It is not by chance that hell is solitude, reduction to self, in a word, the negation of love. Paradise, on the other hand, is love: total, full and infinite; it is unity and agreement with the world, with yourself and with God.

'Above all paradise is reconciling man and nature, that means with material. That is where the profusion of material that is Janna* comes from. It is a feast in all its senses. We have seen what role is accorded to sight in the Islamic vision of sexuality. Now, seeing is the central tenet of existence and it is also an integral part of the human essence. Everything also starts with seeing and ends the same. Is it not sight that gives the houris† everything down to their name? See and be seen, contemplate, *watch, this is a form of happiness. Utter joy is ocular and from this luminosity is precious. Hyacinths and gold, diamonds and topazes, pearls and emeralds, sapphires and coral compose a unique palette for the elect. These precious stones that make up paradise work in the mystical way like the pearl, in which Arab alchemy likes to recognize the purest substitute for sperm with its magical and metaphysical qualities.'*

This dreamy, sensual vision of paradise is described with a great superabundance of vivid details and besides it awards a big role to the seminal liquor contained in the testicles. And so it is that when it rains in paradise, it rains sperm! 'In paradise the sight of God is the summit of happiness and perfection and only occurs after the series of orgasms. Rain in paradise is universal sperm.' (op.cit.) All the same, it is easy to err, as Abdelwahab Bouhdiba explains again:

'We see that everything happens as if the reconciliation of God and man were the same as the reconciliation of man and nature. That is the sense of the joy that is the realization of the body and the end of frustration. And the texts indicate the indubitable manner in which the delights of paradise while sensual are by no means material. It is not that paradise is made material, it is that the material is taken away from the nature of man so that he is reduced to pleasure and the ultimate sensation.

'It is certain that you are supposed to take your body seriously and that is the sense of paradisiacal joy. Far from debunking our pleasures, Islam teaches us to achieve them better. The evocation of paradise is a vigilant dreaminess. It is not theology that is under discussion here but psychology. The image of Muslim paradise is positive and affirmative in itself. Islam does not suppress the libido. In paradise our desires are taken seriously. That means that the peace of paradise represents self-accomplishment. Because paradise is above all a meeting with a beyond-self, love is in some way reduced by the presence not only of wives but of houris. That pluralization of love implies its own transcendence in self-negation.'

* Janna is paradise in Arabic. The word comes from jân (djinn and invisible creature) and means 'the hidden, the invisible.'

† Houris are the 'wives in paradise', eternally young and virgins, evoked in the Koran as a sort of reward for the most pious Muslims. Abdelwahab Bouhdiba makes it clear that the word houri comes from h'ûr al'ain, which means literally 'one who has the eye of the hour', that is the black eye of the faun, that we might translate as 'doe-eyed'. In his Encyclopédie de l'amour en Islam (2003), Malek Chebel states on the other hand that 'The term houri, which the Arabs have known from the start, even if its probable origin is Iran, is still muddied by an imprecise etymology which prevents us from establishing the precise sex of the persons involved.'

A SHORT ETYMOLOGY

Testicules and testicles

The word *testicules* first appeared in French in the fourteenth century.* It derives from the Latin *testis* meaning 'witness'. For the etymological derivatives, see what I have written on page 30 below, in the paragraph headed 'Three?'

Pope Joan's balls

'According to certain sources, it is because of Pope Joan that the word "testicle" possibly derives from the word "witness". According to a thirteenth-century legend, she was an Englishwoman born in Mainz and living in Rome wearing the habits of a monk. She fraudulently obtained the title of pope at the death of Leo IV in AD 855 and reigned for two years. In reality, there was only a pause of a few weeks between the death of Leo IV and the accession of Benedict III.'

Dictionnaire des noms propres Le Petit Robert, 1995

Still, according to the legend, it is because of this slip-up that the dignitaries of the Church made sure thereafter that all popes were of the male sex. To do this, the newly elected pope had to place himself on a chaise percée while an official proved, by reaching his hand under the pope, that he did indeed possess testicles by 'witnessing' his virility. Following this examination, the officer was obliged to pronounce the legendary formula: 'Duos habet et bene pendentes', meaning, 'he has two of them and they hang well'.

Cullions

Couilles is the most popular word in French for testicles, having been first used in the twelfth century in its primitive version *coil*, deriving from the Latin *colea* which in turn came from the classical Latin *coleus* (plur. *colei*) meaning a leather bag.†

Purses

From the French *bourses*, which also appeared in the twelfth century, and means 'a little round bag, generally with tucks and gathering, which is used to keep

---

* The first recorded use of 'testicule' in English was in 1425. By 1597, the word had become 'testicle' (*OED*). *Translator.*
† 'Cullions' are rather more obscure in English. The first recorded use is by Chaucer in *The Pardoner's Tale* of 1386. *Translator.*

money', but can also be a 'little skin' in the sense of a wine skin. Because of the similarity of form, a purse signifies the envelope of the scrotum or, by extension, the balls it contains.*

EUPHEMISMS AND PRUDISH EXPRESSIONS

The symbolism of silence: Are they things or not? All or nothing?

In the Middle Ages, the French word *rien* (nothing) was a feminine noun which, when used in the plural, was a euphemism to describe the brazen bits of a man. The etymology of *rien* is from the dog-Latin *rem* (the accusative of *res*) which paradoxically means 'thing'. On the other hand, the plural *rerum,* 'things', can also signify 'all' according to the context. This is clear from the poet Ovid: '*Tempus edax rerum*' (Time destroys everything).

By calling testicles 'nothings', however, you are entering the realm of the 'not said' – euphemisms – but without being in denial. There is no pejorative connotation. It is just a word that is supremely politically correct (above all when one considers the word political from the point of view of its etymology as well – it comes from the Greek *polis,* meaning town). It is a social word, chosen not to shock, but which says everything without appearing to do so. The immensely popular '*les choses*' (see the lexicon below) used by Georges Brassens in his song *Le Gorille* (The Gorilla) is in the same vein. It is frank, may be placed in any mouth and heard by every ear. In a word, these are the words that allow everyone to come to nothing, in language as in symbolism.

There is much that is more euphemistic still, with a few elliptical formulae where no word, however sweetened, figures and yet, where the sense is quite clear even to the most chaste ears. This is true when they are replaced by the plural pronoun 'them' in a variety of expressions, and where they are alluded to but not named. And in many cases they are the more eloquent for all that.

Less than nothing and 'non sunt'

For the Romans, castrated or impotent men were *non sunt*: 'they are not'. In this instance the negation is pure and hard. The language says crudely that without his knackers a man ceases to exist, at least from a social point of view, relegating him to the status of 'less than nothing'.

---

* This is only rarely used in English, and most often for animals – rams in particular. It is first used to denote a scrotum in 1250. Chaucer's Wife of Bath is keen on purses. *Translator.*

Scientific terms

Using technical words is another way to mask the rudeness of reality. Even though the word testicle is anatomical and academic, it is so evocative that people often prefer popular or even slang words, either because they seem more appropriate or are in the end more fitting. In the eighteenth and nineteenth centuries, it was common to seek advice on one's *oïdia* (medical jargon and Greek for eggs) rather than balls or testicles. Latin words or phrases like *genitalia, pudenda, arma virilia* or *vilia membra* were often used in certain circles to describe male organs (above all by the wealthy *bourgeoisie*, what we would call the *nouveaux riches* today), where politeness separated the social wheat from the chaff and kept the plebs at a distance, especially by eschewing any vulgar language that might betray their origins.

Common and facetious nicknames

There are those who baptize their testicles with charming little names such as 'frivolities', 'waltzers' or 'joyfuls'.* These are still euphemisms, despite the coarseness of the idiom. It is interesting to note it's mostly men who use these names, just as in the past they were used in the butchers' guilds. Abattoir workers and market porters used to sit down together to eat *mignardises* (delicacies) for their morning snack. Although they never lacked for the saucy aside, their quips remained politically correct despite all appearance to the contrary.

THE SYMBOLISM OF NUMBERS

One is better than nothing but hardly Christian

As the old adage has it, two makes a pair, it is the law of nature that enjoins the symmetry of the human body: two arms, two legs, two hands, two feet, two eyes, two ears, two nostrils, two lips, two breasts, two lungs, two buttocks, two kidneys, two testicles and so forth. Even the heart has two ventricles and the brain two spheres. It is therefore to flaunt nature – or you could say, be deformed – if you only have the one; even if that singleton is quite sufficient to allow you to reproduce. When it comes to natural properties, the proverb 'a bird in the hand is worth two in the bush,' is hardly applicable!

---

* *Frivolités, valseuses,* and *joyeuses* – French words without resonance in the English language. The French film, *Les Valseuses* (1974), starring Gérard Depardieu, Patrick Dewaere and Miou-Miou explored the various meanings of the word in French slang.

This notion of physical integrity (two is good, one is bad) is insisted on by the Old Testament, not exactly a charitable point of view, one might say (at least, not for the Judeo-Christian religions). It raises a blush to admit that the holy writ thinks it a solecism to approach God, the absolute perfection (mental and physical), when lacking all your attributes. Can it be true that God cannot bear the sight of an imperfect creature because it offends his vision of creation? Who is he who praises the spiritual life but only accepts as his servants earthly creatures who conform to his physical ideal?

We regret that this is indeed the case:

> And the LORD spake unto Moses, saying,
>
> Speak unto Aaron, saying, Whosoever he be of thy seed in their generations that hath any blemish, let him not approach to offer the bread of his God.
>
> For whatsoever man he be that hath a blemish, he shall not approach: a blind man, or a lame, or he that hath a flat nose, or any thing superfluous,
>
> Or a man that is brokenfooted, or brokenhanded,
>
> Or crookbackt, or a dwarf, or that hath a blemish in his eye, or be scurvy, or scabbed, or hath his stones broken;*
>
> No man that hath a blemish of the seed of Aaron the priest shall come nigh to offer the offerings of the LORD made by fire: he hath a blemish; he shall not come nigh to offer the bread of his God.
>
> He shall eat the bread of his God, both of the most holy, and of the holy.
>
> Only he shall not go in unto the vail, nor come nigh unto the altar, because he hath a blemish; that he profane not my sanctuaries: for I the LORD do sanctify them.
>
> Leviticus, 21 16–23 (King James Bible)

These divine precepts, in Judaism at least, have been applied to the real world. This point is taken up by Mary Douglas in her book *Purity and Danger: An Analysis of Concepts of Pollution and Taboo* (1966): 'The culture of the Israelites attained its plenitude in prayer and in combat. The army could not win without the blessing and to keep the blessing in the camp they had to be specially holy.[†] The camp had to be protected from all impurity, just like the Temple.' The body therefore had to be whole. Once again: 'The notion of wholeness, or totality, extended so that it encompassed, in a social context, the idea of completion.' Any infirmity, therefore, compromised that integrity and completion.

We may regret it, but today this inconvenient view is still widely accepted. Two thousand years later – if you'll allow me to make the jump – we presume, as a

---

* Some translations talk of crushed testicles or eunuchs at this point.

† Mary Douglas makes it clear, 'If it is admitted that the root of the word holy or sanctified [the Greek *hagios*] means 'state of separation', the notion of holiness also includes that of totality and plenitude.'

matter of course, that someone we approve of has 'SOME balls', while at the other extreme of (dis)likeability, opprobrium is vented on 'a little pillock'. The demotic describes an animal as 'whole' when it has not been castrated, still having integrity. Sometimes we find the same applied to men, albeit in trivia:

> J'ai tout ce qu'exige saint Pierre,
> Oui de Cythère vieux routier,
> Je suis entier.

> (I have all Saint Peter demands
> Cythera's old driver, me
> I am whole, see)

> *Béranger chansons, quoted in Louis de Landes (the pseudonym of Auguste Scheler),* Glossaire érotique de la langue française *(Erotic Glossary of the French Language, 1861)*

That said, Napoleon was reputed monorchid. Without indulging in too many 'what-ifs', were his virility, his empire, his destiny because of, or thanks to, this small anomaly?

Two, and binary symbolism

In *Les Sept Merveilles, les expressions chiffrées* (The Seven Wonders, Figures and Numbers, 1994), Jean-Claude Bologne tells us: 'Two is the first number to break away from unity, and for that reason it symbolizes sin.' And when you know that in Judeo-Christian symbolism and tradition, picking the forbidden fruit from the tree of knowledge was committing a sin of the flesh in learning the truth about sex, you can easily guess why you need to hide the two precious tabernacles that contain the seed – and thereby life – that are your testicles, and why Noah's son Ham was cursed for setting eyes upon the nudity of his father.

At the other end of the scale, in other civilizations (notably in the thinking of the Dogon people of Mali), everything pure – that means just and adjusted – is double.

Each to his own symbols …

More prosaically, popular speech loves nicknames that stress duplication and twinning: the pair, twins, binaries, co-directors, acolytes, co-presenters, brothers and sisters, Siamese twins and various dolly sisters.

Three?

It might seem strange that I should name the number three when talking of testicles, even if that anomaly certainly exists in some people. The history of words is full of wit. As René Garrus recounts in his *Curiosités étymologiques* (1996),

Three is *tres,* both masculine and feminine in Latin. The neuter is *tria.* *Tres* is the origin of the French *trois.* In certain conditions, *tri-* was modified to *ter-,* which gives us the adjectives *ternarius* (containing three elements), and which was at the root of ternary, and *tertius,* which spawns the French *tiers* while the feminine *tertia* gives us *tierce.* But in other cases it remained *trini-* (numbering three), from which derives *trinitas* (group of three), from which hails our trinity. From *trini-* comes the vulgar *trinicare* (cut in three) which is the father of the French *trancher* and *tranche* (to slice, and the noun, cut) which gives us the old English 'trencher' for a plate, and 'trencherman' for an epicure.

At the outset there was the derivative *tristis* (which has nothing to do with the French word for sad [*triste*], the source of which is unknown). *Tristis* became *terstis* and then *testis.* The proper meaning of the word was 'who occupies the third position'. *Testis* served the Latin language to mean a witness at a trial, that is a 'third party' who theoretically was not there to support either of the parties in the action. *Testimonium,* derived from *testis,* means a witness report. In French it becomes *témoin* which was more in the sense of a witness report until it came to mean 'the person who bears witness.' *Testis* corresponded to the verb *testari* meaning 'to witness' or 'take as witness' but above all 'make a will'. This act was initially oral, but demanded the presence of witnesses. It was called *testamentum* and became *testament* in French [and English].

Stranger and stranger, and still from René Garrus:

It is surprising that the word testicle should be connected to the root that means 'three'. It is, however, almost certainly the case. In Latin, testicles were called *testes,* and there are strong reasons to believe that to start with the Romans compared them to witnesses. Were they imagining two witnesses, in appearance idle, placed somewhere behind the lawyer? We don't know. To avoid confusion and puns – which was the last thing the comic poet Plautus wished to do – in the end when the Romans wanted to talk about anatomy and not justice, they preferred to use the diminutive *testiculus.*

METAPHORS

They are often basic. The coarsest allude to the testicle's round and pendulous form. The most elaborate harp on details of their physical appearance or bring in other parameters such as the texture, gourmandise and possibly the noise made by rubbing or swinging them, in a word, four out of a possible five senses. The one left out, smell, is not evoked in the popular view of testicles. And yet, according to Marcel Rouet,

> Even when there has been no exercise, certain regions of the body give off to a greater extent the smells that emanate from the sweat glands. In men, these are above all the scrotum, which gives off a characteristic smell, and the perineum; after that it is the torso and, in certain individuals, feet and hands.
> Le paradis sexuel des aphrodisiaques *(The Sexual Heaven of Aphrodisiacs,* 1971)

It is as if a sort of collective self-censorship empirically approved the language. Among the most common metaphors, the following are worth noting:

Balls (French: *boules*)

The most obvious name, and the most widespread in French and in English, with a number of variants created by adding a complement to the noun (Christmas baubles, rubber balls, lottery balls…).* In France in recent times, the word has begun to replace terms now perceived as too vulgar, particularly by the media. For example, in France '*films de cul*' [literally, 'arse films', i.e. pornographic] have become '*films de boules*' ('ball films'). This is also true for magazines of a particular type.

You have lovely nuts, you know?[†]

In France the oval form of testicles has caused many people to nickname them 'eggs'. This was also the case in antiquity, when they used the Greek word *oïdia*, and is true today in many countries round the Mediterranean, North Africa in particular. Here they baptize the testicles thus of all male mammals, be they edible animals such as cocks or rams, or men. This form of egg is revealed once the testicles have been skinned and thereby resemble eggs with their shells off.

---

* These are all French expressions: *boules de noël, de gomme, de pétanque, de loto…* English does not use complements for balls: the word is simply of itself. *Translator.*
† In French this is 'eggs' rather than nuts. In English we do not talk of eggs, but in German 'eggs' are also a common term for testicles. *Translator.*

Epicurean metaphors*

In France there is a vast store of words drawn from the culinary and edible lexicon deployed as synonyms of testicles. They may allude to the look of the thing, but as often as not they refer to the taste as well. There is a distinct idea of gluttony, and of the sin of gluttony.

They can be put into three categories:

— the long litany of fruits, some to flatter the male ego, others to mock: apples (*pommes d'amour* [tomatoes], *reinettes*†), pears, plums of all sorts (pretty well all varieties), peaches, nectarines, olives, chestnuts, cherries, figs, watermelons, walnuts, hazelnuts, raisins, peanuts and other cucurbits;

— sweets and titbits, starting with sweets themselves: sugared almonds, *berlingots*, gum balls, chammalows, chupa chups, pralines, etc. It is unnecessary to add that these epithets stress the implicit pleasure of sucking them, and carry a more sexual connotation than the last category;

— finally, cakes, little and round of course: *petits fours*, choux buns, *chouquettes*, *croquembouches*, *croquignolles*, *pomponettes*, *profiteroles*, etc.§ Don't forget that most of them are filled with cream and are therefore metonymic metaphors, the symbolism of which will be lost on no one. It is curious to note that none of them is used much now.

Metonyms: when the container becomes the contents

These are words that describe container and contents all at once, for example the skin bag or scrotum which contains the glands producing sperm and the contents themselves, the precious treasure indeed. The words purse (*bourse*) and cullions (*couillons*) both evoke etymologically the function of a bag just as do the French terms involving 'bag' (of oats, of seed, of provisions, or an overnight valise⁵), *aumônières* [a purse once worn by ladies on their girdles], *burettes* [a flask that held and dispensed holy oil, drop by drop], containers, little bags, suitcases, luggage, pockets, poacher's bags, gourds, jerrycans, etc. Others allude – without beating about the bush – to the seminal liquor contained in the bags: sperm

---

* It is worth noting that the only gastronomic metaphor associated with testicles in English is nuts, and that is probably American. Despite recent very real advances in food culture, food is still not a subject where ordinary Britons feel at ease. The only organ that is compared with a fruit in English is the female breast or buttock. *Translator.*

† This is the standard sweet apple used in tarts etc. *Translator.*

§ None of these biscuits, buns or cream buns has a convincing English translation, and to the best of the translator's knowledge, they are not used to denote testicles in English. The metaphor stresses a different – perhaps less hidebound – oral approach to sex in France. Apart from choux pastry, with its cream fillings, the words emphasize crunchiness or, in the case of *pomponettes*, there is an allusion to pumping. *Translator.*

⁵ The only one of these having an echo in English is 'oats', in the sense of 'getting your oats', which means 'having sex'. *Translator.*

cartridges, sperm vases, honey bottles, milk pots, little bottles of almond milk, miniatures of aquavitae, jelly bags, etc.

Hangers and other baubles

Nicknames suggesting that testicles hang or swing also constitute a family of images, even if some of them are a little rusty these days: swingers, dongers, hangers, meat-hooks, flappers, clappers, beads, *pastrailles*, dancers, bales, bundles – essentially old-fashioned words now rarely heard.

Musical instruments, big dongs and little clanging dongers

Far less out of date are the nicknames associated with swinging and shaking, the murmuring and clanking that testicles are supposed to make when lightly touched. These are on the little and playful side by contrast to the last group. Here are some examples: the bells (of Notre Dame), little bells, cowbells, peals, doorbells, castanets, cymbals, maracas, or the tasty jingle balls of Old England.

Accessories and old friends

Finally there is a whole series of words that conjure up man's natural attributes as if they were the tool-kit or equipment of one trade or profession or another. The man, therefore, comes laden with his appendices, instruments, tools, equipment, tackle, *batterie* [*de cuisine*], gear or even outfit.

TESTICLES AND VIRILITY

Testicles are the true source of virility – real or imaginary. It stands to reason that men afford them some veneration.

In *Le Pénis dans tous ses états* (The Penis in all its Manifestations, 2000), Maggie Paley writes, 'In many ancient civilizations, the enemy's virility resided in their penises and testicles, and virility lay at the root of all wars.' She reminds us too, that certain sects practised self-castration.

In antiquity (notably during the reign of Alexander the Great), victors and heroes were rewarded with plates of offal, which were considered eminently virile, to reward their prowess. It was a privilege to eat them, because innards – not just testicles but liver, heart, brains and tongues too – have always symbolized virility, potency and, by extension, power.

Talking about calf's liver in *La Table et l'amour, nouveau traité des excitants modernes* (The Table and Love, a New Treatise on Modern Aphrodisiacs, with André Saint-Georges, 1950), Curnonsky recounts, 'Our forefathers used to say of a man of courage that he was not "lily-livered". This conjured up the primitive

---

Charms à la Milanaise

One of the most popular places for a stroll in Milan is the covered Gallery Vittorio-Emanuele in the heart of the city. It provides a link from the splendid cathedral or Duomo to the no less celebrated opera house of La Scala. Famous for its luxury shops and tea saloons, the gallery is also popular for the mosaics worked into the pavement under the rotunda of the central octagon. The Italians like most the image of the bull with its generous testicles. Putting your heel on the organs and spinning around apparently allows for a wish to come true. The wear and tear inflicted on the mosaic at this spot proves that most people believe in the superstition, to such an extent that periodic renewal is essential..*

* In Budapest, students facing final exams repair to the equestrian statue of the Pandur general Hadik, scourge of Frederick the Great, in the citadel in Buda and touch the testicles of the horse. Translator.

---

custom of the victor eating the liver of the vanquished. "Not being lily-livered" was the same as "having b[alls]." '

In China, popular belief, buttressed by traditional medicine, has it that you take on the virtues of whatever part of an animal that you consume; in effect that the animal part is good for the corresponding part of your own body. Pig's trotters, for example, are recommended for those with bad feet. Testicles are eaten to enhance virility, those of the stag, in particular, reputed to cure impotence.

Closer to home, Marie Rouanet tells us in her *Petit traité romanesque de la cuisine* (Kitchen Stories, 1997) that in the old days in south-west France, when a boar pig was castrated to fatten it, the testicles were given to little boys on a slice of bread. It was like an initiation rite, on the one hand it was thought they would symbolically acquire virility (albeit of an animal) while the children saw that

---

Initiation Belgian-style

The Parc d'Avroy is a splash of green in the city of Liège. At its widest point there is a grassy esplanade that looks down on the River Meuse. The balustrade is decorated with four sculptures, one of which – 'Li Torê' – represents a man leading a proud bull whose gonads leave you in no doubt of its sex. During the annual student festival in the city young people parade through the streets and by tradition gather in this place where they daub the attributes of the bull with red paint: a student ritual or the survival of a pagan rite that is much more ancient? .

eating the flesh of a still-living beast was a bridge to adult life. It was an act that proved his capacity, that he was a man.

It was therefore logical that a whole cornucopia of names should have ripened around this cultus, but the two waves clash: on the one hand, there are the words that stress the symbolic worth of testicles, either in the form of metaphors evoking their preciousness – this is the biggest category of the two – or, in the form of superlatives which have the possible virtue of being reassuring even if they fail to convince. The other group of words plays down their importance, making them worthless, but with a sort of false modesty that fools no one.

Words to evoke value

Great words to suit great fantasies: testicles become nuggets, the family jewels, jewel-caskets, the crown jewels. You have to make excuses! The same tendency exists in English where balls are upgraded to 'crystals' or 'diamonds'.

Holy cullions [French: *couilles*]: St Maclou, St Macouille, St Couillard, St Couillebaut, St Coquilbaut

Sterile women in the Department of the Vienne used to invoke St Maclou or St Macou at the Cramard Chapel at Chalandray and for that reason he was also named St Bedou, as bédou or bedon means 'belly'. At the same time, because of his function, St Maclou was also nicknamed St Macouille or even St Couillard.* Young women seeking his intervention rubbed their lower abdomens with one hand and the statue with the other, reciting all the time 'Oh good St Maclou, give me a big bedou,' hence the coexistence of the two nicknames.

Couillebaut was dreamed up in the thirteenth century by Douin de Lavesne in a verse fable called Trubert. Trubert is a commoner who wants to cuckold the Duke of Burgundy, and to that end, presents himself disguised as a woman called 'Coillebaude', a name that means 'merry bollock' or 'most passionate bollock' or – by extension – 'virile member'. As was the custom of the time, other authors took up the name and, out of mockery, they went so far as to sanctify it.

St Coquilbaut, otherwise known as St Couille-le-Beau,[†] is a make-believe phallic saint, who was first seen at the beginning of the sixteenth century in a comic drama, La Farce du chaudronnier (The Boilermaker's Farce).

    from Jacques E. Merceron, Dictionnaire des saints imaginaires et
        facétieux (A Dictionary of Imaginary and Farcical Saints, 2002)

* *St Myball or St Pillock. Translator.*
[†] *St Handsomeballs. Translator.*

Superlatives

Still out of orbit, but to hit the nail squarely on the head (or should I say 'roundly'?) these border on the megalomaniac: *lyonnaises* (the largest size of ball for the French game of *boules* or *pétanque*), watermelons, hot-air balloons.

Sweet Nothings

Members of this family include little nothings that spawn nicknames by association of ideas: peppercorns, trinkets, baubles, pompoms, shavings, *dandrilles* [worthless bits of cloth], rags, tatters. It should be noted that many of these words are linked to textiles, rags and cloths that are soft and gentle; like cuddly toys, so…

Trophy

There was a crescendo of insults, while the deceased, stretched out on his back, stared impassively from his wide eyes at the great sky and the onset of night. The earth that was stuffed into his mouth was the bread he had refused. He would eat no more of that particular bread. It had not brought him good fortune, to starve the poor world.

But the women had other acts of revenge in store for him. They walked round sniffing at him, like wolves. They were all looking for a suitable outrage, some act of savagery that would give them satisfaction. You could hear the bitter tones of the woman Brûlé.

'We should cut him like a tomcat!'

'Yeah, yeah! Let's neuter him! He put it about a bit too much, the shit!'

The woman Mouquette was already debagging him, pulling off his trousers, while the Levaque lifted his legs. With the desiccated hands of a crone, La Brûlé pushed his naked thighs apart and stabbed that dead virility. She held on to the lot, with an effort that tensed her scrawny back and made her big arms crackle. The soft skin resisted and she needed to have another go before she managed to tear off the strip: a rough and bloody packet of flesh that she brandished with a triumphant laugh:

'I've got it! I've got it!'

Screeches of abuse hailed the ghastly trophy.

'You bugger, you won't be stuffing our daughters no more!'

'Yeah, there'll be no more paying in kind, we won't have to line up no more, and present our arses to get a loaf of bread.'

'Oy! I owe you six francs. Do you want me to sub you some? I'm happy if you can still manage it!'

That ribaldry made them shake with terrible gaiety. They dangled the gory morsel in front of one another, treating it like an evil beast that each of them had had to suffer and which they had finally managed to crush and which was now there for all to see, inert and in their power. They spat at it, they stuck out their jaws, repeating in a furious burst of contempt:

'He can't do it anymore! He can't do it no more! He's just a stiff you stuff in the earth. Go and rot, you good for nothing!'

Then the woman Brûlé stuck the whole packet on the end of a stick; and holding it high, carried it aloft like a flag and walked out onto the road followed by the bellowing gaggle of women. It rained drops of blood and that miserable flesh hung like a hunk of meat on a butcher's hook. At the window upstairs, Madame Maigrat had still not moved, but the last glow of the sunset together with the opaque flaws in the panes deformed her white face so that she seemed to be laughing. Crushed, betrayed morning, noon and night, her shoulders permanently bent over the accounts, maybe she was laughing when the band of women came galloping by with the evil beast, the slaughtered beast, on the end of a stick.

This frightful mutilation had been performed in cold horror. Neither Etienne or Mathieu or any of the others had been able to intervene: they remained rooted to the spot before the ride of the furies. Heads popped out of Tison's pub. Rasseneur was pale from nausea and Zacherie and Philomène were struck dumb by what they had seen. The two old men, Bonnemort and Moque, were nodding their heads gravely. Only Jeanlain giggled, digging Bébert in the ribs with his elbow and forcing Lydie to lift her nose. The women were already coming back, however, passing under the windows of the office, and behind the blinds the women and girls stuck out their necks. They could not make out the scene, as it was obscured by the wall, they saw badly in the black of night.

'What do you think they have on the end of that stick?' asked Cécile who had been brazen enough to look.

Lucie and Jeanne stated that it must have been a rabbit skin.

'No, no,' muttered Madame Hennebeau. 'They will have plundered the charcuterie, it looks more like a hunk of pork.'

At that moment she shivered and fell silent. Madame Grégoire had prodded her with her knee. Both women sat open-mouthed. The girls had turned wan and asked no more questions. They watched wide-eyed as the red apparition disappeared into the darkness.

Émile Zola, Germinal, vol. II, Part 5, Chapter VI.

REPRODUCTIVE ORGANS

Virility is also (perhaps first and foremost) a reproductive function, and in some ways the justification for the existence of the organ. It is therefore impossible not to render homage to it through a few terms the sense of which could not be more limpid. These include notably the appropriately named glands or gonads, genitors, genitals, the more poetic 'germinals', and the most concise (we know that *concise* comes from the Latin *concisus* meaning cut!): patrimony.

Castration

Make no mistake: that profusion of words to describe the thing, or rather the things, emerges mostly from the great primal fear that men have of losing their bits. To invoke something is to make it real, and therefore to reassure.

At the other end of the scale, nothing comes of saying nothing, nothing amounts to impotence or castration. We have discussed this before: the Romans called them *non sunt* (they are not), castrated or impotent men. And in the end, nothing has changed much.

If you accept this, you understand better why the terminology for testicles is so rich and diverse. The words act as substitutes, placebos or *Ersatz*. They are fantastical spare parts, little supplements to the soul.

TESTES IN THE KITCHEN: SYMBOL AND MYTH

Nowadays, cocks' testes and rams' purses are neglected at our aseptic tables. But they had their time of glory as ingredient of choice in France's *cuisine ancienne*. As early as the sixteenth century, Rabelais' Gargantuan fantasy has them aplenty. The tradition of eating them probably goes back to Rome, where they were much given to licentious feasts – that in turn had their origins in Greece. Later on, by virtue of their supposed aphrodisiac qualities, testicles were *de rigueur* at royal and princely tables, above all those of Louis XIV in the seventeenth century and Louis XV in the eighteenth. In the nineteenth they made their appearance in the canon of classical and bourgeois cooking where *sauce financière* (in which they are a vital ingredient) topped – or rather drowned – all the savoury pastries like *bouchées à la reine* and *vol-au-vent* (see the recipes) not to mention more highly seasoned dishes of fowl or game. Nearer our own time, they delighted the fine palates of the Belle Époque and were one of the favourite morning snacks associated with the guild of butchers and tripe cooks in the golden days of the Halles market and the abattoirs of La Villette. In a word, in the old days, you could not have a great meal without their presence.

A brace of balls for Castor and Pollux

In the Satyricon, Petronius invites us to the celebrated 'Trimalchio's supper', the longest episode that has come down to us from this novel, a major work of Latin literature, written around AD 60. Trimalchio is an illiterate upstart and this dinner, where the guests eat in the recumbent manner then in force among Roman patricians, is a pretext for a lively description of the manners and characters of the time (of all sorts and class). Witticisms jostle with eroticisms in a succulent tableau that mixes the vices and the absurdity of the period. It is above all a model for all satire written since – which should be obvious enough from the title Satyricon. But let's not forget the original meaning: the word satire comes from the Latin satira which comes in turn from the ancient Latin satura – 'mixed dish', macédoine or even Russian salad.

In the course of the dinner, one of the first dishes to be served is a visual treat based on the signs of the zodiac. The twins (Castor and Pollux) were represented by those organs that go in pairs, hence justly symbolized by testicles which are also delicacies:

This funereal offering was followed by a dish which, without doubt, was rather smaller than we were expecting, but the novelty of the object attracted all our attention. It was a circular tray, inscribed with all twelve zodiacal signs, and on each of the signs the cook had placed a sympathetic, corresponding dish: on Aries the ram, a horned chickpea; on Taurus the bull, a piece of beef; on the Twins, testicles and kidneys; on Cancer the crab a crown; on Leo the lion some African figs; on Virgo the virgin an unbroken sow's vulva; on Libra the scales a balance containing on the one hand a dish bearing a cheese tart and on the other a cake; on Scorpio the scorpion a scorpion fish; on Sagittarius a sea bream; on Capricorn a rock lobster; on Aquarius a goose; on Pisces the fishes two mullet. In the centre there was a mound sown with grass and there was a honeycomb. An Egyptian valet served all the guests bread from a silver oven.'

Later on, Trimalchio labours the point: 'Under the twins are born pairs-in-hand, teams of oxen, big testicles and those who hunt with the hound and run with the hare.' It is not for nothing that Trimalchio reminds us of Monsieur Jourdain [from Molière's Bourgeois Gentilhomme] and his malapropisms.

The orgies of ancient Rome

'At the banquets of Athens or Rome, described for us by Petronius in "Trimalchio's Supper", tables overflowed with spiced wild meats and evocative ragoûts of sows' vulvas and rams' or bulls' testicles which inspired a frenzy of stuffing and drinking that came in the end to an orgy', Claudine Brécourt-Villars reminds us in the new edition of Curnonsky and Saint-Georges' *La Table et l'amour*.

These were dishes consumed for their sexual symbolism rather than any true gastronomic interest, even if they were prepared to be tasty enough at the time.

Rabelaisian repasts

Feasts in Rabelais don't play second fiddle to those of ancient Rome. It's not just the kettles filled with steaming tripe, or gutted piglets and scalded calves' heads; it's the innards subjected to almost alchemical processes to become sausages or strings of *andouilles*.* Among the foods, guts assume pride of place, not least the rams' purses and sows' vulvas which Rabelais has his gluttons scoffing with immense gusto. Rabelaisian orgies, however, don't have the symbolism of their Roman equivalent. They don't revolve around sex, but are more scatological. Rabelais' reasoning is more irreverent and the grand display of tripe is a catalyst aimed at physical disgust in the first place and in the second at provoking social and political reflection. This last is the essence of Rabelais.

Court dinners and the high-water mark of testicles

Many courtiers, kings, queens, favourites and courtesans are famous for the extravagance of their tables. Catherine de Medici, married to Henri II in the sixteenth century, was the most celebrated of all and introduced the French to many new products and recipes from her native Italy – in particular dishes that were believed to be aphrodisiac. Other examples are Marie de Medici, wife to Henri IV at the outset of the seventeenth century and, after her, the famous royal mistresses, Madame de Maintenon (Louis XIV) and Mesdames de Pompadour and Dubarry (Louis XV) to name but three.

In her preface to *La Table et l'amour, nouveau traité des excitants modernes,* Claudine Brécourt-Villars tells us,

> We also owe to La Maintenon the powerful recipe for lamb chops that bears her name. It is a clever combination of mushrooms, smoked tongue and white truffles – which Heraclitus called symbols of spermatozoa and which, in the words of Brillat-Savarin, have the power to 'render women more tender and men more pleasant.'

---

* Slicing sausage made of rolled pig's intestines, not to be confused with the looser and vastly more pungent *andouillette*, which is eaten hot. The epithet *andouille* is also a gentle reproach for someone who has done something foolish. *Translator.*

Countess Dubarry knew what was expected of her at the table and in the bedroom. To these ends she had acquired certain recipes from Madame Gourdan, bawd to a famous brothel. She invented a dish of plovers' eggs for Louis XV. The plover was reputed for its hot blood, like the pigeon, or the dove, the symbol of indefatigable lechery which, according to Aristotle, can copulate eighty-three times in the course of an hour. This recipe is a cocktail of all the ingredients considered most effective at the time: hard-boiled eggs (recommended to voluptuaries for their richness in phosphorus) garnished with a forcemeat composed of foie gras, truffles (to aid the digestion) and chicken with its proven fortifying qualities; the stuffing is seasoned with lots of pepper (which was then sold under the name of 'grains of paradise'), grated nutmeg ('the spice of ecstasy'*), then basted with a demi-glaze sauce, strengthened with game stock and finally decorated with cocks' testicles. This dish is served on hearts of artichoke[†] – of which plant apothecaries used to sell the preserved stems to 'loosen corset strings'[¶] …

Still in the same work, Curnonsky and André Saint-Georges remind us that (according to them), 'Louis XV criticized Madame de Pompadour for being as cold as a fish[#] and made her eat testicles. Madame de Pompadour used every which way to remove an impediment that could have cost her the position as queen in all but name.' She was indeed endowed with an inexhaustible imagination when it came to surprising her royal lover.

We therefore see that if testicles were much in vogue at the royal tables, it was for their refinement and their flavour, but much more for their alleged medicinal capacity to arouse hitherto somnolent organs.

The turn of the eighteenth and nineteenth centuries: sex and gastronomy hang together

'Prince of cooks and cook of princes',** was how Talleyrand, himself no mean gastronome, baptized Carême, who would ennoble cooking and create the art of cookery. More and more, the contents of the plate were meant to tickle the taste buds as much as they were conceived to feast the eyes. It was the apogee of puff

---

* And used in the preparation of the 'love pill', Ecstasy.
[†] In France the 'hearts' of these edible thistles are often called 'culs' meaning bottoms or arses. *Translator.*
[¶] '*Pour dénouer les aiguillettes.*' This phrase can only be rendered into English by some coarse locution like 'getting her knickers off.' *Translator.*
[#] The French is 'macreuse' or scoter duck, but in English this animal is not known to be as frigid as a fish. *Translator.*
** Talleyrand was, of course, also a prince, and Carême was at one time his cook. *Translator.*

pastry, with *bouchées, croûtes*, savoury pies, *vol-au-vent* and *pâtés en croûte* stuffed with a profusion of truffles, cock's combs and cock's stones, subsumed within countless sauces, but principally *financière* and *suprême*.

With the birth of restaurants and the rise of the professional chef, there was a further departure: fine cookery ceased to be the preserve of royal and noble tables and became accessible to the bourgeoisie. And this bourgeoisie wanted to spend its freshly minted coin not only on gross appetite, but in aping the epicene creations of the aristocracy as well as its libertine imagination.

> When such dishes land on bourgeois tables in the nineteenth century, it is to display the fact that they have reached a position of equality. They were not only lavish in the abundance of food – a sign of wealth – but in the rarity and the aristocratic reputation of the dishes. Thus they required venison, the symbol of power or potency* and wildness, and cultivated birds such as the turkey, which had a libidinous reputation: 'a spicy brunette', according to that pathfinder of gastronomic eloquence, Balthazar Grimod de la Reynière. And assuredly, the truffle had never been so prestigious, as was observed by the author of a *Nouveau guide des dîneurs* (New Guide for Diners) published in 1828.
>
> Claudine Brécourt-Villars

It is indeed a fact that the great wind of libertinage blows through the cookery of the period. As the Marquis de Sade, that creator of louche suppers designed to restore strength and sexual libidos, wrote at the time: 'I know nothing that tickles my stomach and head so voluptuously as the redolence of succulent dishes that stroke my brain, preparing it to receive the impression of lechery' (*La Nouvelle Justine*).

In the nineteenth-century kitchen, testicles were highly prized. They were sought for their delicacy and finesse, and their aphrodisiac qualities. In his introduction to *La Table et l'amour* Curnonsky pronounces this encomium to the table:

> We have asked one of the best Parisian restaurateurs, who is also an educated man, for some information on cooking for lovers or, let's make it even clearer, aphrodisiac cookery.

Léandre (the name of the friend) tells him, *inter alia*:

> Alexandre Dumas, who was not only a prodigious novelist but also a perfect cook, reveals a recipe for amorous gastronomy which appears to me to be Voronoff † before his time. It is a recipe for purses.
> 'Purses... What do you mean Léandre?'

---

* Until 1789, hunting had been a privilege of the nobility. *Translator.*
† Serge or Sergei Voronoff (1866–1951) was a physician famous for his advocacy of grafting monkeys' testicles on to men's to rejuvenate the patient. *Translator.*

'What? Don't you know what purses are? They are rams' testicles. In Tuscany, Spain and Provence they are utterly convinced that purses provide an effective aphrodisiac. Rams' are the most highly sought-after in Italy, bulls' in Spain, and in Algeria and Morocco they swear by lions' testicles. As I have never eaten food of this type myself, I will reserve judgement on its efficacy. One of my friends, however, who tried the recipe for purses written by Alexandre Dumas,* assured me that it really had reinvigorating qualities.'

The rise and fall of *cucina povera*

At the end of the nineteenth and the start of the twentieth centuries testicles enjoyed a relative and literal popularity. Like other forms of offal, they found their place at most tables. One reason for this was the Halles covered market in Paris which had its own section or *pavillon* dedicated to offal. It was an earthy dish served in restaurants that were otherwise reputed for their fine cooking. The market porters at Les Halles were happy to eat them for their mid-morning snack, just like the butchers at the abattoir in La Villette, but that popular approach stressed the demotic or coarser connotations of testicles.

At the dawn of the 1970s, a new way of eating came into being. Now, it seemed, differences in class and background were exemplified by people's diet; the rich decided that offal was 'common' and they swapped it for dishes they esteemed more delicate. For their part, the poor refused to eat 'disgusting' things that were disdained by the rich because they were too cheap. Industrialized food was on the march, and folk in general preferred foods that hailed from factories. Testicles were not the only fancy meats that fell out of favour. At the end of the twentieth century nearly all offal was on the wane, not just testicles but calves' heads and feet, mutton trotters, ox heart, spleen, calves' caul, liver and lights, etc. Now only the real offal-lovers continue to eat them, sometimes in secret.

Elsewhere, lascivious frolics have given way in the imagination to common-or-garden sex, and hence the connection between the flesh you eat and the flesh that excites the sexual imagination has been rent asunder.[†] The aphrodisiac alibi [of testicles] is no longer tenable except by a few. Curnonsky confirms it:

> It seems that the French have an animus against this choice morsel. Women in particular make faces at the mere thought of eating it. When they discover that this act [almost, of sacrilege] doesn't result in the world collapsing about their heads, they begin to reassess this dish so dear to Jews and connoisseurs alike.
>
> In truth the texture of a testicle resembles that of sweetbreads[¶] and any recipe for the one will suit the other.

---

* See the recipe for Fries in the manner of Alexandre Dumas in the recipe section, below.
† Madame Vié juxtaposes '*la chère*' (good food – cheer) and '*la chair*' (flesh, meat). *Translator.*
¶ In England, many people assume sweetbreads to be testicles. They are thyroid glands. *Translator.*

La Peña Criadillas: the Society of Knacker Noshers

At the end of the 1980s, French journalist and food-writer Léon Mazzella got together with a group of testicular friends to create – as he puts it – 'a band of aficionados a los toros* who think only of laughing, eating well and drinking.' It is called 'La Peña Criadillas' (The Society of Knacker Noshers). Among their number was Guy Suire, a well-known journalist and broadcaster; an offal-butcher who enjoyed the privilege of receiving all the criadillas taken from bulls after fights in south-west France; and Michel Carrère, a distinguished restaurateur now based at Saint-Justin in the Landes but who was at the time running La Chamade in Bordeaux with two Michelin stars. Every two months or so they met up at La Chamade. There was always an even number of guests (it had to be pairs), sitting at one table holding a maximum of twelve. There was a ritual: the meal kicked off with a dish of cock's stones [called rognons blancs or white kidneys in French] often with a blanquette[†] of cock's combs, followed by a dish of Pauillac lamb's fry and a serving of criadillas which came each time from a different farm. The manner of cooking was different every time and the testicles were always served up in twos. After that, tradition decreed that there would be a daube[¶] of bulls' cheek or ortolans[#] in season. The crowning glory of this totemic meal was a bottle of Château d'Yquem in the guise of dessert! This group of happy chaps met like this for two or three years until the early 1990s: now memorialized by an azulejo** from Seville fixed to the wall of the vaulted basement of La Chamade.

* *Bull fanciers. Translator.*

[†] *A sauce whipped up with the stock from the dish, egg yolks and cream. Translator.*

[¶] *A Provençal stew made with wine. Translator.*

[#] *Buntings, netted, fattened and drowned in armagnac. They are eaten whole. Translator.*

** *A decorative tile. Translator.*

Much worse, perhaps, the rise of psychoanalysis – with its baggage of existential questions which never troubled our predecessors – may have persuaded some into thinking eating testicles induces fear of castration. But in north Africa they think the reverse: ram's 'eggs' are thought to be eminently virile and that part of the *méchoui** is reserved for the guest of honour. Then again, every civilization has its codes and symbols.

---

* The roasting of a lamb that is a festive meal across north Africa and, since independence from France, has become a commonplace among the expelled Pied Noir communities in the south of France. *Translator*

CONCLUSION

I will conclude by saying that at the dawn of this twenty-first century which prides itself on its sexual 'liberty' – which has little of the gallant about it – the naming and display of male parts remain taboo, whatever some may say. We add to an ever-growing surplus of euphemisms with various forms of provocation (by good boys or naughty boys, depending) such as the spate of calendars of naked men produced by sports clubs of all types, or the constant exposure of individuals in the media – which only leaves them more distant and untouchable – all of which reflect the eternal fascination of the *fascinus,* across time and *milieu.*

This means it's all the more the case that dining on the male parts – even if the penis is rarely invited to the feast – is invariably transgressive.

Eating testicles, be they cocks', rams' or bulls', is not an neutral act. It is more a sort of transfer. When tasting these attributes – the quintessence of masculinity – we endow them with a mental image: as love-potions, aphrodisiac food, peasant food, or food to enhance one's virility. In other words, we consume them to appropriate their inherent virtues. However, not everyone sees them in this light: some view them with repulsion, or find they induce a fear of castration.

While testicles have enjoyed* (if I can use the word) genuine popularity in days gone by, now their consumption is mostly subject of anecdote and legend. Maybe this fact is as powerful a sign as any that the erotic 'dissolution' of our society is no more than spin and in truth is rather feeble.

The purpose of this book is to honour them and rehabilitate them to their rightful place at table.

---

* The author here uses the word *jouir,* means a much greater form of enjoyment in French – to the degree of orgasmic pleasure. *Translator.*

WORDS AND EXPRESSIONS THAT FEATURE 'THEM'*

Avoir des couilles (au cul) / **To have balls**

To be brave, daring and reassuring. In French the words '*au cul*' (meaning 'on one's arse') are added, inaccurately (because it is well known that a man's balls do not hang from his bottom) but euphemistically (signifying the sexual organs). Even in slang, there is an element of censure. It can be used in the negative ('*il n'a pas de couilles*'): he has no balls; he's lost his balls; where are his balls? has the man no balls? etc.

Avoir les boules / **To have balls**

Boules in French is another word for *couilles*. This is a phrase indicating that you have balls and 'you've had it (or them) up to here'. To this end, the expression is often accompanied by a lewd gesture whereby the man places two fingers under his chin, which stresses the coarseness of the expression. The phrase, in other words, indicates annoyance.

Avoir des glandes

The same as *avoir des boules*.

Baiser à couilles rabattues / **Fuck with bargain balls**

Fuck non-stop, like a rabbit.

Ça m'en a touché une sans bouger l'autre / **That touches one of them without moving the other**

Another way of saying '*je m'en fous / fiche*' (I don't give a damn / fuck). It was one of the favourite expressions of the puppet version of President Jacques Chirac in the television programme *Guignols de l'Info*. There is no English equivalent beyond 'It leaves me cold.'

Ça m'fout les boules / **That fucks my balls**

See '*avoir des boules*'.

---

* Very few of Madame Vié's expressions find echoes in English, they are none the less presented here together with a few native variants. *Translator.*

Casser les couilles / Briser les couilles / **Bust or break my balls**

Tire someone, wear them out, generally by talking too much. The nearest English equivalent would be to talk the balls off someone, which is more politely rendered as talking the hind legs off a donkey.

Casser les noix / Briser les noix / **Crack or break my nuts**

See above.

C'est de la couille en barre / **It's a ball in pure gold (see goldenballs, below)**

Meaning something special. English-speaking people are more self-deprecating about testicles.

C'est de la couille en branche / **It's a sub-station of balls**

Something worthless.

Couille molle / **Pillock**

In French, as in other languages, someone who lacks courage or is a coward. A pillock is more a '*couillon*' which is the diminutive form ('little bollock'). A pillock is an arse in English, or an arsehole. In the US it would be an asshole.

Couillu / **Ballsy**

An adjective that means he 'has them', either in the proper sense (he has big bollocks) or in the figurative sense of 'he has no fear, he is brave, he is a real chap/guy'. By extension, it has come to mean a wine that has guts. We should also mention the expression '*plus il est poilu, plus il est couillu*' (the hairier he is, the bigger his balls) which, according to popular prejudice, means that hairy men have manifest virility, or even justifies the name '*poilus*' (hairy men) given to soldiers in the First World War. In English, 'ballsy' is often used to describe women who have the sort of attitude associated with men.

Courir sur le haricot / **Run on the bean**

Annoy someone, similar to '*casser les couilles*'. '*Haricot*' is an old word for testicle. The word '*haricocèle*' means an atrophied testicle, as explained in *Dictionnaire historique Le Robert* and which is discussed by Bernard C. Galey, *Du coq à l'âne, l'etymo-jolie 2* (From Cock to Donkey, Word Games 2), 1995.

De mes deux / Of my two

Meaning of my two balls. It is used to express doubt, or doubt of the veracity of a person's functions: *professeur de mes deux, commissaire de mes deux...* In English, the nearest equivalent is the harmless 'my foot', 'my eye', or 'my arse'.

Écouillement

A neologism conceived by the brothers Goncourt to signify opinions and consciences lacking in courage, vigour or balls. In English it would be 'spinelessness': 'It is in the current literary world and in the highest councils of the land that one finds a flattening of judgment, a spinelessness (*écouillement*) of opinion and conscience' (Edmond and Jules Goncourt, *Journal*).

En avoir... (ou pas) / To have them... (or not)

Meaning balls.

Avoir ferme les rognons / To have hard kidneys

To be keen on sex. The English equivalent would talk of 'loins', as in 'the higher the brows, the lower the loins…'.

Finir en couille(s) / Make a balls-up

End up doing badly by making too much of an effort. The English is more specifically to make a mess of things. In Ireland it would be: 'Make a bollocks of things…'.*

Foutre les boules / Fuck the balls

A more extreme version of the phrase (above) *'avoir les boules'*.

J'ai le grandpère qui colle aux bonbons / My grandad is sticking to the toffees

A picturesque expression meaning someone is uncomfortable in his underclothes or too hot. There is no obvious English equivalent.

J'me bouffe les couilles / I am eating my bollocks

Expression of panic used in critical situations, for example footballers who have lost a match. The nearest English would be to eat shit, suffer humiliation.

---

* Ireland's use of the word bollocks is of interest: The [dog's] bollocks is the best, the *ne plus ultra*, whereas 'a bollocks' is a very nasty man, a cunt. The article, definite or indefinite, decides for good or bad. *Translator.*

J'm'en bats les couilles / I'm beating my balls

To absolutely not care about something. More commonly this would be expressed by the French verb for to fuck – *foutre* – '*je m'en fous*' or 'I don't give a fuck.' Although that expression is used by people of both genders, the verb *foutre* is essentially masculine because only men are supposed to have balls and to fuck. There is a discussion of these variables, in French and other languages, in Florence Montreynaud's *Appeler une chatte… Mots et plaisirs du sexe* (Call it a Pussy … The Words and Pleasures of Sex) 2004. [It should be added that in the past generation, in English-speaking countries at least, women have been made to 'fuck' too as part of sexual liberation. So a woman might say, 'I fucked him last night', without implying any great perversity in the act. *Translator.*]

La peau de mes rouleaux / The skin of my bollocks

In other words, nothing at all, see also '*peau de balles*', below. There is no English equivalent. *Rouleaux* is slang for testicles (see the glossary below), although literally it means rollers or rolls of coin wrapped in papers, or toilet rolls, or rolling pins. The phrase *au bout de son rouleau* means at the end of one's tether.

Ma couille / My bollock

A popular term of affection (used a lot by the actor Gérard Depardieu), meaning a person one likes a great deal: 'Good morning bollock, how are you, my little bollock?' It appeared first in Jean-Marie Poiré's film *Les Visiteurs* of 1993. Needless to say, it would go down badly in an English-speaking country.

It is possibly related to the word *couillard,* meaning 'having testicles', which was used first in the sixteenth century. This was a word of friendship too, '*Eh! bien, couillard, que dis-tu de ceci?*'* (Béroalde de Verville, quoted in Louis de Landes, *Glossaire érotique de la langue française*)

Partir en couille / Se barrer en couille / Make a balls-up

In French slang the word *couille* is synonymous with *emmerdement* (trouble or nuisance), often used in relation to a *couillonnade* or a balls-up.

Peau de balle(s) / Pillock skin

Meaning 'worth absolutely nothing'. In this phrase *balle* has two meanings: it is the French slang or *argot* for *testicules* or testicles; and it also means the chaff of wheat or grain. The phrase in this latter case is therefore a pleonasm, where one of the words is redundant ('the skin of skin').

---

* 'OK, big balls, what do you say to that?' *Translator.*

Quand ma tante aura des couilles / **When my aunt grows balls**

Meaning never, or 'when the cows come home.'

Se faire des couilles en or / **Have golden balls**

To make a lot of money. In England James Goldsmith was baptized 'Goldenballs' by the magazine *Private Eye*.

Tenir (quelqu'un) par les couilles / **Have someone by the balls**

Have power over someone: one of the few French phrases that translates perfectly into English.

Tu me les gonfles / *Ça me les gonfle* / **That makes them swell up**

That is, my balls. The phrase underlines the connection between sex and aggression, given that the testes nigh-on double in volume at the height of arousal. In France, the expression is often accompanied by an excitable gesture to the head (but obviously really meaning to the balls) as described under *'avoir les boules'*, above.

Y a une couille (dans le potage) / **There's a pillock in my soup**

Meaning something has gone wrong. In England: a balls-up.

Y a une couille dans le potlatch / **There is a pillock in the works**

This is a development of the preceding phrase, for *potlatch* is a paronym of *potage*. It means that something is not working in a family structure, or a hierarchy, caused by a lack or loyalty or respect, a failure to be honest or to tell the truth. There is no English equivalent, although in Austrian German *'eine Hinterfotze'* (an inverted cunt, adjective *Hinterfotzig*) has something of the same sense even if the word is rather more explicit. In politics, it may indicate that an individual's actions do not match his or her public statements.

A LOAD OF OLD BOLLOCKS*

Odd

'He is born of a mother and an unknown pair.'
> San-Antonio (Frédéric Dard), Réflexions poivrées sur la jactance
> (Spicy Thoughts on Blather, 1999)

The French is, '*Il est né de mère et de paire inconnues.*' The pun is on the word *paire* (pair [of balls]), a homophone of the word *père* (father).

Ballsy vowels

The French word *tréma* comes from the Greek *trêma*, meaning stop. In English, it translates as diaeresis, being a double point placed horizontally over the vowels e, i, and u, to indicate that the preceding one should be pronounced separately, as in Moët (& Chandon) and Perrier Jouët. In the mischievous jargon employed by French printers, these two little dots have been christened 'balls'.

Balls-ups

The following anecdote is attributed to a number of writers, but it seems most likely that the perpetrator (and victim) was Armand Silvestre (d. 1901), a famous columnist on the *Journal de Paris*. Wishing to amuse his readers, he wrote a humorous article composed of all the most amusing *coquilles* (typos) that he had had the occasion to see in the course of his career, notably in his own pieces. He gave the piece the title *Mes Coquilles* (My Typos). When the article appeared, however, there was a typo in the title: intentionally or otherwise, the letter q had been omitted. The title read *Mes Couilles* (My Balls).

Françoise Sagan's squishy Kools

Everyone knows how, once she'd upset the literary apple-cart with her celebrated novel *Bonjour tristesse*, the author Françoise Sagan was for ever in the news for her enthusiastic nighttime frolics and excess of all sorts – notably drink and fags. An inveterate smoker, she was often short of her favourite brand: soft paper packs of Kool Menthol. Marie-Thérèse Bartoli, who was her personal assistant from 1982 to

---

* In this little section, the author indulges in French wordplay. The explanations in English are necessarily plodding. *Translator.*

1998, tells us in her kiss-and-tell memoir (*Chère Madame Sagan*, 2002) that when this happened in the course of an all-nighter, the two women would set off on the prowl for an open tobacconist, screaming as they went, '*Je veux des Kool molles. Je veux des Kool molles!*' ('I want soft Kools. I want soft Kools!') [The pun here is on Kool for *couilles* (balls), and *molle*, i.e. soft or squishy, for the more precise *paquet souple* or soft paper cigarette packs as opposed to card, see *couille molle*, above.]

A hermaphrodite Porsche

In *Le Pire des mondes* (The Worst of Worlds, 2003), the French novelist Ann Scott describes how her hero bags plenty of status by buying a loft and a Porsche. She describes the car as having 'seen from above, the shapely curve of a woman's hips, and sporting a mammoth pair of bollocks with its motor at the back.'

The hazards of *criadillas*

Here is a little joke told me by the late Olivier Nanteau [a French radio journalist and gastronomic chronicler], who was something of an expert.

> It is the story of a tourist who went to Andalusia for his holidays. One day he went to a restaurant and while he was eating the food on his plate, he saw a dish arrive at the next table containing two impressive looking balls.
> '*Por favor*, could you tell me what that dish is?' He asked the waiter.
> '*Señor*, those are *criadillas*, the bollocks of a *toro bravo* or fighting bull that has been killed in the ring.'
> The next day, the tourist returned to the same restaurant and he too ordered the famous *criadillas*. But oh! what disappointment came over him when he saw the dish come to his table, featuring two little balls of modest dimensions!
> '*Por favor*, why are these *criadillas* so much smaller than those you served the gentleman next to me last night?' He asked at once.
> '*Señor*, we are really sorry, but this time it was the *toro* who won, and it is the *torero* who died in the ring!'

A well-stuffed purse or how to acquire golden balls

> A nice old lady arrived at the head office of the Bank of Canada with a bag brimming with Canadian dollars. She made it clear that she wanted to meet the chairman of the bank in person in order to make her deposit. Despite their protestations, and taking the old lady's insistence into account, the staff finally agreed to disturb the chairman (after all, the customer is always right).
> The chairman asked the old lady how much she had in her bag. She replied, 'I have $200,000 that I want to pay in.'

The chairman was curious, and asked her how she came by such a sum in cash.

'It was a bet.' She said.

'What sort of bet?'

'Well, for example, if I were to bet you $25,000 you had square balls.'

The chairman roared with laughter, exclaiming 'What a daft bet!'

At this point she said 'Do you want to make a bet with me?'

'Of course!' He thought the odds in his favour, as he was convinced that his balls were round.

'Given the amount of money at stake, I would like my lawyer to be present to verify matters tomorrow morning at ten,' said the old lady. The chairman instantly agreed.

That evening, the chairman was a little nervous and apprehensive as he examined his testicles, juggling them in his hands and checking their roundness with close attention. Once he had reassured himself, he smiled. The very thought of making money from his balls!

The next day, at ten o'clock on the dot, the old lady arrived at the bank with her lawyer and the two of them headed for the chairman's office. She asked the chairman to drop his trousers. He did so at once.

The old lady asked him if she could touch them to check them herself.

'OK, for $25,000 I understand that you would like to be certain. Go ahead,' the chairman agreed.

He was suddenly aware, however, that the lawyer was bashing his head violently against the wall and asked the old lady why he was doing such a thing.

She replied, 'Oh, that's nothing serious! He has just lost his bet. I wagered $100,000 that I would have the Chairman of the Bank of Canada by the balls!'

(A little story found on the Internet)

Testi cucul es / A pillock's tale

Steve-O, alias Stephen Glover, a twenty-nine-year-old British-born American, is the brightest member of *Jackass*, the most highly rated trash-show on MTV. Master of stupid and risky stunts, he is frank about being a professional idiot and cites in his defence the fact that he was on the move throughout his childhood, and that he needed to play the buffoon to be noticed. Among the eight most imbecilic tricks he claims to like the best (in fact number two on the list) is stapling his testicles to his thigh! 'And I don't treat them, I let them get better by themselves,' he adds.

Article by Florence Trédez in Elle, *5 January 2004*

Your bollocks or your life

Some exclamation is in order when it is stated that pharmacies sell condoms at prices beyond most purses. [The *double entendre* here being purses, i.e. *bourses*, i.e. ball-bags.]

Philippe Vandel, Le Dico des paradoxes *(The Dictionary of Paradoxes, 1993), citing a reader's letter in* Sud-Ouest Bordeaux *of 11 May 1990*

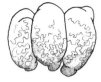

METHOD

The Underbelly of Culinary Curiosity:
Fries, *Criadillas*, Gonads, White Kidneys and Other Little 'Things'

Can you offer a woman anything more succulent?

Marie Rouanet, Petit traité romanesque de cuisine

A LITTLE KNOWLEDGE

A lexicon of anatomical, culinary and fantastic terms to describe edible testicals

Âmes / Souls

I have never heard the word *âmes* used in this sense anywhere else than in the Brasserie Thoumieux in Paris, run by Jean Bassalert and his wife Françoise, but this might be the moment to give them a pat on the back for regularly offering cock's stones and lamb's fry on their *à la carte* menu and even occasionally on the daily *table d'hôte*. They inform me that they have always used the epithet *âmes* for cock's and lamb's testicles in their family, which comes from the Limousin, where they have been restaurateurs, man and boy, for four generations. I am convinced that the derivation is similar to that of *animelles* (see below).

Amourette(s) / Passing fancies

In the singular, the term means the spinal cord of bovines (or more rarely of ovines) when it is used in cooking. Some authors only give it this name when it is cooked. Veal marrow is more refined than ox. Used in the plural, the word describes a mix of different delicate garnishes (marrow, *animelles*, cock's combs and cock's stones) served in a savoury pie or a vol-au-vent. Some authors are confused between the two usages and wrongly use *amourettes* to mean *animelles* (see below). *Amourettes* is sometimes used in the Middle East (the Lebanon in particular) to mean lamb's fry in books on oriental cookery.

Amoureuses / Lovers

In her book *L'Agneau, des mots et des saveurs* (Lamb, Words and Flavours), Sophie Denis uses this word as a synonym for *animelles*. I have been unable to find it in any other cookery manual.

Animelles* / Testicle as butcher's meat

The name of the 'disbursed'† glands (testicles) of a male animal destined to be sold as butcher's meat. The best loved in France, North Africa and the Middle

---

* *Animelle* (n.f. plur.) means sweetbreads in Italian. *Translator.*
† i.e. removed from the scrotum. *Translator.*

East are taken from rams, while in Spain they prefer those from bulls. The word is always used in the plural. It is particularly interesting to note that the word *animelles* comes from the Latin for breath, *anima*, which gives us our own animal (because it is animated or alive), as well as the French word *âme* (i.e. soul) because the soul is the breath of the spirit that animated man. [The English word soul is of Germanic origin, ultimately perhaps derived from Greek rather than Latin.] As regards *animelles*, they naturally contain the seed of life, therefore the breath.*

Banes /Bull's testicles

A rare anatomical term used for bull's testicles. In French conversation the word *gonades* is preferred, while in cooking the Spanish *criadillas* is usual.

> Argomuche was a picturesque language stuffed with words drawn from street slang (*argot*) known to everyone, and jargon specific to the slaughterhouses of La Villette. A virile man, for example, was called a *banard* from *banes*, a bull's testicles, and they said that a man had marrowbone, when they meant courage.
>
> Guy Shemla, Les Ventres de Paris, les Halles, la Villette, Rungis, l'histoire du plus grand marché du monde *(The Bellies of Paris … the History of the World's Biggest Market, 1994)*

Béatilles

Béatilles is the French for the cocktail of different delicate garnishes (veal or lamb's sweetbreads, *amourettes*, *animelles*, cock's combs and cock's stones) that are used to decorate a pie or a vol-au-vent. [There is no precise English equivalent, although see Batalia pie, described by the author Robert May in 1660, below.] As a general usage, *amourettes* may be preferable because *béatilles* usually includes sweetbreads. Some authors use *béatilles* as a synonym for *animelles*, which is false. Etymologically, the word derives from *béat* (in the Greek sense of contented) and was used first to mean 'objects created by beatific nuns; and, by extension, in around 1500 it was used for the ornaments in ladies' hair, and then for sweetmeats (1585), specially used in cooking for delicate morsels used to garnish *pâtés* or which are served on the side (1680)' (*Dictionnaire historique de la langue française*, Le Robert).

> Do you know what *béatilles* are? By jove, it's a pretty old word. Our fathers called *béatilles* those delicate little meats such as sweetbreads, cock's combs and testes. They were served separately, sautéed, or put into *pâtés*. In some regions, they were also cooked in restorative

---

*   The stuff of life to knit me
      Blew hither: here am I.
      Now – for a breath I tarry…
           A.E. Houseman, *A Shropshire Lad. Translator.*

broths for young married couples on the day after their wedding. Our forefathers knew what they were doing.

Curnonsky and André Saint-Georges, La Table et l'amour, nouveau traité des excitants modernes

By this name in the past were designated a collection of little bits like cock's combs and testes, lamb's sweetbreads and mushrooms that were used as garnishes to vol-au-vents, *bouchées* and pies. These little things were usually bound by a *sauce velouté* or a *sauce supreme*.

Prosper Montagné, Larousse gastronomique, *1938*

The family jewels

An expression that refers to male genital organs (see the lexicon), but which is also used by the Belgian star chef Pierre Wynants at his restaurant Comme Chez Soi in Brussels to designate bull's testicles (young bull's gonads) which are indispensable for the making of *choesels* (see below).

Bourses / Purses

Used in the plural, the word *bourses* is used both to denote the skin covering the testes, the scrotum, and, metonymically, the glands contained therein. The verb *débourser* (disburse) is therefore used when the contents are separated from the container and the glands removed from their outside envelope.

Caillettes / Cauls*

In the sixteenth century the word was used for the sack that contained a ram's balls, its scrotum.

Caprices de femmes / Women's caprices

A fantasy name for rams' purses, it was a favourite Iranian euphemism when the Pahlavis were shahs (before the Islamic revolution), a moment perhaps when Persian gastronomy reached a high-water mark.

Choesels

A word that means bull's testicles in Belgian slang. See also '*chosettes*' and the more wide-ranging description in the recipe section.

---

* Caul or omentum is the thin fatty membrane that wraps itself round the greater intestine and internal organs of mammmals. Often taken from a pig, it is used to bind faggots and other meat confections that require wrapping. Faggots are often called *caillettes* in French. *Translator.*

Chosettes

This word (*choesels* in Belgium) is a prudish expression to denote a bull's 'things' [*choses* is French for things]. Some disagree. For a more detailed explanation see the recipe on p. 113.

Criadillas

See below, in foreign words.

Daintiers*

Nowadays a technical word denoting a stag's testicles. They look like big black eggs and are highly sought-after in Chinese medicine (often served with the animal's penis as well) to heighten sexuality. They are thought effective in combating male impotence. Stags are endangered in the wild in China and they are being farmed in ever-greater numbers, notably because of the popularity of this dish.

Désirs / Desires

A fantasy name used by the great chef Escoffier for cock's stones.

Faux ris / False sweetbreads

A name that used to be used a lot instead of *animelles* as their fine, appetizing texture, and even their appearance, was reminiscent of veal sweetbreads.

Friture de veau / Calf's fry

A prudish name by which Canadian cowboys [Well, actually American, but Canadians speak French, Americans don't. *Translator.*] refer to the testicles of a young bull, understood by everyone because they are always eaten fried. (See also 'Rocky mountain oysters' and 'Prairie oysters'.)

Frivolités / Frivolities

A fantasy name by which butchers, offal merchants and other industry professionals used to refer to lamb's testicles (in particular at the abattoirs at La

---

* In English, *OED* has dowset or doucet (evidently from the French *doux*) for the testicles of a deer. A more familiar word for all the entrails of a deer is umbles, which gives us humble pie: the lords ate a magnificent venison pasty, and the plebs ate the offal. The French *daintiers* is an old hunter's word and doubtless related to *dainteau*, a young fallow deer (Cotgrave, *A Dictionarie of the French and English Tongues*, 1611). *Translator.*

Villette in Paris). Another favoured word was *joyeuses* (see below) often used by cookery writers of the same period.

Frivolités de la reine / The queen's frivolities

In her book *L'Agneau, des mots et des saveurs*, Sophie Denis tells us, 'Lamb's fries were also referred to as the queen's frivolities, in memory of the dish with which – it seems – Louis XV treated Madame de Pompadour in order to stimulate her amorous appetites.' It is certainly true that the court of Louis XV (1710–1774, he reigned from 1715) was very partial to offal, notably lamb's fry and cock's stones, and it is also claimed that he made his mistress eat them to kindle her ardour (see Mythology). Madame de Pompadour, however, was his mistress, not his queen. She indeed was Marie Leszczynska (1703–1768), who married Louis in 1725 and was very fond of her food, inspiring a great many recipes which are styled *à la reine*: chicken, consommé, minced chicken, and above all the celebrated *bouchées à la reine* (the queen's morsels). The authentic form of this last is made from a garnish *à la financière*, based on cock's combs and cock's stones. It seems to me the 'frivolities' are more likely to have been a tribute to the queen than the mistress, an opinion shared by Prosper Montagné in the original edition of *Larousse Gastronomique* of 1938 (see also *Morceau de la reine* below).

Gonade(s) / Gonad(s)

From the Greek *gône* meaning seed, the word gonad denotes the sexual glands that produce gametes and secrete hormones. The male gonad is the testicle and the female is the ovary. In the language of the French butcher, particularly in the north of France, the term is applied specifically to bull's or bullock's testicles. It is also used to designate the coral tongues that are found inside sea urchins and which are no less than the sexual organs of this mollusc (they are yellow for males and pink or red for females). The latter can represent up to twelve per cent of the adult animal. It is a proportion that would make a mammal's eyes boggle.

Honneurs / Honours

A fantasy term for rams' purses, not used much now.

Huîtres de montagne / Mountain oysters

One of the homely sobriquets applied by cowboys to bullock's gonads castrated on the ranches of North America – the United States (especially Virginia) and Canada. After castration, the bullock's testicles are generally fried with herbs and served with marinated cloves of wild garlic. It is a seasonal dish, consumed above all in the spring when the beasts are being branded (see Mountain oysters in the lexicon of foreign terms, below).

Huîtres des montagnes Rocheuses / Rocky mountain oysters

Another name American cowboys give to bullock's testicles.

Huîtres des prairies / Prairie oysters

Yet another name conferred on bullock's testicles by American cowboys.*

Joyeuses (or joyeusetés) / Joys

A saucy euphemism, *joyeuses* was used for a long time by butchers, offal dealers and meat professionals (particularly in abattoirs) to mean rams' purses, and they were happy to eat them for their morning snack [*casse-croûte matinal*]. In popular speech the term is also used to describe a man's testicles and was common between the wars and even into the 1970s, that is, until the closing of Les Halles and the transfer of the market to Rungis.† The celebrated chef, the late Alain Chapel, went so far as to create a 'Confrérie des joyeuses' (see recipe for *Les joyeuses de l'ami Roger*). Some Middle Eastern cookbooks use the word *joyeuseté* to describe lamb's fry.

Morceau de la reine / The queen's morsel

This is the name Marie Rouannet gives cock's stones in her *Petit traité romanesque de la cuisine* of 1997. She reminds us that 'these used to garnish the celebrated *bouchée à la reine.*'

Oeufs de mouton / Rams' eggs

Arabs call testicles in general and sheeps' in particular 'eggs' or *baïdh*. In literary Arabic the word has essentially these two meanings (see the lexicon below). The epithet is used in other countries too: for example Spain (*huevos*) and Germany (*Eier*).

> And this one looked at me, and that one smiled at me, and one drove me mad with her eyes, and another recited verse, and that one there

---

* For males of the roughest hue, cowboys are strangely attracted by euphemisms for bollocks. Rocky mountain oysters are but half of them. A brief trawl of the Internet will yield 'cowboy caviar', 'Montana tendergroins', 'dusted nuts', 'bull fries' or 'swinging beef' among others. *Translator.*

† Paris's magnificent central market at was pulled down and new buildings were created close to Orly Airport in the southern suburbs. With the demolition of Les Halles, an entire popular culture went too. *Translator.*

opened her arms to me, and that one said 'Oh you my eye!' and the other 'Oh you my soul!' and another 'Oh flame of heart!' And then they all came towards me and began to caress me... Once the meal was over, after we had feasted on the finest foods – birds' tongues, brains, rams' balls (*oeufs de mouton*) – and we had all had our share of the honey cake; after the dances and the songs, they said to me:

> Oh my darling, now is the time for solid pleasure and in bed; choose between us the one who attracts you the most, and without fear that you will offend us, for each of us will have our turn during the night, we forty sisters, and afterwards the turn of every one of us will come again to play with you in the bed, every night.

The Thousand and One Nights *(Story of the Third Saâlouk, Fifteenth Night)*

Rognons blancs / Lamb's fries

These are ovine testicles, removed from their natural packaging. Sheep don't generally have them, for it is indeed theirs that one eats, once lambs have been castrated [in the process, when fully grown, becoming wethers]. Ram lambs (non-castrated males) or rams (breeding males) [sometimes called bucks or tups] still have them. *Rognons blancs* (white kidneys) is the French term for fries most commonly used today, and the accepted usage within the butchery trade, for what were once called *animelles*, a word that has fallen from use. The euphemism stems from their similarity in shape to kidneys, which paradoxically butchers now call *rognons de chair* (flesh kidneys) to distinguish them from fries. Fry is included in the fifth 'quarter', what the French call *triperie* (tripe) and we call offal – the other four quarters being the two front legs and the two hind legs of a beast. The Arabs are particularly fond of them, as are the inhabitants of Iceland. While once the common coin of restaurant menus in France, they are now the stuff of legend.

Rognons (blancs) de coq / Cock's stones

The French term is euphemistic: these are cock's testicles, and they are found inside the bird. Chickens are castrated before they become cockerels; the result being a capon. At the time of the Renaissance in Rome, they said that the operation turned the vulgar chicken into two exceptional dishes. Gastronomy makes no mention of the testes of any other birds, despite the fact that ducks, turkey cocks, ostriches (to name but three) must have them too. In one of his songs, *Le Coq et la Pendule* (The Cock and the Clock), the French singer–songwriter Claude Nougaro dubs his amorous cockerel a 'cock's comb with testicles.'

Oh, Aziz, come with me, I will cook cock's combs and testes and other delicious things. Be aware that I have been overcome with desire for you, night and day.

The Thousand and One Nights

Rognons blancs de mouton / Sheep's balls or lamb's fry

An expression used to denote ovine testicles when, paradoxically, the sheep is no longer in possession of his prowess! It can mean the those of sheep following castration (practised at different ages according to custom), or they might have belonged to a young buck or tup following slaughter. As regards rams, they hang on to theirs as they have business to do! (See *rognons blancs*.)

Ronds / Lamb's fry

In his *200 recettes secrètes de la cuisine française* (200 Secret Recipes of French Cooking, 1965), the pseudonymous author Bifrons gives two recipes for *frivolités* (frivolities or lamb's fry) which he calls *ronds* (see the recipe below for frivolities in tomato sauce). I have seen this word nowhere else.

Sac(s) / Bags

Name given to the testicles of a living bullock.

'And you, when she asked the castrator for the bullock's bags for you to scoff in a salad!'

And later:

'Without forgetting the balls,' Lebrac said in conclusion, 'we are going to see if you have any!'
'You'll need to tie up the bag before cutting them, like they do with bullocks,' Gambette threw in; he had obviously witnessed this sort of thing.

Louis Pergaud, La Guerre des boutons *(War of the Buttons, 1912)*

Suites

A French anatomical term for wild boar's testicles.* I should point out that several dictionaries of synonyms put out by different publishers incorrectly give the word as *luites* rather than *suites*. We need to know now who copied whom!

---

* The word was included in Randle Cotgrave's *Dictionarie of the French and English Tongues*, 1611, where he translated it as 'the cods of a wild bore'. *Translator.*

Testicules / Testicles

Anatomically speaking, these are male genital glands (gonads) situated inside the scrotum, which is still called a *bourse* (purse) in French, which constitutes their external cutaneous envelope. Ignoring these details, the word testicle is generally used metonymically to denote both content and container. It is the testicles that produce spermatozoa and secrete the male hormone testosterone. The testicles of all male animals that we butcher are edible and eaten, as are those taken from cockerels. Also consumed, but in tiny quantities, are the testicles of foals and boar pigs or indeed those of a semi-mature male pig that has been castrated. These last used to be much appreciated in country districts in the old days. It is not beyond the stretch of the imagination to think that other in other latitudes they eat the testicles of different animals: donkeys, camels (the meat of the 'ship of the desert' – above all the young camel – is prized south of the Sahara, a region where it was first introduced at the beginning of the first millennium), gazelles, buffalos, bison, red deer, stags, reindeer, caribous, bears, lions (see Mythology) and kangaroos (they must pack something in their pouch!) – without even mentioning dogs in China, etc. In a word, every animal that we eat or the meat of which we consume. On the other hand, despite the proud reputation of the 'jack rabbit' as a prolific breeder, no one has ever found anywhere any trace of the rodent's balls.

Truffes / Truffles

A name given in France to bull's testicles, above all when the skin is black.

In other languages

Animelle

The Italian word *animelle* is a false friend that means 'sweetbreads', but there is often confusion between lamb's fry, bone marrow and sweetbreads, probably because they are often sold together in Italy. Proper fry are sold under the name of *granelli* (see below).

Baïdh

Name for eggs and testicles in literary Arabic, where the word means both. Other words used in speech are *soualah* and *hab echbab* (see below).

Balas

Testicles and fry in Provençal.

Batalia or Battalia pie

This was a dish described by the English author Robert May in his *Accomplisht Cook* of 1660. Its name derives from the French *béatilles* (see above). There were later English recipes, such as by John Nott (1726), Charles Carter (1730) and Eliza Smith (1730) and they all incorporate the juicy morsels implied by the word *béatilles* (the Spanish is *beatilla*). However, there is a further layer of allusion to the name inasmuch as some of these pies were dressed up in the manner of fortifications, giving the dish, and the word, a military connotation. *Translator.*

Criadillas

The word applies to all animal testicles sold by Spanish butchers.* It is not, as often thought, restricted to bull's balls. The Spaniards are very fond of this sort of food and bull's slabs (*criadillas de toro*), bullock's or calf's testicles (*criadillas de beccero*) and pig's or boar's testicles (*criadillas de cerdo*) are traditionally eaten all over Spain. My friend Isabel Calvache Gisbert tells me that the meat of the *toro de lidia* (fighting bull) is not eaten immediately away after the *corrida*, but left to rest for a few days after it has been butchered in order to rid it of both blood and toxins. The word *criadillas* comes from the verb *criar*, meaning 'create, produce, engender, feed, and breed.' The verb also gives the words *cria* (breeding farm, hatchery, litter or babe in arms), *criada* (maidservant), *criadero* (nursery, oyster-bed, stock farm, seam, deposit; and 'fertile' when employed as an adjective), and finally *criador* (creator, producer, breeder, wet-nurse). The term *criadillas* is also used for a wild mushroom typically found in the Estramadura in summer – the *jarera* or *jariega* – which is popularly called *criadilla de tierra* or *criadilla del campo* (that is, truffle or field truffle). The botanical name is *Choiromyces gangliformis* (plant in the form of a gland) and has clearly no connection with the black truffle (*Tuber melanosporum*) or indeed with the *criadillas* of a bull. The word *criadillas* is also used in French, where it has superseded old terms like *banes* and even the more usual word gonads, which has always been popular in the north of the country. It should be noted that the meat of fighting bulls has now been banned from sale in France.

Frivolity

A culinary name for lamb's fry in English [a sense not recorded in the *OED*, *Translator*].

---

* The word also means potato in Spanish, as well as truffle – see later in the paragraph. *Translator.*

Fry

Culinary name for a testicle in English, testicle being strictly anatomical. The plural is fries.

Granelli

Culinary epithet conferred on cock's stones in Italy, as well as the testicles of rams, lambs, bulls and calves. *Granelli* means little grains, and is therefore a metaphor. They are mostly eaten in the north of Italy, but in the southern Mezzogiorno lamb's fries are used in the preparation of lamb faggots. Sicilians are also fond of them.

Hab echbab

Name for lamb's fries or ram's purses in Arabic (particularly in Algeria). The word *soualah* is also used.

Huevos

A word that means eggs in Spanish, and is a synonym of *criadillas* (see above). This metaphorical usage is found extensively through the Mediterranean region (Italy, Spain and North Africa) as well as in other countries such as Germany.

Lamb's fry

Culinary term for lamb's testicles in English.

Mountain oysters

The name given by Virginian farmers in the United States to fried calf's testicles. This was confirmed for me by Valérie de Lescure, a friend of Jean Coyner, whose parents own a large ranch in Virginia. Virginia is a scattered with beef farms and crossed by a chain of mountains. They are eaten by the cowboys after the castration of the calves.

Ovette di pollo

An Italian metaphorical term for cock's stones (*ovette* means eggs), especially in Piedmont where they are often sold together with cock's combs and wattles (*creste, ovette e babigli di pollo*). In fact it would be more appropriate to say *ovette di gallo*, the testes being culled from a cock (*gallo*), not a chicken (*pollo*).

Prairie oyster

A calf's testicle in the United States. It is the preferred Canadian usage. In parts of Texas and Oklahoma, they may be called calf fries. [The *OED* records its first use as 1941. *Translator.*]

Rocky mountain oyster

As prairie oyster, above, but used more in the United States than Canada. [The *OED* records its first use as 1889. *Translator.*]

Soualah

The name given by Arabs to designate lamb's fry, particularly in Algeria. (See also *hab echbab*, above.)

Testicoli di gallo

The more usual name for cock's stones in Italian.

A little supplementary vocabulary for a better understanding of... those things!

Albuginea

The tunica albuginea is one of the two cutaneous envelopes around the testicles, more precisely the subcutaneous envelope which covers each testicle inside the scrotum, which is the external envelope, dermis or skin (cf. dermatitis). It is in fact a whitish double skin (a thick tunic reinforced by a fine membrane). In the first instance, this adjective described colour (from the Latin *albus* or white) but was recorded as an anatomical term in 1751.

Belin / Tup

A male sheep that has not yet been castrated but is not going to be used as a ram for reproductive purposes. The American word is 'buck'.

Castration / Castration

An operation which removes the testicles of a young animal in order that it will fatten more readily in consequence of his loss of virility and, therefore, his aggressive drive. In this way, its meat becomes both more tender and more abundant. In the case of mankind, the castration of a youth tends to make him obese, but was done in past centuries to inhibit his voice from breaking. This was the reason it was practised among opera singers who then became *castrati*. (See also the word 'eunuch', and the box at the end of this section.)

Chapon / Capon

A chicken that has been intentionally castrated at around four months-old to prevent him from becoming a cock and to make him fatten more readily.

Chaponner / Caponize

To emasculate a male. Generally used for chickens (see above) but can be extended to other beasts, even men.

Châtrer / Castrate, geld, neuter

In English, the verb to neuter is generally used for domestic pets such as cats and dogs. The French *châtrer* refers, as do our castrate and geld, to any animal, even a man. An exception to the rule: *châtrer* is also used to refer to the removal of the black vein in crayfish, this being the digestive tract, not its sexual organs.

Couillard / Tup

Another French epithet for an intact male sheep (see tup, above). Rabelais uses the word 'couillart' to describe a donkey:

> … voyant un âne couillart qui mangeait des chardons…
> (Seeing a big-bollocked donkey which was eating thistles…)
>
> Gargantua *(Chapter XX) 5th ed., 1542*

Dessous (les)

> The mass of fat that fills ox scrotums after castration is called the *dessous* [in French]. The *dessous* are examined as part of those tests which allow us to evaluate the living beast. Butchers pronounce the word *d'sous* ('cet animal a des d'sous!' There's some fat on this beast).
>
> Georges Chaudieu, Pour le boucher, nouveau manuel de la boucherie *(For the Butcher. A New Manual of Butchery, 1963)*

Emasculate

A synonym for castrate, and generally used for men rather than beasts. In French literature there are two verbs that owe their existence to the fate of Abelard – *abailardiser* and *abélardiser*: a reference to the state in which Canon Fulbert left Abelard:

> D'un colonel vous courtisez la femme,
> S'il vous prend, il vous abailardisera.
>
> (You court the colonel's wife, If he catches you, he'll have your balls.)
>
> *Pommereul,* Poésies, *quoted in Louis de Lande*

Epididymis

From the Greek *epi*, meaning 'on' and *didumos* or testicle: a long, narrow structure that runs along the side of the testicle that contains a serpentine canal though which spermatozoa pass. It looks like a great big vein which sticks out and runs along the testicle, but it is not a vein.

Eunuch

In the old days, there were among the Arabs and certain peoples in the Middle East and in China, men who had been willingly castrated so that they might grow up without risk of their committing adultery with women, in particular women in harems. The removal may be partial or total. There are three sorts of eunuchs: complete eunuchs (castrated in infancy), partial eunuchs (castrated after the onset of puberty) and false eunuchs (who have had their testicles removed but may still copulate). Muslims never carry out the act of castration, and the eunuchs are never Muslims themselves as Islamic law forbids castration. It is for this reason that in Islamic literature such as the *Thousand and One Nights* – we might add, the second most read Islamic book after the Koran – they speak of eunuchs having dark or black skin – not Muslims, but rather Egyptians, Somalis from Barbary, or Abyssinians.

Gamete

From the Greek *gamos*, meaning marriage, it is a reproductive cell, either male or female, at the core of which is a single chromosome of each sort and which can unite with the gamete of the opposite sex to form a zygote, but cannot do anything by itself.

Gland

An organ, the function of which is to create certain substances and secrete them either on the surface of the organism (exocrine glands) or directly into the bloodstream (endocrine glands). Testicles are male genital glands, they produce spermatozoa and secrete the male hormone called testosterone.

Neuter

In zoology or butchery, an animal that has no sex or which has lost it as a result of castration, such as an ox or a sheep.

Opotherapy or organotherapy

Is the therapeutic use of glands and animal organs in the form of pharmaceutical extracts. When this discipline first emerged, the butcher's trade furnished many opotherapeutic products, in particular, kidneys and testicles.

Raphe

The dictionary definition of the word is, 'A groove, ridge, or seam in an organ or tissue, esp. one marking a line of fusion between two halves or parts' (*NSOED*). In the case of the scrotum, it is the narrow fold which runs vertically up the middle of the outer skin.

Scrotum

The cutaneous envelope (of exterior skin or dermis) that contains the male genital organs. Each one of the glands contained within is itself covered with a subcutaneous envelope called tunica albuginea (see above).

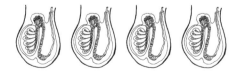

CASTRATION

He bawled like a bull that a vet was preparing to turn into an ox.
San-Antonio (Frédéric Dard), Réflexions jubilatoires sur l'existence
(Happy Thoughts on Life, 2000)

C'est Noël au harem; les eunuques rassemblés,
Écoutent les demoiselles si belles, qui gazouillent,
Le sultan entre alors et lance à l'assemblée:
Qu'elle cadeau pour Noël? Et les eunuques: Des couilles!
(It's Yuletide in the harem, the eunuchs are so glum,
Listening to the odalisques who lisp in pillared halls.
The sultan enters then and shouts to all and one
'What d'you want for Christmas?' The eunuchs say 'some balls'.)
Traditional, quoted in Maggie Paley, Le Pénis dans tous ses états (2000)

OF THE CASTRATION OF RAMS

*Beasts are castrated to make them fatten more readily and to remove the
wild and obnoxious taste of the ram; to make the flesh more tender, and
finally to obtain a wool that is at once thicker and finer.*

*Rams are castrated at any age, but it is better to do it when they are
lambs as early as the second week because the earlier you perform the
operation the smaller the risk of the animal dying. It is simply a question of
cutting open the purses and removing the testicles one after the other by
twisting the spermatic cord which is easily done. Some people then rub the
purses with lard, others simply bind the wound. It heals quite quickly. This
method is not suitable for rams of three or four years of age. They would not
survive. These you castrate by twisting the cord or by tying with a ligature.*

*The method of castration called bistournage which is achieved by
rupturing the spermatic cord is performed by seizing the testicles and
twisting them inside the scrotum two or three times, and with some force,
in such a way as to bring the bottom part of the testicle up to the top and
the top part down to the bottom. The purses are then tied up beneath
the testicles to prevent them from dropping and reassuming their natural
position. This method, which is very painful, is not without danger for the
beast.*

*Using a ligature (fouetter) is an easy method which has none of the
drawbacks of bistournage. Monsieur Bourgeois, the director of the sheep
farm at Rambouillet, recommends it highly to farmers. He has produced the
following description:*

"Rams are always treated in the morning, before feeding; it is also

better if they are not damp. The procedure is best performed in March or October.

"Having captured the ram you want to operate on, you bind his four legs in such a way that the hind legs are as close as possible to the forelegs, but without causing the beast too much pain. The ram is then laid on his back on his straw in the pen; then, with the fingers, you pull out the wool above the testicles which would otherwise obstruct the knot of the ligature. The string you use should be tough and be roughly twice as thick as an ordinary whipcord. If you have a lot of rams to castrate, it is wise to prepare the ligatures in advance. You take about two feet of cord and attach a piece of wood measuring five or six inches by two-thirds of an inch diameter to each end. Using the cord as a loop, the operator makes a tourniquet around the purse, the knot being tied one or two inches above the testes. Now, two men are placed on each side of the ram while a third holds it down. The two then pull simultaneously on each end of the ligature, holding the piece of wood in their hands and placing their feet against each other to give themselves more force; you must tighten the knot firmly and gradually, but not so hard that you sever anything but merely cut off the circulation above the ligature. After this, to make sure of the first knot, a second is tied, simply done and equally well, and the cord is cut an inch and a half from the knot; after which the beast is untied, its penis is pulled out from its sheath and the ram is made to stand on its feet. Sometimes the ligature breaks; in this case you will need to have another one ready, and apply it without removing the first. When you see rams shake themselves after this operation, it is an indication that it has been well performed. Three days later you may cut off the testicles an inch below the knot."

The flesh of sheep which have had their testicles removed when still young is a lot more pleasant that that of tups that have been castrated or corded.*

Jules Trousset, Un million de recettes, Grande encyclopédie nationale et illustrée d'économie domestique et rurale *(A Million Recipes. Complete National and Illustrated Encyclopedia of Domestic and Rural Economy), vol. II, end of the 19th century.*

* Nowadays, most male lambs are ringed not long after birth. The rings impede the blood flow to the testes, which atrophy. The modern version of the ligature is the Burdizzo clamp, an ingenious device which crushes the spermatic cord by external pressure, meaning no breaking of the skin, no blood loss and no infection. Again, deprived of their blood supply, the testes atrophy. In England, it is not permitted that the Burdizzo clamp be used on sheep more than four months old.

CASTRATING COCKS*

We owe the art of caponizing cocks to the Romans, here is how: the inhabitants of the island of Cos had shown the Romans how to fatten fowl in dark, enclosed places, and when the repute of these fattened chickens reached Rome, everyone had to have one, which forced the Consul Caius Fanius to issue a decree (as a public health measure) obliging people to rear their chickens in the streets and not inside their houses. The hens left out in the open air did not fatten up. To satisfy gourmands, a Roman veterinarian dreamt up the idea of caponizing them, which worked a treat. It is done at the age of four months, at the end of spring or the beginning of summer, and you need to choose a cool spell that is more damp than dry to castrate the chickens. The operation always takes place in the morning before the chickens have been fed. You need to equip yourself with a lancet, or some well-sharpened scissors and a needle threaded with waxed cotton. Everything should be in good condition. An assistant places the chicken on the castrator's lap on its back, with its head nearest the ground. The wings are clamped between the knees and the assistant holds it firmly with its right leg aligned along the body and the left thrown backwards, in order to expose the left side in which the incision is to be made. Then you pull out the feathers at the end of the wishbone or sternum and, using the needle as assistance, you lift the skin that runs along the inside of the thigh. Here you make a transverse incision of about four centimetres. As soon as the cut has been made, you uncover the muscle and, with a little metal hook called a surgeon's tenaculum, you lift it to separate it from the intestines. Cutting with the lancet, you can then see the peritoneum, a thin, slack, transparent membrane which covers the intestine and you make a cut big enough for you to put your finger into the belly.

If part of the intestine pops out, you need to carefully push it back into the belly, then, put your greased right-hand index finger under the intestines in the region of the kidneys, a little to the right above the croup, at the site of the final vertebra. There the finger will come across two glands the size of haricot beans. They are smooth and moveable, even if sticky. These are carefully torn off and rolled back towards the incision. It is this action that requires the greatest skill and experience, as the gland occasionally gets lost before it can be brought out and it is very difficult to find it again. If they have been taken off properly, they can stay inside the animal without too much inconvenience, but it is better to get them out.

Having sewn up the edges with a few deft stitches of waxed thread, the scar is washed with some alcohol or it can be gently rubbed with some camphor. Every time that you attempt a stitch, you need to pull out the skin with the tip of the needle in such a way as to avoid pricking the intestine, which can lead to mortal accidents. At the same time as depriving the cock of his organs, it is the practice to rid him of his other attributes, that is to say, cut off his cock's comb and his wattles.

The cock is then placed in a big open cage in a quiet spot and for the next few hours he will be given no other food than a little white bread soaked in wine. For the first few days these young capons should sleep on clean straw: if he tries to find a perch he will delay the wound's healing. The birds are kept apart for three or four days while they are being looked after, then they can be returned to their normal existence…

Farmers in Le Mans, the Maine, Bresse, Périgord and Normandy have been able to provide the best capons in Europe for many years. The breeds which should be best suited to caponization are the black chicken of Crèvecoeur, the high-legged chicken of La Flèche, the small-headed chicken of Campine, the Bresse chicken, the Spanish chicken, the Darking [Dorking] chicken and finally the red crested chicken of Houdan.

Joseph Favre, Dictionnaire universel de la cuisine, encyclopédie illustrée d'hygiène alimentaire (Universal Dictionary of Cookery, an Illustrated Encyclopedia of Dietary Hygiene, 1884)

Do you want to know how they remove them? In the Lauragais it is work they give the women. They split the skin with a razor-blade, above the anus, between the croup and the cloaca. They stick in two fingers – the index and the ring finger – which are first of all dipped in brandy. The fingers follow the spinal column until they reach the kidneys, then they seize the testicles with the finger-tips and pull. The operation is very painful and the cock, in the hands of the woman, seems to be quite dead at the end of it: its eyes half-closed, hardly breathing. This is what birds do when things are going very badly.

The cock is sewn up again with a big needle using strong thread. They apply a pommade made from charcoal to the scar.

Then they cut off the cock's comb and the wattles and cauterize the scars with a hot iron. You might ask why they do this, as the cock's comb withers away naturally with the disappearance of the sexual organs? The truth is that it is good to eat, but on the other hand, isn't it right to make a further sign that marks out those cocks that are no longer male?

Marie Rouanet, 'Le morceau de la reine' (The Queen's Morsel) in Petit traité romanesque de cuisine (1997)

---

* Surgical castration of chickens is no longer legal in Britain; nor is the chemical alternative (an oestrogen implant). Translator.

A LITTLE SAVOIR-FAIRE

A summary description

Before we begin, it should be understood that the size of testicles, fry and other *criadillas* can vary from one individual to another, just like those of men! Obviously it all depends on the age at which the beast is slaughtered.

Lamb's fries

They are ovoid and can vary in size from a small olive (when the lamb is castrated at around ten days of age) to a pigeon's egg (a lamb that has been weaned), or even a big hen's egg (a tup). They have a soft texture and can be slightly elastic. Their ivory-white colour reminds many people of lamb or veal sweetbreads. They are soft in texture and quite delicate in taste. In France, they can be bought fresh from the offal dealer (sadly, more and more rarely) or ordered in advance from an Arab butcher. I should emphasize that in order to qualify as halal* (permitted for Muslims), animals prepared for human consumption are never castrated, Islam forbidding castration for man and beast alike, because one must never denature Allah's creation.† The testicles of these halal animals are therefore always bigger – having belonged to their owner until the moment of slaughter – than those of castrated beasts which were deprived of them when their virility was in its infancy. The weight of a butchered lamb's testicle may vary by a hundred per cent: from an average 75–80 grams to 175 grams for the biggest. It should be noted that on peeling, the fry can lose anything from a quarter to a half of its weight and then a further half its weight in cooking. That means that the usual fry of 80 grams will weigh 45–50 grams when peeled and only 25–30 grams once poached. This obviously needs to be taken into account when you are thinking of quantities.

Kid's testicles

Very similar to those from a lamb, if slightly smaller. You rarely see them on sale. Kid (*cabri*) is eaten in all the scrublands where goats are bred (Poitou, Corsica, the Italian Mezzogiorno), Sardinia, etc.

---

* Or, indeed, kosher. *Translator.*
† As Abdelwahab Bouhdiba says in his thrilling essay, *La Sexualité en Islam* (Sex in Islam, 1975), 'An attack against a man's sexual faculties is as serious as an attack on life itself.'

IF IT ISN'T YOU IT WILL BE YOUR BROTHER...

There are three sorts of lamb found on the butcher's slab:

— Milk-fed lamb, not yet weaned, slaughtered at six weeks, which appears on tables around Easter-tide. The gestation occurs in the winter months, on the return from transhumance, and the births occur around February, for this reason it is still called 'Easter' or 'Paschal' lamb. It weighs seven to nine kilos.
—Spring lamb or house lamb, slaughtered between 100 and 110 days, it is fed by its mother, then by bottle. It weighs twelve to fifteen kilos.
—Grass-fed lamb, because it has begun to graze. It is slaughtered at four or five months according to breed. This is what you roast or grill in the summer. It weighs from fifteen to eighteen kilos.

As regards mutton (the adult sheep, most often castrated, except when slaughtered according to the Muslim method), it is called:

—Hog, hogget or teg, is up to eighteen months old and fed on grass, cereals and cake. It weighs twenty-five to thirty kilos. It is a young sheep and at its best in the autumn.
—A two-tooth is aged from eighteen months to two years and is fed on grass, cereals and cake. It weighs between eighteen and twenty-five kilos. It is the 'lamb' we eat in winter.
—Mutton describes the animal from its maturity to six years of age (the maximum permitted for sale in France). The carcase doesn't get bigger, but the meat is stronger and more characterful and can smell of lanolin and taste of tallow. It has its aficionados, but there is less and less of it about.

Bull's or calf's slabs,* gonads or *criadillas*

They are a little rounder and bigger than sheep's fry. Their flesh is pinkish and slightly spongy, but they are delicate and very tender to eat. They were highly esteemed in Spain (and in all countries that enjoyed the *corrida*), but now their consumption is minuscule.[†] In France, the law has banned eating the *criadillas* of any fighting bull (*toro bravo*) since 2004, on the pretext that their blood is full of toxins from the stress of the *corrida*. Bullock's testicles were also popular in

---

* Slabs (balls backwards) is an example of British butchers' slang. In the 1950s, Caribbean immigrants of the 'Windrush generation' were partial to 'cock and balls': the genital organs of bullocks, which they apparently stewed. It seems, however, that the taste for such things is now lost. *Translator.*
† They are normally to be found among the offerings of the tapas bars of Jerez de la Frontera in the far south of Spain. *Translator.*

northern France and Belgium but there, too, they are fast becoming a thing of myth, even for the celebrated *choesels* (see recipe) which is as nothing without them.

Foals' testicles

These are very difficult to find, as they are not sold in France, even in horse butchers* (it seems that you may find them in Italy in the regions where horses are bred). The reason for this is due to the fact that, in France, there is no breeding of horses for human consumption, something deplored by Michel Beaubois.[†] As he explains, 'Horses are the subject of careful breeding, but not for their meat as other animals. Yet the meat has value and not a single case of BSE has been recorded as a result of eating horse.[¶] As far as testicles are concerned, in the first place 98 per cent of the French stock that ends up on the plate is from culled animals, the majority of which are either geldings[#] or mares. This means that 85 per cent of the stock of *boucheries chevalines* is fattened abroad and imported ready-butchered. In the second place, the castration technique practised is a traditional one which does not involve the removal of the live testes. Rather, they are tied with a ligature and crushed and then you wait for them to fall off, which means you cannot eat them.' Jean-Marc Delcourt** explains for his part that the young foals are slaughtered often before their testicles have dropped (between six and eighteen months) – they are not 'ripe' – and thus cannot be recovered. It is only from the age of fifteen months (when the testicles have dropped) that stallions are selected and the other foals castrated. But at that age they are usually being brought on in other countries (in Italy and eastern Europe). Michel Beaubois does recall having occasion to eat them and found their flavour very fine.

Boar's or pig's fries

When taken from piglets, they are spherical and about the size of a large olive. They are pink, leaning to red, almost crimson in colour and they appear pearl-like and almost varnished, something that evokes cowrie shells for Valérie de Lescure.[††] They are not sold commercially in France, but in the Midi-Pyrénées

---

* *Les boucheries chevalines.* They have the advantage of being open on Mondays, when the conventional butcher is closed. They sell only horsemeat. *Translator.*
† President of the Interbev-Équins and FBHF (French Federation of Hippophagic Butchers).
¶ BSE: Bovine Spongiform Encephalopathy, or Mad Cow Disease.
# The French word for a gelding is *hongre.* The word comes from *Hongrie* or Hungary whence, it is suggested, came the custom of gelding itself. The 'h' of *hongre* is aspirated; the word is of 15th century origin. *Translator.*
** An agricultural technician specializing in heavy horses and vice-president of the FNC (Fédération national du cheval, National Horse Federation).
†† A winewriter friend of the author's.

region there is a custom whereby they are given to small boys on toast when the time comes to castrate the male piglets (see Mythology, above).* On the other hand, they are popular in Spain, where they are called *criadillas de cerdo*.

Wild boar's balls

Very similar to the testicles of a domesticated pig, but bigger, because these boars are wild and, as a result, no one castrates them. The balls of a wild boar, therefore, are almost invariably a dish cooked by sportsmen or hunters.

Cock's stones

White and smooth, they look like pigeons' eggs; to such an extent that you could almost imagine them having shells. Or you could say they resemble peeled quail eggs. The meat melts in the mouth and is very delicate. They used to be highly prized in court cookery, notably that of Louis XV's reign, and subsequently entered the canon of *cuisine bourgeoise*. Today, they have fallen from grace and are never seen, even in the making of *bouchées à la reine* and other vol-au-vent for which they were the prime ingredient in the old days.

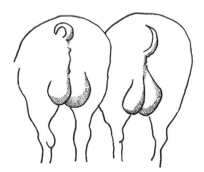

---

* They may be ordered in British butchers' shops. *Translator.*

PRELIMINARIES

Lamb's fries

Before any sort of cooking gets under way, the testicles need to be skinned (some Middle Eastern handbooks call the process 'taking the top off'). To do this, the first thing is to pull of the rather thick outer covering of skin (it turns inside out like a glove) and then the fine membrane that encases them, cutting and pulling to get it off. You can grasp it with a thin wet cloth, which makes the job easier [this is a little like the process of skinning a sole, when a cloth comes in handy too]. Once the testis is stripped, it looks like an egg. For some dishes it may be necessary to soak the fries in a mixture of vinegar and water or lemon and water, for longer or shorter depending on the recipe, or indeed simply marinate them. In some instances it may be wise to blanch them before embarking on the final cooking so that you can handle them more easily or so that they stiffen and do not break up in the dish (whether a fricassee, ragout, pâté or pie), or even to poach them in lemony water or white wine so that they become whiter and hold their form when the recipe calls for longer cooking. To blanch them, the best is to put the fries in a saucepan, cover them in cold salted water, heat them on a gentle flame and take them off the stove as soon as they begin to boil. They can also be plunged quickly in boiling water for one or two minutes before draining and refreshing in cold water, then drying them in a tea towel. To poach them, place in cold water, take them off the stove as soon as the pan begins to boil and let them poach off the heat.

You need to allot a pair of fries per person (about 100–125 grams once they have been peeled). These could serve as an hors d'oeuvre or *tapa* or a light main course. Allow two pairs (200–250 grams per person) to garnish a risotto or a main course like a tajine. Before their final preparation, they should be dried with a cloth or kitchen paper, then cut into more or less thick slices (in order to sauté them) or cut in quarters (fillings) or chop them (to grill or simmer). To turn them in the pan during cooking, I recommend a flexible spatula because they might be broken by a fork.

Criadillas

Since 2004, French law has banned the the sale of *criadillas* that derive from fighting bulls (*toros bravos*) due to the toxins (principally adrenaline) secreted during the *corrida*. The *criadillas* that you buy in Spain are sold pre-prepared and ready to cook.

Wild boar's balls

Boar's balls are not sold commercially, and one might suppose that they contain toxins too, as the animal also experiences stress during the hunt. That in no way prevents hunters from consuming them 'at gun point' during hunting trips, not even bleeding them first.

Cock's stones

In some earlier cookery books for example *Le livre de cuisine de Madame E. Saint-Ange* (1927; translated by Paul Aratow in 2005 as *La Bonne Cuisine de Madame de Saint-Ange*) it is said that the gonads should be allowed to soak in cold water for 24 hours and there is no need to skin them, but simply to remove the stringy bits. Nowadays, they are generally ready to cook when you find them. They are also sold in tins (by good grocers in France) generally mixed with cock's combs and with veal or lamb sweetbreads, either properly labelled or simply called 'garnish for bouchées à la reine'. I would advise you to look at the ingredients on the label, however, as lots of brands substitute the testes with little egg dumplings.

FREEZING BALLS

It is not easy to find lamb's fry in the shops, but if you order them, it may be that you manage to procure a decent quantity in one go. If this happens, don't hesitate to freeze them by wrapping each testicle individually in clingfilm.

To use them, all you need do is pop them out of their wrappers, put them in a saucepan of cold water and heat them without boiling. As soon as the water is hot (no hotter than you can stand when testing it with your finger), take the saucepan off the stove and let the fries defrost in the water. In this way they recover their natural state without being actually cooked. Now drain them and peel them.

Some prefer to prepare them before freezing. To do this, once you have removed their skin, cut them in slices, dice or batons, and spread them on a large plate or tray. Cover with aluminium foil and put them into a freezer for three hours. After that, put them in a suitable storage box, separating each layer with a piece of greaseproof, or Cellophane such as you use for jam jars, or clingfilm. Seal the box, label it and return it to the freezer. When you have done them this way, you don't need to defrost as a preliminary but can proceed to frying in some butter, on a fairly high heat, for about a minute each side, and then again for two or three minutes, without forgetting to season them.

COOKING IN FLOUR OR BREADCRUMBS

You can simply sauté the fries in butter in a pan, and this is very good, particularly if you develop it into a fricassee by basting the offal with stock, white wine, sherry, beer, vermouth or vinegar, which will then form the basis for a sauce. While we are on the subject, I would advise that you do not stint on butter – doing the same as you would for all delicate foods – lest they dry out. A good hunk of foaming butter is much better than a little knob which will blacken too quickly, and all you need to do is eliminate the excess at the end of the cooking. In the north of France or in Belgium, where they like bullock's bollocks, they are happy to use lard which has the advantage of not blackening.

To dry their surface before frying, the usual thing is to dredge them in a little flour. However, flour has a tendency to stick, and it colours in cooking. This can leave a bitter taste.

It is perhaps better to follow the Asian technique of dredging them with potato flour. This is lighter than wheat flour and doesn't discolour.

Some prefer a coating of breadcrumbs before frying. For me, this is the best. In one fell swoop you keep a delicacy of flavour and a succulent texture.

The classic method is to dip the fries in beaten egg, then in home-made soft breadcrumbs (please avoid ready-made breadcrumbs which taste of rusk and make for a crude coating which lumps up and blackens in the pan). You can mix something extra into the breadcrumbs according to taste: spices, chopped parsley and garlic [persillade à la française], crumbled dried chilli, freshly grated Parmesan, lemon or orange zest (not waxed), powdered almonds, chopped herbs, etc.

For myself, I would advise a method somewhere between the two – neither flour nor breadcrumbs. Dredge the fries in some fine semolina, and use the old Italian method (see recipe). The result is astonishing: the fries themselves are juicy and melt in the mouth, while at the same time protected by a delicately crunchy crust which adds another level of subtlety.

RECIPES

Sheep's testicles or lamb's fries

Almost all recipes for lamb's fries can also be made with calf's testicles, or even cock's stones.

Fries *à l'italienne* (with a semolina coating)

Slice two pairs of prepared fries in half-centimetre thick pieces. Put them in a terrine along with salt, chopped parsley, thyme, onions cut in rounds, crushed black pepper, oil and lemon, let them marinate for several hours stirring them from time to time.

Dry them in a cloth, dredge them in semolina, pressing to make sure that it sticks to the fries. Place them on a saucepan lid, and just before the time comes to serve them, fry them in some reasonably hot oil. Scatter them with salt and drain them in a cloth, serve in a napkin as for a *croustade*. Top them with fried sprig of parsley and a lemon.

Joseph Favre, Dictionnaire universel de cuisine

Fries *à la crème*

Cut them into thin slices. Season them with salt and pepper. Cook them in butter. When they are cooked, add a few spoonfuls of cream sauce. Let them simmer on a low flame. At the last moment, add a little crème fraîche and fresh butter. Mix well. Prepared in this way, the fries are generally used as part of the garnish for *bouchées*, *croustades*, pies or vol-au-vent. When that is indeed the case, you may add mushrooms or truffles.

Prosper Montagné, Larousse gastronomique

Fries *à la crème* with freshly grated truffles

To turn this hors d'oeuvre into a main course, double the proportions and, if needs be, stretch the fries by adding lamb's sweetbreads. They can be served in a nest of fresh pasta or a risotto (in this case, grate some white truffle over it and serve with some fresh shavings of Parmesan).

Serves two: 3 pairs of prepared lamb's fries
100 g butter
200 ml single cream
1 fresh truffle
nutmeg, fine salt, and pepper from the mill

Blanch the testicles by putting them in a saucepan filled with cold salted water, bring to the boil, remove from the heat at once and drain them. Refresh them in cold water, wipe dry and cut them in chunks or cubes.

Melt some butter in a sauteuse, toss in the fries, add salt and pepper and let them cook in gently foaming butter for 5 minutes, turning them from time to time. Meanwhile, pour the cream into a small saucepan with some salt, pepper and nutmeg and reduce over a low heat until a velvety consistency.

To serve, arrange the fries on a very hot plate (dish them with a slotted spoon to avoid taking the butter with them), and crown them straight away with the cream. Carefully mix in order to properly coat them.

Grate a carefully brushed truffle (don't bother to peel it) over the plate. It will be the task of the first guest to gently mix the dish before it is served.

Fries in the manner of Alexandre Dumas

Have ready two sets of fries, of which you have removed the skins, cut in fillets the length of a little finger but only half as thick; marinate them in lemon juice, salt, pepper, some sprigs of parsley and some spring onions; drain them when you are ready, dredge them in flour, fry them until they are crisp and serve.

Alexandre Dumas, Grand dictionnaire de la cuisine *(Great Dictionary of Cookery, 1873)*

Fries *à la vinaigrette, ravigotée* or not

Cooking them in a 'blanc' brightens up fries, which otherwise tend to be a bit grey. Even simpler would be to poach them in boiling water with or without lemon juice.

Serves four:	6 pairs of prepared lamb's fries	a sprig of thyme
	2 tbsp white wine vinegar	a bay leaf
	or lemon juice	a small branch of celery
	an onion	3 sprigs flat-leaf parsley
	2 cloves	1 tbsp rock salt
	the white part of a leek	a dozen peppercorns
	a carrot	
Vinaigrette:	2 tbsp vinegar	
	6 tbsp oil	
	sea salt and a twist of black pepper	

Vinaigrette ravigotée:

the vinaigrette
1 little onion or 2 shallots, chopped
1 tbsp capers
1 tbsp chopped mixed herbs (parsley, chervil, tarragon and chives)

First of all make a 'blanc', i.e. a *court-bouillon* thickened with flour. Bring two litres of water to the boil in a large saucepan (you need to use a wide pan because when it boils the blanc rises and boils over like milk, thick aluminium is generally recommended). While the water heats, whisk together the flour and the white wine vinegar or the juice of a lemon with 100 ml cold water. Make sure you don't leave any lumps. Pour the mixture into the boiling water through a sieve, beating vigorously for 5 minutes, which is the time required to ensure that the flour, cooking all the while, remains in suspension in the liquid rather than falling to the bottom of the pan. The emulsion must be very light. Add the onion cut into quarters, one of which must be studded with the cloves, the chopped up leek, the carrot cut into slices, the celery, thyme, bay, parsley, salt and pepper. Cook for 20 minutes then allow it to cool.

When it is tepid, whisk it again to maintain the emulsion and then add the testicles. Heat it until it is just beginning to boil then take it off the flame and allow them to cool down in the blanc.

To make the vinaigrette, in a big bowl or a little salad bowl, first dissolve a good pinch of salt in the vinegar. Pour in the oil in a thin stream beating at the same time to make an emulsion. Finish off by adding a few twists of pepper. Mix again before serving.

To make a vinaigrette ravigotée, add the very finely chopped onion or the shallots, the capers and the herbs to the vinaigrette and allow it to sit for 30 minutes.

To serve: strain the fries carefully (take them out with a slotted spoon and dry them on a cloth) and cut them up into batons, cubes or slices, as you like. Put them in a salad bowl and baste them with the sauce you have chosen. Mix them carefully and serve at once,

Note 1: the *court-bouillon* can be flavoured with a glass of white wine, some dry or fino sherry or even white or dry vermouth. Whatever, you will need to do this before you add the fries.

Note 2: for the vinaigrette it is important to start with the salt so that it can dissolve in the vinegar. If you do it later the crystals will remain on the tongue.

Lamb's fries with ham *à l'italienne*

The testicles can be mixed with lamb's brain or sweetbreads. This little ragout is served with a garnish of peas or artichoke hearts cooked in butter.

Serves four:

4–6 pairs of prepared lamb or milk-fed lamb fries	1 small onion
80 g prosciutto or Parma ham	100 ml veal or chicken stock
100 g butter	salt, freshly ground black pepper

To blanch the fries, put them in a saucepan filled with salted water, bring to the boil and then remove from the heat and drain. Refresh with cold water, dry the fries with kitchen paper and cut into large pieces.

Melt 80 g butter in a sauteuse and sweat the coarsely chopped ham and the finely sliced onion. Add the fries, salt and pepper, cover and let it cook over a gentle flame for 10 minutes, turning from time to time. During the cooking, baste the fries with a little hot stock to prevent the dish from drying out. When they are ready, arrange them on a hot serving dish and keep it warm.

Using a whisk, beat the cooking juices with the rest of the butter added in small knobs. If the consistency of the sauce is too fluid, add a pinch of flour, if it is too thick, on the other hand, mix in a bit of stock. When it begins to bubble, pour it over the fries. Serve at once, if possible with its customary garnish of peas or artichokes.

Lamb's fries with green peppercorns

Serves four: 4–6 pairs of prepared lamb's fries
200 ml meat or very concentrated chicken stock (if possible
add meat or chicken jus)
2 tbsp green peppercorns (either fresh or in brine)
100 ml crème fraîche
100 g butter
fine sea salt

Pour the stock into a saucepan and heat it until it begins to boil; add the peppercorns (draining them if in brine and removing the stalks if necessary) and the cream. Let it reduce over a medium heat until the texture is velvety.

While the sauce is reducing, cut the fries in two lengthways. Let the butter melt in a sauteuse and quickly brown them on both sides, then strain them and put them aside while you rinse and dry the sauteuse. Replace the fries in the clean pan and cover with the pepper sauce. Let them simmer for 7–8 minutes on a gentle heat. To serve, turn them into a deep, hot dish. They should be accompanied by rice.

Lamb's fries with mushrooms

Cut the fries in slices and cook them in stock to which you have added the necessary seasonings and some white wine.

Make a *blanquette* sauce with the cooking juices and add the essence of fresh mushrooms. Bind the sauce with good butter and egg yolks and pass it through a sieve or a *chinois*. Put the fries and the mushrooms into the sauce.

Cook rice in some stock and put it into a ring mould. Turn the rice out and in the centre pour the blanquette of fries with mushrooms.

Joseph Favre, Dictionnaire universel de cuisine

Sautéed lamb's fries

Prepare the testicles of a young ram, cut them into slices and season them with salt, crushed black peppercorns and lemon juice. Marinate them for ten minutes. Dry them on a kitchen cloth, fry them at a high heat for just two minutes, place them in a sieve and rinse them in very cold water. Place them in a saucepan containing *maître d'hôtel* butter, and add a third of its volume in meat glaze, the juice of a lemon and tiny piece of chilli. Bind it by heating it and serve it on hot plates.

This is a delicious luncheon dish and much better than sautéed kidneys.

Joseph Favre, Dictionnaire universel de cuisine

Lamb's fries marinated and fried, with citrus fruits

Serves four: 3–4 pairs of lamb's fries   oil for deep-frying
               2 lemons   fine sea salt
               1 orange   freshly ground black pepper
               flour

Flatten the prepared fries as if for an escalope, sprinkle them with the juice of one lemon and let them marinate for an hour. Wipe them with a cloth and dust them with flour, just enough to dry them. Drop them one by one into the frier (heated to 175°C), and remove with a slotted spoon as soon as they come to the surface. Drain them on paper towels.

To serve, arrange the fries on a dish, add salt and pepper and ring them with thin slices of well-peeled orange and lemon (pips removed).

Sautéed lamb's fries *en persillade*

Serves four: 4–6 pairs of lamb's fries   100 g butter
               2 cloves garlic   100 ml crème fraîche
               8–12 sprigs of flat-leaf parsley   fine sea salt
               200 ml vinegar   freshly ground black pepper

To prepare the persillade, peel the garlic and chop together with the parsley.

Put a litre of water together with the vinegar into a saucepan, heat it until begins to simmer. Turn down the heat and put in the lamb's fries, blanching them for one minute. Drain them straightaway and refresh them with cold water. Cut them into thick slices and dry them with kitchen paper or a cloth. Rub them with salt and pepper.

Melt some butter in a frying-pan and add the testicles. Cook them for a minute on each side in the foaming butter. Scatter the persillade over the pan and cook for another minute on each side. Pour the cream into the pan, add a little salt and pepper, and let it simmer until you achieve a velvety consistency. During this process, carefully turn the fries once or twice (with a flexible spatula or a fork). Serve on pre-heated plates.

Balas à la provençal, **as an apéritif**

Serves four: 4 lamb's fries [*balas* in Provençal] oil for deep-frying
                200 g fine soft breadcrumbs   2 lemons
                   or dried crumbs   fine sea salt
                2 eggs   freshly ground white pepper
                1 tbsp crème fraîche

Remove the membrane surrounding the testicles and rinse them in cold water in which you have added a dash of vinegar or lemon juice. Drain and dry and cut into slices 5 mm thick. Spread out the breadcrumbs on a flat plate. Beat the eggs as for an omelette in a bowl together with the cream.

Lightly season the slices with salt and pepper, dip them in the egg mixture then turn them in the breadcrumbs, making sure both sides are covered.

Next drop them in the hot oil, which should not be smoking (175°C) and fry them for 2–3 minutes on each side until they are golden. Dry them on paper towels.

To serve, arrange them in a pyramid on a hot plate and surround them with lemon quarters.

Note: double the quantities if you wish to serve the *balas* as a main course. They can be accompanied by a fresh tomato sauce.

'Frivolity Fritters', or beignets of lamb's fries

Serves four to six:
                1 kg prepared lamb's fries
                oil for deep-frying
                2 lemons, in quarters

Marinade: 50 ml olive oil   juice of 1 lemon
                some sprigs of herbs (flat parsley, chervil, tarragon, chives)
                fine sea salt, freshly ground white pepper

Fritter batter: 170 g flour   2 egg whites
                200 ml lager or white wine   20 g butter, melted
                4 egg yolks   fine sea salt, black pepper

Blanch the fries by dropping them in a pan filled with salted cold water. Bring to the boil then remove from the flame, drain and refresh them in cold water. Dry them in a cloth or on kitchen paper and cut them into slices 5 mm thick.

Put the fries in a dish and add salt and pepper, oil, the lemon juice and some finely chopped herbs. Mix well and leave to stand for an hour in a cool place.

To make the fritter batter: sieve the flour into a mixing bowl and add a good pinch of salt. Make an indentation in the centre and pour in the melted butter and the egg yolks. Working with a wooden spoon, gradually incorporate the wine or beer until you have a smooth paste of coating consistency. Leave it to rest until you need it.

When you have a moment, beat the egg whites until stiff and fold them into the fritter batter.

Heat the oil in the fryer until it is boiling but not smoking (175°C).

One by one, dip the testicle slices in the batter, and drop them into the hot oil. Let them turn golden on both sides. When the fritters are properly golden, take them out with a slotted spoon and dry them on kitchen paper.

Serve them hot with lemon quarters.

Blanquette of lamb's fries with mushrooms

Serves four:
6 pairs of prepared fries	the white of a leek
a dash of vinegar	1 carrot
200 ml dry white wine	80 g butter
1 small onion	juice of 2 lemons
1 clove	1 level tbsp flour
bouquet garni (a sprig of thyme, half a bay leaf, a little branch of celery, four sprigs of flat-leaf parsley)	2 egg yolks
	200 ml crème fraîche
	8 sprigs of flat-leaf parsley
	nutmeg
250 g button mushrooms	fine sea salt and freshly ground white pepper

Prepare the fries and soak them for 10 minutes in a bowlful of cold water with a dash of vinegar.

Put the fries in a saucepan with the white wine and the bouquet garni. Add the onion cut into in quarters (one studded with the clove). Add just enough water to cover them (not more) and gently heat until it begins to boil. Take it off the flame at once and allow it to continue cooking for 10 minutes off the heat.

Clean the mushrooms and cut them into pieces, put them in a pan with half the butter and the juice of 1 lemon, cover and allow to stew for 10 minutes, shaking the pan from time to time.

Peel and wash the leek and carrot. Chop the leek finely and grate the carrot.

Melt the rest of the butter in a casserole. Sweat the leek and carrot without letting them colour, but enough to soften. Add salt, pepper and a little grated nutmeg.

Meanwhile, drain the fries, reserving the cooking liquid, wipe them dry, then cut them into large dice. Pass the stock through a sieve.

Add the flour to the vegetables, mix and cook without letting it colour, pour in the strained cooking liquid, stir and simmer it until it has a velvety consistency (the sauce should not be as thick as a béchamel), stirring constantly with a wooden spoon.

Off the heat, add the lamb's fries together with the drained mushrooms. Mix well. Take a bowl and make a liaison of the egg yolks with the cream and the juice of the second lemon. Stir in the chopped parsley. Add this to the casserole, put it back on a gentle heat and warm it through thoroughly. Do not let it boil.

Present the blanquette in a hot deep bowl.

Note: you may use anything left over to garnish ramekins (see the recipe below, p. 103).

Tuscan-style kebabs of lamb's fries

Serves four:
4 pairs of prepared fries	juice of 1 lemon
8 chicken livers	a sprig of fresh thyme
fine sea salt	freshly ground black pepper
100 ml olive oil	32 sage leaves

Blanch the fries by putting them in a pan filled with salted cold water which you bring to the boil before taking it off the heat. Drain the fries and refresh them in cold water. Dab them dry with a cloth or kitchen paper and cut them into two or three pieces.

Prepare the chicken livers and quarter or halve them.

Put the fries in a bowl with half the oil, the lemon juice, salt and pepper. Turn them in the marinade. Put the chicken livers in another dish with the rest of the oil, the leaves of the thyme and some pepper (do not add salt as that will draw the blood out of the livers). Turn these over likewise. Leave the dishes to marinate for an hour in a cool place.

Remove the fries and the livers from their respective marinades and put them on the skewers separating them with sage leaves.

Cook the skewers for 6 minutes on hot coals, but not too hot. Turn the skewers from time to time to prevent the meats from becoming rubbery. Serve once they are cooked.

Note: you can wrap each piece of liver in a thin slice of bacon.

'Brochettes of Honour' of sheep's balls as in the Maghreb

In North Africa, the testicles (the sheep's 'eggs' or *oeufs*) are thought the daintiest morsel, often reserved for the guest of honour. This is especially the case when the whole beast is cooked in a *méchoui* or when there is someone at the feast to whom they wish to show their respect.

Serves four: 4 pairs of prepared lamb's fries   ½ tsp ground black pepper
              3 tbsp olive oil   ½ tsp ground cumin
              juice of 1 lemon   4 sprigs flat-leaf parsley
              ½ tsp fine sea salt   4 sprigs fresh coriander

Cut the fries into cubes roughly 4 cm square.

Put them in a dish with the olive oil, the lemon juice, salt, pepper, cumin, parsley and finely chopped coriander. Mix well and allow to stand for an hour in a cool place.

When the hour is up, put the dice on skewers (about 8 or 12 on each skewer)

Cook these for 5–6 minutes on hot coals, turning them often in the course of the cooking so that the 'eggs' remain juicy.

Serve hot with little salads and vegetable '*méchouia*' (grilled vegetables).

Note: if you want you may put a tiny bit of chilli with the spices in the marinade.

Skewers of lamb's fries cooked in the Iranian style

Serves four: 4 pairs of prepared lamb's fries
              fine sea salt and freshly ground black pepper

Cut the fries into 4 cm cubes, rinse and drain them and put them on skewers.

Add generous amounts of salt and pepper.

Cook the skewers for about 6 minutes on hot coals turning from time to time in the course of the cooking.

Serve piping hot.

It is the simplest of things, without artifice, but is delicious.

Skewers of marinated and grilled lamb's fries *à la marocaine*

Serves eight: 1 kg of prepared lamb's fries   1 tbsp sweet paprika or *pimentón*
50 ml olive oil   ¼ tsp hot *pimentón*
1 bunch of flat-leaf parsley   1 tbsp ground cumin
3 cloves of garlic   ½ tsp salt

Cut the prepared lamb's fry into cubes of 2 centimetres.

Put them in a dish with the oil, finely chopped parsley, the peeled and crushed garlic and all the spices (mild and strong *pimentón*, cumin and salt), mix well and leave to stand for 2 hours in a cool place. When this time has elapsed, thread the fries onto skewers (approximately 8–12 on each skewer). Cook the skewers on hot coals, but not too hot, turning them from time to time in the course of the cooking, which should take 5 minutes at the most. The fries should seize and become firm, but should still be juicy in the middle.

Serve hot with little vegetable salads and mint tea.

'Bollocks in the nest' (an appetizer)

Serves two: 1 pair of lamb's fries   2 tbsp crème fraîche
100 ml strong veal or chicken   1 small jar of truffle peelings
stock (if possible, beef it up   (optional)
with a soupspoon of chicken   1 tbsp grated Parmesan
jus from the roasting pan)   1 egg yolk
50 ml Sauternes or sweet wine   nutmeg, fine sea salt
20 g butter   freshly ground white pepper
1 tsp flour   2 little *brioches à tête**

Place the fries in a saucepan with the stock. Bring to the boil then take it off the flame and let them poach for a further 10 minutes in the hot stock. Remove them with a slotted spoon, dry them and cut them into little cubes. Strain the stock through a chinois or sieve.

Rinse the pan and pour the stock back in, add the Sauternes and reduce by half.

Preheat the oven to 180°C (Gas 6).

Melt the butter over a gentle flame in a small pan. Toss in the fries and stir to cover them with melted butter. Sprinkle them with flour, stir them gently without letting them brown. Pour the stock over them and stir carefully until it thickens.

---

* *Brioches à tête* are the classic Parisian shape for brioche buns, rather akin to the cottage loaf shape that used to be a favourite of British bakery; in other words, with a topknot. *Translator.*

Taking the dish off the heat, fold in the cream and adjust the seasoning with salt and pepper; grate a little nutmeg and finally add in the roughly chopped truffle peelings (if you are using them), the grated Parmesan and the egg yolk.

Remove the tops of the brioches and excavate the crumb, leaving a shell a couple of centimetres round their perimeters. Add some of this excavated crumb to the mixture, but not too much to make it stodgy or too thick. Fill the brioches with the mixture. Do not put the heads back on (but they can be heated at the same time). Pack the brioches in a little oven dish.

Place them in the middle of the oven and allow them to bake for just 5 minutes.

When you take them out of the oven, put a brioche (and possibly a hat) on each plate. Eat at once.

Fricassee of fries and sweetbreads with *vin jaune* and morels

To make an even more festive meal, add some green asparagus tips quickly seized in butter and a dozen large oysters, drained and likewise quickly seized in butter. If you wish, the *vin jaune* can be replaced by any white wine, or even by champagne.* You may also make the fricassee into a pie-filling but you will need to thicken the roux by using a tablespoonful of flour instead of a teaspoonful.

Serves four:	500 g prepared lamb's fries	juice of 2 lemons
	500 g lamb's sweetbreads	200 ml *vin jaune*
	250 g fresh morels or	a little flour
	125 g dried ones	200 ml thick crème fraîche
	the white part of a leek	2 egg yolks
	4 shallots	8 sprigs flat-leaved parsley
	150 g butter	nutmeg, fine sea salt
		freshly ground white pepper

If you are using dried morels, put them in a bowl filled with warm water and rehydrate them until you are ready to use them. If they are fresh, they need to be properly cleaned: wash them in several waters, cutting them into four if they are big. Put to one side.

The sweetbreads should have been soaked in water for a couple of hours to get rid of any blood. Blanch them separately: put thee fries and sweetbreads in pans filled with cold salted water and bring to a simmer. Take off the stove immediately and drain them before refreshing them in cold water. Drain the testicles, dry with kitchen paper and cut them into large dice. Dredge the sweetbreads in a little flour to dry them.

---

* *Vin jaune* is a white wine from the Jura region that resembles sherry, although it is not fortified. It is made from the Savagnin grape and matures under a veil of yeast like the *flor* of sherry. *Translator.*

Melt 50 g of butter in a pan and lightly brown the sweetbreads. Drain them and put them to one side.

Put the morels (fresh or drained and rinsed) in a pot with 50 g of butter and the juice of a lemon, cover and stew for 10 minutes, shaking the pan from time to time.

Peel and wash the leek, slice it finely, along with the shallots. Sweat them together in a casserole with 50 g butter. Don't let them colour.

Add the fries to the pan and cook them on all sides, then add the sweetbreads. Sprinkle in a level teaspoonful of flour and stir gently with a wooden spoon. Moisten with the *vin jaune*, add the morels and their juices, and allow to simmer until you have a velvety texture (the sauce should be runny and not as thick as a béchamel). Keep stirring with the wooden spoon.

Take a bowl and make a liaison with the cream, egg yolks, salt, pepper, nutmeg and the juice of the second lemon. Fold in the chopped parsley.

Add this to the casserole and stir it until it just begins to simmer, but on no account let it boil.

To serve, pour it into a preheated bowl and make sure the plates are also hot.

Fritters* of lamb's fries with tartar sauce or *sauce gribiche*

Serve these fritters with a crunchy crouton salad. The croutons can be rubbed with garlic. An alternative is to serve them with a tomato sauce.

Serves six:	12 prepared fries	juice of 1 lemon
	2 shallots	oil for deep-frying
	12 sprigs flat-leaf parsley	fine sea salt
	50 ml olive oil	freshly ground black pepper
Fritter batter:	200 g flour	1 tsp vegetable oil
	pinch of fine sea salt	1 egg
	½ sachet instant yeast	200 ml water
Tartar sauce:	1 very fresh egg yolk	fine sea salt
	1 tsp strong Dijon mustard	freshly ground black pepper
	150–200 ml vegetable oil	6 middle-sized gherkins
	1 tbsp wine vinegar or	2 tbsp small capers
	lemon juice	a few blades of chives

---

* Typically, the French have a specialized word for these fritters: *fritots*. *Larousse Gastronomique* defines *fritots* as a sort of beignet made with small pieces of meat (escalopes of chicken, sweetbreads, lamb's fry, etc.) which have usually been cooked and marinated beforehand. *Translator.*

Sauce gribiche: 1 bowl of tartar sauce
              1 hard-boiled egg
              a few leaves of tarragon.

Cut each lamb's fry into four slices and put them in a terrine with chopped shallots and parsley. Add the oil, lemon juice, salt and pepper. Mix well and leave to marinate for an hour.

To make the batter, blend the flour, salt and yeast in a mixing bowl and make a well in the centre. Separate the white and yolk of one egg. Set aside the white and add the yolk and the oil to the flour. Then pour into the well 200 ml of lukewarm water and gradually mix all this into the flour, working with a fork. Put to one side until needed.

To make the tartar sauce: mix together the egg yolk and the mustard in a bowl then, as if making a mayonnaise, add the oil drop by drop at first and then in a thin stream, whisking all the while (in the same direction) until you reach saturation point. When the mayonnaise is properly stiff, add salt, pepper and the vinegar or lemon juice (which will whiten and slightly liquefy the mayonnaise). Then add the coarsely chopped gherkins, the capers (which should be properly dry) and the finely chopped chives. Mix and keep in a cool place.

For the *sauce gribiche,* prepare a bowl of tartar sauce. Chop up a hard-boiled egg and a few tarragon leaves. Mix these in, leave in a cool place.

When the moment arrives, heat the oil in the deep-fryer so that it is boiling but not smoking (175°C). While the oil is heating, fold the egg-white (beaten to a stiff foam) into the batter, and strain the fries from the marinade.

Dip each side of the fries in the batter, and then drop into the oil. Let each slice brown on both sides, remove with a slotted spoon and drain on kitchen paper. Do about six fritters at a time so as not to let the oil get cold.

Serve with the sauce you have chosen.

'Frivolities' with tomato sauce

From your butcher or offal butcher buy some sheep's testicles. Get rid of the membrane attached to them and the nerve [or sinew] that is sometimes still connected. Cut them in two. Put them in rock salt for half an hour. Rinse. Then, in a copper-bottomed sauteuse, make a proper white roux (oil, onion, flour, and a drop of water). Turn up the heat and slowly cook a skinned and pipped tomato. Now put in the 'balls', adding the juice of two lemons. Add salt and pepper and cover with lukewarm water. Let it simmer until it is well reduced.

Balls* are far more delicate than calf's sweetbreads.

Bifrons, 200 recettes secrètes de la cuisine française

'Frivolities' of La Villette (Lamb's fries crumbed and fried)

'Frivolities' were one of the favourite mid-morning snacks of the butchers working in the main Paris abattoir at La Villette, along with some other offal dishes such as calf's head or tripe.

Serves two:	2 pairs of prepared lamb's fries	100 g butter
	flour	fine sea salt
	soft crumbs from stale bread	freshly ground black pepper
	2 eggs	1 lemon

The fries can be blanched or not, a question of taste.

Cut the fries into escalopes 3–4 mm thick. Rub each one with salt and pepper and then dredge them in flour to dry them.

Make some breadcrumbs and spread them on a dish. In another bowl, beat the eggs as for an omelette, adding a little salt and pepper.

Dip the fries twice in the eggs and then twice in the breadcrumbs to make sure they are thickly coated.

Heat the butter in a biggish frying-pan on a medium flame, but don't let it colour. Quickly fry the escalopes on both sides, a minute on each, then repeat until the coating is golden. To turn the slices, it is best to use a flexible spatula because you might break them with a fork.

Serve very hot, with lemon quarters.

---

* The word Bifrons uses is *ronds*. Usually, the noun means a disc or circle, although the adjective may have spherical as well as circular connotations. *Translator.*

Joyeuses de l'ami Roger (Alain Chapel's recipe)

The celebrated chef, the late Alain Chapel, created the Confrérie des joyeuses (The Brotherhood of Joys) under the aegis of his friend Roger Reuther, a miller by profession, who maintains that he performed the duties of 'Grand Chamberlain'. It was the custom for the members to meet around 8 o'clock on a Saturday morning to eat testicles [the *joyeuses* of the title] when the chef returned from the market. They were cooked according to the recipe given by Chapel in his book *La Cuisine, c'est beaucoup plus que des recettes* (Cooking, it's More than Recipes, 1980).

Serves three: 6 sheep's fries   2 lemons
              a sprig of thyme   salt, pepper
              a bay leaf   200 g butter

Remove the membrane surrounding the fries (or ask your butcher); blanch them for a minute in boiling water.

Refresh them, then poach gently for 15 minutes in a saucepan of salted water, with the thyme, bay, and a few slices of lemon. Dry them on a kitchen towel then cook them like fish, in a small porcelain dish such as you would use for eggs en cocotte, in butter for 5 minutes.

At the moment of serving, add the juice of a lemon; they can also be served with chopped parsley or a few capers.

Red and white kidney kebabs

[The name of the dish depends on the French euphemisim for lamb's fry, *rognons blancs* (white kidneys), here combined with real (red) kidneys (*rognons rouges*). *Translator.*]

Serves four: 500 g prepared lamb's kidneys   8 sprigs of fresh coriander
            500 g prepared lamb's fries   ½ tsp fine sea salt
            250 g lamb's kidney suet   ½ tsp ground black pepper
            2 tbsp olive oil   grated nutmeg
            8 sprigs of flat-leaf parsley

Chop the kidneys, fries and suet in 2-cm dice. Mix them all up in a bowl, add the oil, the finely chopped herbs and the seasonings (salt, pepper and a generous grating of nutmeg). Mix thoroughly and let it stand in a cool place for 2 hours. When the time has elapsed, thread the squares onto skewers, alternating fries, kidneys and suet. Cook for 5–6 minutes on charcoal, which should not be too hot, turning them often so that the fat coats the kidneys and fries and stops them drying out. Serve very hot.

Lamb's fry as cooked in the Lebanon

Serves six:
600 g lamb's fries
3 tbsp olive oil
fine sea salt, freshly ground black pepper

Sauce:
3 tbsp olive oil
juice of 1 lemon
1 clove of garlic

a pinch of chilli or cayenne
4 sprigs of flat-leaf parsley
1 sprig of fresh mint

Skin the lamb's fry, cut them in two lengthways and then in two widthways.

Heat the oil in a frying-pan. Toss in the fry and sauté, adding salt and pepper.

When they are done, dry them on kitchen paper and put them in a bowl.

Finish them with the oil, lemon juice, the peeled and crushed garlic and the chilli powder or cayenne pepper, mix well and scatter with parsley and mint, both finely chopped.

Lamb's fry grilled with garlic and lemon, Lebanese style

Serves six:
600 g lamb's fries
vinegar

olive oil
fine sea salt
freshly ground black pepper

Sauce:
2 garlic cloves
6 tbsp olive oil
juice of 1 lemon

fine sea salt
freshly ground black pepper
fresh mint leaves

Skin the lamb's fries. Soak them in water acidulated with vinegar for 2 hours. When this time has elapsed, drain them and toss them into a pan filled with lightly salted boiling water. Poach them for a few minutes at a simmer.

Drain the fries, refresh them in cold water and then carefully dry them. Cut them in two lengthways and brush them with olive oil before putting them onto skewers.

Grill the skewers on hot coals, turning them often in the course of the cooking to stop them from drying out. Add salt and pepper in moderation.

While you are grilling the skewers, make the sauce: peel and crush the garlic cloves in a bowl and add salt and pepper. Add the oil and the juice of a lemon. Whisk well to make an emulsion.

To serve, present the skewers piping hot together with the sauce and the mint leaves.

Poached lamb's fry with tahini, Lebanese style

Serves six: 600 g lamb's fries
                 vinegar
                 fine sea salt

Sauce: 3–4 tbsp tahini   fresh mint leaves
                 1 lemon (optional)

Skin the lamb's fry. Soak them in water acidulated with vinegar for 2 hours. When this time has elapsed, drain them and toss them into a pan filled with lightly salted boiling water. Poach them for a few minutes at a simmer.

Drain the fries, refresh them in cold water and then carefully dry them. Cut them into big cubes and put them in a bowl.

Season with a little salt and pepper, turn them over in the tahini (the quantity will depend on taste). The mix can be acidified with lemon juice. Mix gently.

Serve lukewarm or cold with mint leaves on the side.

The Marquis de Sade's little salad of ram's balls, with artichoke hearts and truffles

It should be noted that the ingredients for this salad (rocket, truffles, artichokes and nasturtium flowers) are all reputed aphrodisiacs. Crack open the champagne.

Serves 2 lovers: 2 fresh or frozen artichoke hearts
                    1 lemon (if fresh artichokes are used)
                    4 pairs of ram's testicles, prepared and soaked
                    3 tbsp neutral oil, such as peanut, grapeseed, vegetable, etc.
                    2 tbsp sherry vinegar
                    a handful of rocket
                    a brace of truffles (30 g each)
                    1 tbsp safflower oil.
                    fine sea salt, freshly ground black pepper.
                    optional: two nasturtium flowers (not sprayed with chemicals)

If you are using fresh artichoke hearts, turn them in lemon juice to prevent them from going black, then steam them for 15–20 minutes (more if needs be). If they are deep-frozen, they will need to be steamed as well. Drain them, dry them and cut them into fine strips.

Slice the raw ram's testicles and fry them on both sides in a tablespoonful of hot oil. Season with salt and pepper. At the end of this very fast frying, pour a tablespoonful of sherry vinegar into the pan and boil at a high heat to make it evaporate. Shake the pan hard, turning the fries in the juice so that it coats them. Strain. Pick over the rocket and throw away any large stalks, wash it and spin dry.

Peel the truffles, chop up the peelings and put them in a bowl. Cut the prepared truffles into slices or into julienne strips, as you prefer.

Prepare a vinaigrette in the bowl containing the truffle peelings with what remains of the vegetable oil, the safflower oil, the remainder of the sherry vinegar, salt and pepper. Beat into an emulsion.

Put the rocket in a bowl together with the ram's fries; add the truffles, pour the vinaigrette over it, and gently mix.

To serve, share out the salad between two plates and decorate each of them with a nasturtium flower (these are edible but you need to take out the pistils and sepals).

Lamb's fry ramekins

Serves eight: 1 kg lamb's fries
1 tbsp wine vinegar
1 litre strong chicken stock

Sauce:

20 g flour	2 tbsp white port, sherry
20 g butter	or Madeira
250 ml single cream	1 tbsp grated Parmesan
1 little tin of truffle peelings	1 egg yolk
(optional)	fine sea salt, freshly ground white
	pepper, nutmeg

Skin the lamb's fries, soak them in cold water with a little vinegar for 10 minutes, strain and dry them on kitchen paper.

Pour the cold stock into a pan and add the fries, bring just to the boil, take off the heat at once and let the fries poach for a further 5 minutes in the hot stock.

To make the sauce, combine the butter and flour in a saucepan over a low heat. Once the mixture begins to foam, add the cream, and season with salt, pepper and a little grated nutmeg; let it cook until it thickens, stirring continually with a wooden spoon. Take it off the stove and let it cool. Heat the oven to 180°C (gas 6).

Drain the fries and cut them into cubes. If you are using truffles, cut them coarsely and put them into the lukewarm sauce together with the port (or sherry or Madeira), the grated Parmesan and finally the egg yolk. Adjust the seasoning.

Put the fries and the sauce into little ramekins, place in the middle of the oven and cook for 15–20 minutes. Serve hot.

Note: this dish could also be used as a garnish for little *bouchées* or for filling little pastry cases.

Lamb's fries with cumin, Tunisian-style

Serves four:
1 kg prepared lamb's fries	½ tsp tomato purée
100 ml olive oil	½ tsp mild *pimentón*
8 cloves of garlic	1 tsp ground cumin
1 tsp harissa	1 tsp salt
	some lemons

Put the oil in a heavy pan and heat it on a medium flame; peel and crush the cloves of garlic and put them into the oil, letting them cook for a few seconds while turning them. Quickly add 500 ml of water and mix in the harissa, the tomato purée, the *pimentón*, the cumin, salt and the juice of half a lemon. Let it simmer gently.

At the same time cut the fries into 3 cm cubes and add them into the sauce, stir, cover and simmer for 20 minutes over a gentle flame so that the sauce reduces properly (it should be thick).

Serve hot, arranging the fries on a dish, with quartered lemons round the rim.

Note: the harissa is not essential.

White kidneys poached with mild spices, Moroccan fashion

Serves eight:
2 kg lamb's fries	1 tsp ground cinnamon
1 tsp mild *pimentón*	200 g butter
1 tsp ground cumin	fine sea salt

Make a slit in the fries so you can strip off the membrane that covers them. Carefully roll them in salt, while taking care not to crush them, then wash them several times in cold water. Drain them and cut into large cubes.

Put the fries in a pan with the butter and spices. Add a small amount of salt and enough water to cover. Bring to a simmer on a gentle heat so that the flesh firms up. Remove with a slotted spoon and keep hot.

Adjust the seasoning of the cooking juices and reduce by boiling until thickened.

To serve, arrange the fries in a very hot bowl and cover with the sauce.

Note: a delicious variant of this recipe consists of making a mixture of fries, brains and sweetbreads in equal measure, all prepared and blanched.

Les animelles fried *à l'Algérienne,* with or without tomato sauce

Serves four:
4 pairs lamb's fries	½ tsp ground mignonette pepper
½ tsp fine sea salt	100 ml vegetable oil
2 tbsp flour	8 sprigs of flat-leaf parsley

Skin the testicles and cut them into small pieces; salt them and toss them in flour.

Add them to hot oil in a frying-pan, turning them without letting them brown. Stop cooking as soon as they become a pinky beige.

To serve, add pepper and some finely chopped flat-leaf parsley.

These may be served with a tomato sauce.

Lamb's fry *en persillade,* Algerian fashion

Serves four:
4 pairs lamb's fries	100 ml vegetable oil
2 cloves garlic	1 or 2 lemons
12 sprigs flat-leaf parsley	fine sea salt, freshly ground pepper

Prepare the fries and cut them into cubes. Season with salt and pepper.

Heat the oil in a frying-pan. Toss in the fries and cook them on all sides for a few minutes, stirring two or three times.

When they have finished cooking, scatter crushed garlic and finely chopped parsley.

Serve with slices of lemon.

Lamb's fry in batter in the North African style

Serves four:
600 g prepared lamb's fries
200 g of home-made soft breadcrumbs
100 ml vegetable oil
fine sea salt, freshly ground black pepper

Prepare the testicles, wash them and cut them in quarters. Mix the breadcrumbs with salt and plenty of pepper.

Heat the oil in a frying-pan. Coat the lamb's fry in the breadcrumbs and put them to cook in the pan. Fry until they are golden brown on all sides.

Serve hot on the *kemia* table (the Tunisian array of hors d'oeuvre).

Lamb's fries with *sauce piquante* as in Algeria

Serves four: 4 pairs lamb's fries   1 tsp mild *pimentón*
                   6 cloves of garlic   100 ml vegetable oil
                   1 very ripe tomato   fine sea salt, freshly milled pepper
                   1 little dried hot chilli (*felfel driss*)

Prepare the testicles and cut them into cubes.

Peel and crush the garlic in a mortar together with the chilli [*felfel driss* is the very hot dried chilli widely used in Algerian cooking (*Translator*)]. Dilute the paste you make with 50 ml water.

Pour the oil into a frying-pan, add the tomato, peeled, de-pipped and coarsely chopped, together with the garlic mixture and the *pimentón*. Add salt and pepper. Let it simmer for 15–20 minutes on a gentle flame until it achieves the consistency of thick *coulis*. At this point add the testicles, mix and continue cooking for another 20 minutes on a very low heat. Serve very hot.

Lamb's fries, *sauce poulette*

Serves two: 2 pairs lamb's fries   1 level tbsp flour
                  1 lemon   2 egg yolks
                  1 small onion   100 ml crème fraîche
                  200 ml veal stock   a few sprigs parsley and chervil
                     (you could use a cube)   a few chive stalks
                  40 g butter   fine sea salt, white pepper

Blanch the fries in a pan of salted boiling water with the juice of half a lemon for just two minutes. Drain. Peel and chop the onion. Heat the stock.

Melt the butter in a pan and add the onion. Cook until it is opaque then add the flour to make a roux. Moisten it little by little with the stock, stirring constantly.

Cut each of the testicles into 8 matchsticks and add them to the pan. Season with salt and pepper, mix and let it simmer on a gentle flame until the time comes to make the liaison.

Mix the egg yolks and the cream in a bowl. Take two or three spoonfuls of sauce from the pan and add them to the liaison, whisking it until it has a velvety consistency.

Add this back to the pan, stirring gently (to avoid breaking the lamb's fry) and without letting it boil. Then take it off the heat.

Now is the moment to put in the herbs, finely chopped, and the juice of half a lemon.

Mix and correct the seasoning if needs be.

To serve, transfer to a hot serving bowl. Accompany with rice.

Note: you can also add 250 g of button mushrooms to the *sauce poulette* (cut into large dice and stewed in butter). They should be added to the pan at the same time as the lamb's fry. You can also replace the herbs with capers, or use both.

Sautéed lamb's fries with spices in the Moroccan manner

Serves eight: 1 kg prepared lamb's fries ½ tsp ground cumin
100 g butter ½ tsp ground cinnamon
1 tsp mild *pimentón* ½ tsp of fine sea salt

Melt the butter in a pan. Cook the fries quickly on both sides without browning.

Add the spices and continue the cooking for another 10 to 15 minutes, continue stirring with a spatula.

Serve hot as a main course.

Lamb's fries as canapés

Serves four: 3 or 4 pairs lamb's fries 1 or 2 cloves garlic
500 ml *court bouillon* ½ bunch of flat-leaf parsley
200 ml dry white wine 8 slices cut from a small white loaf
150 g butter fine sea salt, ground black pepper

Pour the *court bouillon* (for a recipe see p. 87) and the white wine into a saucepan. Bring to the boil, correcting the seasoning if necessary, then poach the testicles for 2 minutes. Meanwhile, crush the garlic (1 or 2 cloves according to preference) with the chopped parsley.

Drain the fries on a cloth then cut them into slices.

Melt 100 g butter in a frying-pan, sieze the fries in it for a minute on each side, add salt and pepper, then add the garlic and parsley mixture and cook for another minute or two, turning the slices with a soft spatula rather than a fork in case they break. At the same time cut the crusts off the bread and fry on both sides in the remaining butter in another pan. Remove from the fat onto kitchen paper.

To serve, put the bread on a hot plate and immediately pile onto them the testicles with their persillade.

Eat them piping hot with your apéritif or as a first course.

A salad of lamb's fries and brains Moroccan-style

Serves eight: 500 g prepared lamb's fries   1 tsp sweet *pimentón*
              500 g lamb's brains   1 tsp hot chilli powder,
              1 lemon   preferably *felfel driss* (p. 106)
              4 cloves garlic   1 tsp of ground cumin
              ½ bunch flat-leaf parsley,   8 fully ripe tomatoes
                 plus 4 sprigs   fine sea salt and freshly
              ½ bunch fresh coriander   milled black pepper
              8 tbsp olive oil plus a dash

Soak the brains for an hour in cold acidulated (lemon juice or vinegar) water, drain them and remove the bloody filaments and membranes. At the same time, slit the fries to remove their skins and soak them as well in cold water with the juice of half a lemon for around an hour. Drain.

Cut the brains and fries into large cubes. Put them in a saucepan with the garlic cloves (peeled and crushed), the half-bunches of parsley and coriander (finely chopped), the 8 tbsp of olive oil and all the the spices. Cook on a low flame for 5 minutes, stirring gently.

Peel, de-pip and coarsely chop the tomatoes, add them to the pan and cover with cold water. Continue cooking for 20 minutes, at a very low simmer, until the offal is tender.

At the end of the cooking, add salt and pepper and sprinkle with the juice of the other half of the lemon. Allow the dish to cool.

To serve, place in a salad bowl, moisten it with a dash of olive oil and scatter over it the remaining 4 sprigs of parsley, chopped fine.

Tajine of lamb's white offal with spices

Serves eight: 500 g lamb's sweetbreads   100 ml olive oil
              500 g lamb's brains   1 lemon
              500 g lamb's fries   1 large onion
              1 tbsp ground ginger   8 sprigs flat-leaf parsley
              1 tsp ground turmeric   8 sprigs fresh coriander
              1 tsp hot *pimentón*   fine sea salt, ground black pepper

Soak the brains for an hour in cold acidulated (lemon juice or vinegar) water, drain them and remove the bloody filaments and membranes. At the same time, slit the fries to remove their skins and soak them as well in cold water with the juice of half a lemon for around an hour. Wash all the offal several times in clean cold water, drain them and cut them into large dice. Put them into a pan filled with cold water and bring them just to the boil so as to blanch them, skimming any scum that may rise to the top. Strain them at once, rinse them in cold water and dry them.

To prepare the *chermoula* or sauce, mix the spices in a bowl with half the olive oil and the lemon juice. Add the offal and turn it well in the sauce. Let it stand for an hour.

At the end of this time, heat the rest of the oil in the tajine (if it is a terracotta tajine, you might need to use a heat diffuser). Add the chopped onion and cook it until it is opaque. Now add the offal and the sauce, with some salt and pepper. Stir gently, moisten with 200 ml water, and bring to a gentle boil. Lower the heat slightly and put on the lid of the tajine, then let it simmer for 20 minutes.

Add the finely chopped parsley and coriander, stir gently and continue the cooking for another 5 minutes.

Serve piping hot in the tajine, or cold the next day.

Sacromonte tortilla with lamb's white offal

According to popular legend, a long time ago the canons of the Abbey of Sacromonte – a troglodytic hill to be found in the foothills of the Sierra Nevada in Granada which has been since time immemorial the fiefdom of gypsies and flamenco – held a chapter or business meeting. They found, however, that they had nothing to eat save a few eggs and various bits of sheep's offal. They therefore decided to ask a gypsy by the name of Chorrojumo to do his best 'with that', and that is how this succulent recipe was born. There are a number of variations on this tortilla, now a legend in its own right, and some people mix brains and lamb's fries with kidneys, but don't sanction the chorizo. Everyone, however, agrees on two essentials: that the tortilla should be large and thick, and that it must contain the balls and the brains of sheep. It is very substantial, but has a fine flavour.

Serves eight:		
	2 lamb's brains	200 g Serrano ham
	8 lamb's fries	80 g chorizo
	4 large potatoes (800 g)	16 eggs
	80 g sweet red pepper or	olive oil
	piquillos in a tin	fine sea salt, freshly ground
	80 g cooked peas	white pepper (optional)

Prepare the lamb's offal as in the previous recipe. Blanch them separately for 5 minutes in simmering water. Drain and cut into small dice.

Peel, wash and wipe the potatoes and cut them into slices or large dice.

Put enough oil into a big frying-pan to cook the potatoes. Bring it up to temperature (not too hot) and sauté them on a low flame until they are soft. Cover them during the cooking so that they do not brown too much. Lift them out and drain them well. Dispose of the oil.

Cut the ham and chorizo into small pieces, likewise the peppers (or *piquillos,* which are the small Spanish peppers, already peeled and grilled that are sold in jars or cans).

Beat the eggs as for an omelette in a bowl, adding salt and, if desired, pepper (Spaniards don't). Add the potatoes, the ham and the chorizo, the brains and the testicles, the peas and the peppers. Mix well to make it homogeneous.

Cook as two omelettes, best done simultaneously in two frying-pans. (Alternatively, you can make one very thick one.) To do this, put the pans on the flame with a little oil. As soon as they are hot, share the mixture between them making sure that it spreads out over their entire surface. Shake the pans so that the egg mixture doesn't stick. Cook for 3 minutes on one side then, with great care, lift or slide the tortillas onto a plate or pan lid and reverse or flip them back into the pans to cook for 2 or 3 minutes on the other side, until the eggs are set. Do not let the tortillas dry out. Serve at once.

Kid's testicles

All recipes for lamb's fries can be equally applied to kid's balls and vice versa.

Mixed skewers of kid's balls and kidneys

Serves four: 400 g prepared kid's kidneys   1 sprig savory
                  400 g prepared kid's testicles   2 bay leaves
                  50 ml olive oil   fine sea salt and freshly
                  1 sprig fresh rosemary   ground pepper

Cut the kidneys and the testicles into two or four depending on how big they are. Put them in a dish with the olive oil, rosemary and savory – divested of their stems – crumbled bay leaves and a generous turn of pepper. Do not add salt. Mix thoroughly and leave to stand for an hour or two.

When the time has elapsed, thread alternating pieces of kidney and testicles onto the skewers (if you can find them, the best are sticks of green wood that have been stripped of their bark and sharpened).

Cook them for 5 minutes on hot coals, but not so hot that they dry out the offal, turn them often and season them in the course of the cooking with salt and pepper.

Serve very hot.

Note: a few juniper berries may be added to the marinade.

A little soup of kid's balls

Use the same method as for the 'Clear soup with cock's bits' (see recipe on page 126).

The *criadillas*, slabs or gonads of a bull, bullock or calf

Little pots or *cassolettes* of *criadillas* with chilli

This is a delicious recipe for tapas or for an hors d'oeuvre.

Serves four: 500 g prepared *criadillas*
2 cloves garlic
1 little dried red Espelette pimento
100 ml best extra virgin olive oil
fine sea salt

Once the slabs have been properly prepared (see under lamb's fries in Preliminaries on page 82), cut them into large dice.

Pound the pimento with the garlic in a mortar. [*Piment d'Espelette* is a variety of medium-hot chilli pepper grown in the Basque country, now with its own *appellation contrôlée*. It can be found dried, or it is sold in powdered form throughout south-western France. It would be possible to replace this with a more easily obtained dried chilli, although these are generally hotter in taste. *Translator.*]

Heat the oil in an earthenware dish (use a heat diffuser if needs be), put in the garlic paste, stir about and then add the *criadillas* into the hot oil. Cook them quickly on all sides making sure that they stay juicy. Be very sparing with the salt.

Divide the *criadillas* between little copper pots or terracotta dishes which should be as burning hot as the dish itself, pour some oil on top

Serve red hot, accompanied by toothpicks.

Note: warm the *cassolettes* in the oven or by putting them in boiling water, then drying them just at the moment of serving.

Choesels in Madeira, as they cook it in Brussels

The word *choesels* is an example of *brusseleir*: a sort of Flemish patois that is heavily influenced by French. It means 'little things' – a prudish way of suggesting the bull's testicles, just as we might say 'things' (see the lexicon at the end of the book) to indicate testicles in general. By metonymy the word has been transferred to this dish. The recipe for *choesels* effectively describes a ragout of meats and offal (oxtail, mutton breast and trotters, bullock's balls, ox kidney, ox pancreas, sometimes veal or heifer sweetbreads; sometimes there are also *fricadelles*: little egg dumplings made from veal or veal sweetbreads), slow-cooked with onions and beer. There are, however, several schools of thought and for some of them, the presence of testicles and pancreas (*fagoues*) is the *sine qua non*. For others, only the pancreas is required. In truth, this dish, that had its glory days in the brasseries of Brussels, came down to us from the kitchens of the poor, and was prepared from the cheapest or most spurned cuts: notably the pancreas and the gonads. And the question we might ask is not whether testicles should be included, because that is not in dispute (even if some people affirm the contrary), but if the 'little things' that gave their name to the dish refer to the bull's balls that go into its making, or rather to the entire panoply of 'little things' that make up the recipe, when they are all taken together? One thing is certain, as so often, is that a recipe of the people founded on common sense has been compromised in the course of its evolution. It depended on cheap cuts, some disparate indeed (but brought into a single dish by considerations of expense), but now must answer to different criteria, more culturally correct perhaps, which impose fancier, more sophisticated ingredients. This is a denial of its own origins, which we now think too modest. In a manner of speaking, this is a crime against culture.

Hence today this dish is made principally with sweetbreads while formerly they were only there if you could afford them. As that was rarely the case, sweetbreads formed a tiny proportion of the meats, and usually they made dumplings with them to stretch the dish. This modern tendency (should we call it a heresy?) can be compared to the addition of lobster to a bouillabaisse to 'ennoble' a fish soup that used to be made from the fish that remained unsold at the end of the market (like almost all fish soups that were created along the coasts). It is also worth noting that when this dish became popular in Brussels brasseries, it was only offered on Thursdays, because Wednesday had become the slaughtering day in the abattoirs of Brussels and the suburbs, and the offal required for the making of *choesels* (the pancreas, for example) had to be cooked within twenty-four hours of slaughter. Finally, before we finish with *choesels*, I cannot resist offering you this little hypothesis given to me by a restaurateur in Liège (and a former butcher to boot), through a mutual friend: for him *choesels* are indeed bull's balls… but stuffed! And the ancient recipe consisted of emptying the scrotums of their contents, stuffing them and serving them with a Madeira sauce. Is this an obscure recipe or a Belgian joke?

Serves eight: a handsome oxtail, trimmed   half a mutton breast (more
500 g button mushrooms   likely lamb), weighing
200 g butter   *c.* 500 g; it should be boned
1 lemon   and have its fat removed
500 g onions   5–6 ox pancreas, total
1.5 litres of Gueuze Lambic   weight *c.* 500 g
  – Belgian beer – or lager   500 g bull's balls,
4 sheep's trotters, prepared   skinned and prepared
  and pre-cooked   1 ox kidney
1 *bouquet garni*   1 veal sweetbread (optional)
  (thyme, bayleaf, flat-leaf parsley) 1 dessertspoon potato flour
3 cloves   or cornflour
grated nutmeg   200 ml Madeira
fine sea salt   freshly ground black pepper
1 tbsp black peppercorns

Chop the oxtail into segments and blanch them for 30 minutes in salted water.

Meanwhile, peel the mushrooms (if necessary) and stew them in another pan, covered, with half the butter, a glass of water and the juice of the lemon. Drain and set aside.

Peel the onions and slice them fine. Stew them in the rest of the butter in a wide, shallow and heavy pan [a large sauté pan would be best]. When they begin to change colour, add the carefully drained oxtail pieces and turn them in the fat.

Moisten the pan with a litre of beer, add the mutton trotters cut in four, the herbs (*bouquet garni* and cloves), a little grated nutmeg, salt and peppercorns. Bring to the boil and simmer for 45 minutes, covered, on a low heat.

While this is underway, cut the breast of mutton into squares and prepare the pancreas, bull's balls, ox kidney and, if you are using one, the calf's sweetbread. Cut them into fairly large cubes. Add them to the pan, together with what remains of the beer in order to cover all the meats. Stir gently, cover and simmer for 45 minutes.

Put in the mushrooms, stir, adjust the seasoning and cook for another 15 minutes.

At the end of the cooking, take out the meats and the mushroom with a slotted spoon and put them in a really hot, deep bowl. Take out the *bouquet garni*. Slake the potato flour or cornflour with the Madeira and pour it into the cooking liquid that remains. Bind the sauce by stirring vigorously until it begins to bubble.

To serve, coat the *choesels* with the Madeira sauce.

The tradition is to serve the *choesels* with boiled potatoes, preferably in their skins.

Note that 15 minutes before serving you can add a generous handful of *fricadelles*, *balekes* [the Flemish word for *fricadelles*] or forcemeat balls. These meatballs are made from seasoned and minced veal bound by a whole beaten egg.

[Mme Vié makes a distinction in this recipe between the pancreas of an ox and sweetbreads. Sweetbreads are generally understood to be either the thymus gland or the pancreas of a calf or a lamb (or at a pinch a pig). Hence the ox pancreas is not usually found on refined restaurant menus. Indeed, you will have to be close to a keen and eager butcher (most likely at the abbatoir) to get him to provide the ox pancreas proposed for this recipe. You may, therefore, have to commit the cultural heresy so deplored by the author to fill out your list of ingredients. *Translator*.]

Criadillas coated in breadcrumbs as they cook them in Andalusia (*Criadillas empanadas*)

This recipe can be used for either bull's or bullock's balls and you may also add a fine paste of garlic and parsley to the breadcrumb coating. I myself would include some grated zest of non-treated orange or lemon as well as chopped parsley, or possibly some finely chopped fresh coriander.

Serves four:	4 pairs of *criadillas* 2–3 eggs soft white breadcrumbs	200 g butter or a glass of oil according to taste (for frying) 2 lemons or an orange fine sea salt, freshly ground pepper

After taking the *criadillas* out of their two skins, blanch them for 5 minutes in boiling salted water. Drain and dry them on a kitchen cloth.

Now that they are tender and cooked, cut them in relatively thick slices.

Beat the eggs in a bowl as for an omelette and season with salt and pepper. Grate the bread for the breadcrumbs and spread them out on a tray.

Melt the butter in a large frying-pan (or heat some oil if you prefer).

Dip the slices of *criadillas* in the beaten eggs then the breadcrumbs, making sure that they are well coated. Put them immediately into the pan. Fry them for a minute on one side in the foaming butter, then turn them over (with a soft spatula rather then a fork in order to avoid breaking them). Let them cook for a further 2 or 3 minutes on the other side.

Drain and serve hot with lemon or orange quarters.

Criadillas sautéed with sherry

Serves two: 2 pairs of prepared, blanched *criadillas*
100 g butter
100 ml dry sherry or Montilla fino
an untreated orange
fine sea salt and freshly ground pepper

Cut the *criadillas* into lengths (about 8 pieces) or in large cubes. Add salt and pepper.

Melt some butter in a frying-pan and add the *criadillas*. Seize them for 1–2 minutes, working them well to make sure they are basted with the fat. Moisten them with the sherry or Montilla fino and let them simmer for 5 minutes on a low heat, stirring them gently two or three times.

Meanwhile, wash the orange, finely grate the zest and squeeze the juice.

When the *criadillas* are cooked, take them out gently with a slotted spoon and keep them hot.

Add the orange zest and the juice to the frying-pan and boil it for 2–3 minutes, scraping the pan with the spatula in order to deglaze it thoroughly.

Pour the sauce over the *criadillas*. Serve piping hot.

Daube of *toro bravo* with *criadillas*

Remember that a *toro bravo* is a fighting bull. This recipe comes from Pino Correnti's *Cinq mille ans de cuisine aphrodisiaque* (Five Thousand Years of Aphrodisiac Cookery, 1992). A word of advice: use olive oil to melt the spices and to fry the meat.

Serves two: 500 g oxtail   2 carrots
2 testicles of a *toro bravo*   1 pinch saffron
1 large onion   1 pinch chilli
3 garlic cloves   ½ litre dry white wine
2 well-ripened tomatoes   salt

Cut the oxtail into small pieces and remove any fat. Also cut up the testicles. Cut the up the onion and crush the garlic.

Fry the onion and the garlic in a saucepan then, without waiting for them to brown, add the bits of meat and fry them on all sides.

Meanwhile, chop the tomatoes into pieces and cut the carrots into rounds. Put these ingredients into the pot together with the saffron, the chilli and the white wine. Cover and let it cook for 3 hours. If needs be add a little water.

Once the cooking is finished, let the meat rest in its juices for at least an hour. Mix and put back on the heat for at least 10 minutes (or 20 minutes if there is still a decent amount of stock). Serve with sautéed potatoes, or simply with slices of black bread and butter.

Scrambled eggs with *criadillas* and brains (*Huevos a la porreta*)

This Spanish recipe is typical of the province of La Mancha so dear to Don Quixote.

Serves four: 250 g of prepared *criadillas*   8 eggs
250 g blanched bull's or ox brains 100 g butter
1 lemon   fine sea salt
                                     freshly ground white pepper

Having prepared the *criadillas* and soaked the brains in acidulated water, remove the fine membrane from the latter together with the bloody filaments that hang off it.

Heat a pan of salted water and lemon juice to boiling. Poach the offal for a very few minutes, until scum ceases to rise, then drain and let it cool on a kitchen towel. Cut into large cubes or dice.

Melt half the butter in a frying-pan and sauter the offal until it has firmed. Do not let the butter blacken or burn. The meats should not brown, merely turn a cream colour.

Melt the rest of the butter in a smaller pan (put a heat diffuser underneath it if it is terracotta). Break in the whole eggs and stir them vigorously with a spatula to scramble them, without actually beating them. When they begin to set, add salt and pepper, and continue mixing. Add the meats to the eggs (after having taken them out of their pan with a slotted spoon and patted the offal clean of any cooking fat with kitchen paper). Finish the cooking without letting the eggs dry out, as they must remain moist.

Note: a few strips of truffles (or roughly chopped) can be mixed in at the same time as the offal and will make the dish all the better.

Bull's balls pâté

In the chapter dedicated to gastronomy in her *Bréviaire de l'amour sorcier* (Sorcerer's Handbook of Love, 1969), Ange Bastiani tells us,

> It fell to no less a person than the pope's cook, in this instance Bartolomeo Scappi, who worked the ovens of Pius V, to offer the *ne plus ultra* of what one might make from this salacious gourmandise, that is to say the divine bull's balls pâté, the recipe for which I have here. It is relatively simple:
>
>> Boil half a dozen bull's balls, cut them in slices after having added salt and pepper and garnished them with nutmeg and bay leaves. Intersperse them then with a finely chopped mixture of lamb's kidneys, ham, thyme, garlic and oregano, then serve them hot.

Charcoal-grilled calf's balls as cooked in Marrakesh

This recipe is a firm favourite in Marrakesh, where the people are so partial to the food they obtain from open-air grills that the place is littered with them, notably on Djemaa el-Fna.

Serves four: 4 prepared calf's balls
1 tbsp oil
½ tsp ground cumin
¼ tsp ground black pepper
fine sea salt

Cut the balls into thin slices. Put them on a plate with oil, cumin, pepper and salt. Turn them well in the marinade so that they are covered in spices on both sides.

Grill the balls for a few minutes, best is on a charcoal grill, turning them two or three times during the cooking. This can be done under an electric grill. Serve piping hot.

Salad of warm *criadillas* with pomegranates

I invented this recipe for my friend Isabel Calvache Gisbert whom I met in Spain while I was on a press trip to Andalusia. Isobel was then in charge of foreign press relations for the fino producers of Montilla Alvear [Montilla is a white wine produced along the same lines as sherry from Jerez to the south-west. The fino is the lightest and brightest of the styles. *Translator*]. To help me with this book she has been kind enough to answer my questions about vocabulary and to provide me with a few recipes for *criadillas*.

Serves two:
200 ml Montilla fino	1 pomegranate
grated zest of 1 orange	1 bunch lamb's lettuce
and juice of ½ an orange	1 shallot
1 sprig thyme	4 tbsp olive oil
a bay leaf	2 tbsp Montilla fino vinegar
2 nice pairs of	fine sea salt and freshly
prepared *criadillas*	ground pepper

Pour the fino into a little pan and add the finely grated orange zest together with the thyme and bay leaf. Let it boil for 5 minutes, take off the heat and let it cool.

Drop the *criadillas* into the pan and put it back on the heat. Bring it to the boil and simmer on a low heat for 5 minutes, then allow the *criadillas* to stand in the fino for a further 5 minutes off the flame. After that, remove them with a slotted spoon and cut them into large dice.

Strain the cooking juices and pour back into the pan, together with the juice of half an orange. Reduce by boiling until there remains only around 50 ml of liquid.

Meanwhile peel the pomegranate and extract all the seeds. Take the lamb's lettuce, throw away any nasty leaves, wash it and dry it.

Peel and chop the shallot. Fry it in a pan with a tbsp oil until it is soft. Add the *criadillas* and some salt and pepper then quickly sauté them on both sides. Now add the pomegranate seeds and moisten them with a tbsp of fino Montilla vinegar [sherry vinegar would do just as well], at a high heat to let the liquid evaporate, shaking the pan to ensure that the chunks are properly coated with the juices. Lift them onto a dish and keep them warm. Now add the fino reduction to the pan and let it boil for 2–3 minutes until it is syrupy. Prepare a vinaigrette with the rest of the oil, vinegar and salt and pepper.

Put the lamb's lettuce in a salad bowl and combine this with the *criadillas* and the pomegranate seeds.

Pour the sauce from the frying-pan into the vinaigrette, stir, pour over the *criadillas*, stir again. Serve lukewarm.

The cods of wild boar

The cods of a wild boar sautéed in a black pan

Olivier Nanteau* told me once that he had taken part in a wild boar '*diane*' or hunt, in the course of which he was able to taste the '*suites*' or testicles of the beast. In practice it all takes place like this: as soon as it is killed 'the ginger beast' [a huntsman's term for the wild boar in French is *la bête rousse*] is taken to a convenient place or even butchered on the spot. It is strung up, head uppermost, between two trees so that it can be disembowelled. This operation needs to be performed with the utmost speed – in theory within two hours of the kill – to prevent the flesh from going bad. As soon as the animal has been cut open, and if it is male, the testicles are the first things to go. They are stripped and cut into round escalopes and quickly seized in one of those lovely black iron frying-pans you still find in the country. The only artifice is a little salt and pepper and they are in the pan only for enough time to seize, no more. Just 'fried frothy', as Olivier put it, who found them delicious. They generally form the mid-morning snack of the huntsmen.

---

* The food writer (*La Revue des gourmands*) and author (*Portraits toqués, enquêtes chez les trois étoiles* [Chefs' Portraits; Looking into Three-Stars, 1999]).

Cock's stones

A great many of the recipes for cock's stones given here are drawn from the repertoire of French *haute cuisine*, either classical or bourgeoise. They are offered *in memoriam*: as intellectual nourishment even if you never get the chance to taste them. The choice is deliberate, because it would seem otiose to repeat the recipes for lamb's fry just substituting cock's stones, even though most of them could as well be applied to both.

A sauté of *béatilles**

For 500 g of *béatilles* (of several sorts for preference), which you have diced, put a large knob of butter and a finely chopped onion into your pan. When the onion is all but cooked, but not browned, stir in your *béatilles* which you have generously seasoned with as many St John's herbs† that you can lay your hands on together with nutmeg, a smidgen of ginger and a pinch of pepper. Then add a glass of white wine and salt, and let it simmer until cooked.

Be careful! *Béatilles* are not firm-fleshed and you need to cook them just before eating. The cooking will not take long.

If you enjoy them, give thanks to Marie Touchet who served *béatilles* to her royal lover, Charles IX,§ whenever he, lustily inclined, paid her a visit.

Curnonsky and André Saint-Georges, La Table et l'amour, nouveau traité des excitants modernes

---

* For a discussion of the word *béatilles* and its translation into English, see the earlier paragraphs on page 60. *Translator.*
† St John's herbs refer to herbs that once were collected on St John the Baptist's day, i.e. Midsummer. Bouquets, garlands or wreaths of them would be hung on front doors to bring good fortune and good health. Among those plants considered to fall into the category were thyme, verveine, arnica, camomile, elderflower, dandelion and sage (as many as twenty-seven are listed). In Catalonia, the harvest of these plants is called the '*ramellet de la bonaventura*'. *Translator.*
§ King of France, son of Henri II and Catherine de' Medici (1550–1574).

Bouchées à la reine

For the origin of this dish you should read the earlier paragraphs on pages 63 and 64 under the headings *Frivolités de la reine* and *Morceau de la reine*. The original recipe calls for *bouchées* made from puff pastry which is garnished with a *salpicon*: a ragout of exquisite morsels such as lamb's or veal sweetbreads, veal or lamb's brains, cock's combs and cock's stones, little chicken quenelles, mushrooms, truffles and green olives all of which is bound with a *sauce financière* or *suprême*. I am giving you a slightly simplified version of the recipe here, but it is both authentic and delicious. If you want to make your own *bouchées*, go to the recipe for meat-filled vol-au-vent (below, page 143), but cut the pastry into eight circles instead of one big one. You can roll it out a bit more thinly. Finally, to make a *sauce suprême* (which is the basis for the *financière*) look at the same recipe which gives the version used in classical *haute cuisine* or perhaps that given in the recipe following this one for chicken *bouchées* with cock's stones and a *sauce suprême*. I should repeat that the cock's combs and cock's stones can be replaced by lamb's fries.

Serves eight: 8 puff-pastry *bouchées*, if possible they should be home-made,
                    if not, bought from a pâtissier

Garnish: 1 veal sweetbread
                    3 blanched lamb's brains
                    150 g cock's combs and cock's stones
                    200 g button mushrooms
                    1 litre good veal stock
                    30 g butter
                    2 lemons

Sauce financière:
                    40 g butter
                    40 g flour
                    250 ml good chicken stock
                    100 g pitted green olives
                    1 small tin of truffle peelings
                    200 ml Madeira
                    250 ml crème fraîche
                    3 egg yolks
                    fine sea salt and ground white pepper

Trim the sweetbread and put it to soak in cold acidulated water, then poach it until firm to the touch in three-quarters of the hot veal stock.

Trim the brains of any superfluous membranes, poach them gently in a pan filled with salted water and the juice of a lemon until they are firm to the touch.

Blanch the cock's combs and cock's stones for 2–3 minutes in another pan filled with salted boiling water.

If necessary, peel the mushrooms, cut them in cubes, cover them and stew them with butter and the juice of a lemon.

When the sweetbreads, brains, cock's combs and cock's stones are ready, drain them and cut them into large dice. Keep them warm.

Open the tin of truffle peelings, chop them fine and put them in a little pan with the Madeira and their juice. Reduce by half on a low flame.

Toss the olives into a pan filled with boiling water and blanch them for 2 minutes, carefully drain them and cut them into small pieces.

While all this is going on, start making the *sauce financière*. Stir together the butter and the flour in a pan over a low heat. When the mixture begins to foam, moisten gradually with the rest of the veal stock and the chicken stock, stirring all the while so that lumps do not form, until it has thickened. Remove from the flame at once.

Incorporate the mushrooms and their juices, the sweetbreads, brains, cock's combs and cock's stones, olives, the reduction of truffles and Madeira into the velouté. Stir it carefully. Keep it hot in a bain-marie.

In a bowl, blend the cream and the egg yolks. Pour this into the sauce and stir carefully to bind it. Taste and adjust the seasoning, which will depend enormously on the quality of the stocks you have used. [Many in France, as well as in England, now use dehydrated stock cubes or powders. These are often overseasoned and coarse in flavour. Better pre-prepared (liquid) stocks are available from some shops; otherwise, make your own. *Translator*]

Heat the *bouchées* for 5 minutes in the oven and garnish them with the *salpicon* which should be hot but not still cooking.

Serve at once.

Bouchées of chicken stuffed with cock's stones and a sauce suprême

For ten people, take:
1°) for the envelopes: 500 g concentrated chicken stock – 300 g chicken breast – 200 g flour – 175 g chicken fat – 125 g veal suet – 4 whole eggs – 2 egg whites – 1 egg yolk – nutmeg – salt and pepper;
2°) for the stuffing: 300 g of a mixture of chicken livers cooked in butter, blanched cock's stones and grilled mushrooms;
3°) for the sauce: 150 g jellied veal and chicken stock [i.e. well reduced] – 60 g thick cream – 40 g Sauternes – 25 g butter – 15 g flour – 1 fresh egg yolk – the juice of a lemon – salt and pepper.

Mix the flour and the whole eggs, stir in the hot chicken stock a little at a time; put it on a gentle heat and work it for half an hour in order to achieve a good consistency,

In a pestle and mortar pound, one at a time, the chicken breast, the chicken fat and the veal fat to a paste, then blend them and season with salt, pepper and nutmeg to taste; pound this mixture once more before adding the flour-eggs-and-stock combination, together with two egg whites that have been beaten stiff.

Pass the all this through a sieve; then knead the resulting paste to make it smooth and supple. Roll it out to a thickness of 5–6 mm and cut it into twenty squares.

On each of the squares place one-twentieth of the stuffing; close up the bouchées [so as to make little pastry parcels].

Prepare the sauce: put the butter and flour into a pan; stir it without allowing it to colour, stir in the chicken and veal jelly, moisten it with the Sauternes, let it cook gently for a quarter of an hour, then add the cream. Mix well but don't let it boil; finally bind it with an egg yolk. Taste and complete the seasoning with salt, pepper and lemon juice.

Poach the bouchées in salted boiling water; drain them and gild them with egg yolk. Put them in the oven [to turn a golden brown].

Arrange the bouchées on a dish covered with a napkin; serve them together with the sauce in a sauce boat.

Ali-Bab, Gastronomie pratique *(Practical Gastronomy, 1928)*

Brochettes of cock's stones béarnaise

Choose some good cock's stones, poach them and season them; thread them on seven or eight small silver skewers; baste them with melted butter; scatter them with the finest white breadcrumbs and grill them gently.

Serve them with some Béarnaise sauce in a sauce boat.

Auguste Escoffier, Le Guide culinaire *(Culinary Guide, 1921)*

'*Cibreo*' in the Florentine manner

Cibreo is a dish based on chicken offal which dates from the Renaissance. It doubtless appeared for the first time on the tables of the Medicis. It was for many years a fashionable Florentine speciality but has long fallen from grace. Despite that, the local chef Fabio Picchi named his restaurant Cibreo, opening in 1979, and continued to offer the dish to enthusiasts, although they need to order it in advance. However, he did not want to give me his own recipe, jealously keeping it away from prying eyes. I believe that he has considerably modernized the historic recipe which I give below. He adds chicken hearts and ham, he leaves out the eggs and replaces the butter by oil, he includes garlic paste, sage and rosemary and moistens the dish with white wine. It is a variant that is sometimes turned in to a fricassee by binding the sauce with two egg yolks and half a lemon right at the end of the cooking.

The word cibreo means any sort of mixture, an amalgam of various ingredients. It is a term used only in Tuscany. *Cibreo* is a thoroughly gourmand dish, distinguished, exquisite and very delicate.

Here is the roll-call of ingredients: cock's stones, cock's combs, chicken livers and unlaid eggs. [These are the barely formed eggs found in the carcase of a slaughtered hen. Their use is optional.]

Serves four:
    24 cock's stones (*granelli*)
    24 cock's combs (*creste*)
    24 chicken livers (*fegatini*)
    12 unlaid eggs (*non-nate*)
    50 ml chicken stock
    50 g butter
    8 egg yolks
    the juice of two lemons

Method:
The cock's stones and the eggs – or rather the egg yolks – need to be boiled for a minute to prevent them from bursting.

The cock's combs are treated as if they would be used in a *sauce financière*, they should only be blanched.

The chicken livers should be carefully divested of their bile ducts.

Season the different elements and turn them in the hot butter. Moisten with stock and cook for five minutes, take off the heat and bind it with the egg yolks mixed with a little stock and some lemon juice. Serve at once.

Louis Monod, La Cuisine Florentine *(Florentine Cookery, 1914)*

Clear soup with cock's bits

Take a consommé or strong stock made from chicken or veal, add a little gooseberry juice or verjuice together with some finely chopped mint, marjoram, sorrel and burnet. Now add some breadcrumbs mixed with pounded almonds in such a way as to thicken the stock. Poach the cock's bits [cock's stones] in this at a simmer, turning the several times with a spoon.

This little pottage may be served on sippets.

Bartolomeo Scappi (chef to Pope Pius V, 1566–72), Opera dell'arte del cucinare

Note: this recipe would work well for kid's balls.

Cock's combs and cock's stones *à la grecque*

Make 250 g of pilau rice, adding half a mild chilli cut into small pieces and a pinch of saffron.

Mix in 24 cock's stones that have been previously fried in butter and a dozen nice cock's combs that have been blanched and fried like lamb's sweetbreads.

Arrange them on a silver dish, spoon out the rice onto a layer of aubergine rounds that have been seasoned, dipped in flour and fried in oil.

Auguste Escoffier, Le Guide culinaire

Cock's combs and cock's stones in a white sauce

Once the cock's combs and cock's stones have been soaked in several changes of cold water, as they should be, season them with salt and pepper, and cook them with a bouquet garni in some water whitened with a spoonful of flour. When the cooking is finished, make a white roux which you will moisten with consommé, add a spoonful or two of the juices from a roast chicken; simmer the cock's combs and stones for fifteen minutes in this sauce. At the moment of serving, melt 60 grams of cold butter into which you have worked a pinch of flour and half a spoonful of fresh herbs; squeeze a lemon and add this together with a dash of vinegar. Serve very hot. In great kitchens, after they have cooked cock's combs and stones in a simple *blanc* [a cooking liquor of water and flour, variously seasoned], the dish is finished with a *velouté*, [a rich white sauce] which makes them dearer, but not necessarily better.

Jules Breteuil, Nouveau cuisinier européen *(New European Chef, 9th edition, early twentieth century)*

COCK'S COMBS FIRST WAY

They will be whiter and better if you can let them soak for three or four days in cold water, changing it three or four times a day. Chose the pinkest with the longest points, but not curly.

Having thus soaked them, put them in a little casserole, more or less covered in cold water. Heat them gently. As soon as the water is so hot that you can't stick your finger in it, quickly drain them. If the combs have seized, or if the water boils, they will stay red and be tasteless. There is no cure for this problem. If, on the other hand, the operation is well conducted, the combs will have lost all traces of blood and will be uniformly grey.

Drain them and rub them in a kitchen cloth with some rock salt to take off the skin. Put them back into soak in salted water for at least half a day. Then wash them several times in cold water, pressing them lightly with your hands to remove all the bloody bits. They should now be as pure white as porcelain. Cut off any points that are too thin and trim the side where the combs once stuck to the head.

To cook: put them in a boiling 'blanc'. So, for 150 g of cock's combs: a level spoonful of flour, a litre and ¼ of water, a big pinch of salt, a spoonful of vinegar, and a spoonful of fat skimmed from the stock. Boil on a low heat for 35 minutes.

Madame Saint-Ange, La Cuisine

COCK'S COMBS SECOND WAY

Three quarters of the cock's combs that one eats in Paris are nothing more than bits of ox palate stamped out with cutters. Real cock's combs have rough edges while bogus ones have smooth sides. In order to make sure they are not being duped, people who can afford the luxury of such a garnish prepared their cock's combs themselves in the following manner: clean them, dip them for a few minutes in water that is almost boiling, drain them and rub them between your fingers to get off the skin that covers them, toss them into cold water so that they soak for at least two hours. When they have become properly white, wipe them and cook them in enough water or stock to cover them; add good butter, a dash of vinegar and salt. Boiling for a quarter of an hour is enough. This is how you proceed for pastry garnishes: after soaking you must heat them in salty water them drain them before putting them in a cloth filled with rock salt in which they are rubbed for a moment as if they were being washed with soap. Open the cloth and carefully peel the cock's combs and put them in cold water which should be changed every four hours until they are properly white. They are then drained and cooked in water with a glass of white wine, salt, pepper and a suitable quantity of spices.

Jules Trousset, Un million de recettes (A Million Recipes, published in Paris at the end of the nineteenth century).

Darioles* of cock's stones and foie gras

A variant on the recipe for cock's stones and chicken livers in aspic [see the recipe below, page 138].

You can also make these little jellies in dariole moulds and use them as a garnish for a dish of chicken *chaud-froid*.[†]

Ali-Bab, Gastronomie pratique

Darioles of cock's stones with chicken livers

A variant on the recipe for cock's stones and chicken livers in aspic [see the recipe below, page 138].

You can also make these little jellies in dariole moulds and use them as a garnish for a dish of chicken *chaud-froid*.

Ali-Bab, Gastronomie pratique

Darioles of cock's stones and game livers

A variant on the recipe for cock's stones and chicken livers in aspic [see the recipe below, page 138].

The stones and game livers can be done in the same way, but it will be necessary to flavour both jelly and sauce, which will be a brown *chaud-froid* in this case, with a game stock.

Ali-Bab, Gastronomie pratique

Désirs de Mascotte[§]

Put 24 very fresh cock's stones in 100 g brown butter; season with salt, pepper and a pinch of cayenne and cook for 5 or 6 minutes.

Make 12 round croutons, 8 mm thick and cut out with pastry cutters 2 cm in diameter; fry them in butter at the last minute.

Add 4 good, fresh black truffles cut in thick slices and add them to the amount of reduced demi-glaze sauce you desire; put in the stones as well as the fried croutons, 50 g fine butter, a few drops of lemon, and shuffle the pan so that the whole mixes well together.

Arrange the dish in a silver timbale[#] and serve at once, properly hot.

Auguste Escoffier, Le Guide culinaire

---

* A dariole is a small cup-shaped mould. *Translator.*

[†] A *chaud-froid* is a velouté sauce mixed with aspic so that it sets when cooled. *Translator.*

[§] *À la mascotte* is a recognized garnish for chicken and light meat dishes in French *haute cuisine*. It consists of artichoke hearts, potatoes and truffles. The Victorian *bon viveur* Lt-Col Newnham-Davies was served Désirs de Mascotte in a meal at the Savoy Hotel cooked by Escoffier before 1897.

[#] A timbale is a round dish or mould.

Escalopes of sweetbreads in breadcrumbs with a *salpicon* of truffles, cock's combs and cock's stones and with a *sauce suprême*

For six people, you will need: 250 g jellied veal and chicken stock – 140 g butter – 100 g cream – 60 g Sauternes – 15 g flour – 2 fresh eggs – 2 fresh yolks – 1 nice veal sweetbread – very finely grated soft breadcrumbs – lemon juice – salt and pepper.

Trim the sweetbread and leave it to soak for 1 hour in some slightly salty cold water. Cut it into escalopes, the operation requires some care.

Beat two whole eggs.

Dip the escalopes in the eggs several times and then in the breadcrumbs so that they are properly coated. Cook them gently in 100 g of butter in a frying-pan for 15 minutes; they should not be seasoned.

While they are cooking, prepare the *sauce suprême*: put 30 g of butter and the flour in a saucepan, stir it but don't let it brown, stir in the veal and chicken stocks, moisten with the Sauternes and let it cook for at least a quarter of an hour. At this point add the rest of the butter cut into little pieces, then finish with a liaison of the egg yolks and the cream. Mix well, heat it but do not let it boil, taste it and correct the seasoning with salt, pepper and lemon juice.

Serve the escalopes of sweetbread coated by the sauce, or serve the sauce apart, in a sauceboat.

As variation, you may stud the escalopes with some fine bacon lardons, then, when they are cooked, arrange them in a turban [i.e. a round shape with a hollow in the centre] on a dish. The turban can be garnished with a *salpicon* of truffles, cock's combs and cock's stones in a *sauce suprême*.

Ali-Bab, Gastronomie pratique

Fricassee of cock's stones with sorrel

Serves four:

500 g trimmed cock's stones	200 ml concentrated veal stock
1 good bunch of sorrel	100 g butter
250 g button mushrooms	1 lemon
2 grey shallots	200 ml runny crème fraîche
100 g cured ham	3 egg yolks
	fine salt and freshly milled pepper

Pick over the sorrel and wash. Plunge it for a minute into salted, boiling water to blanch it. Drain and then toss it in cold water (the heat shock will preserve the emerald green colour). Spin-dry and chop it fine with a knife.

Clean the mushrooms. Cut them into large dice. Put them in a pan with half the butter and the lemon juice, cover and stew them for 10 minutes, shaking them from time to time. Strain.

Peel and chop the shallots; take the rinds off the ham and chop it coarsely.

Put the cream in a little pan, reduce it until it has a velvety consistency. Let it cool.

Melt the rest of the butter in a sauteuse. Fry the chopped shallots and the ham. As soon as the shallot starts to soften, add the cock's stones and seize them on all sides, without taking colour. At this point moisten them with hot stock and let them simmer for 5 minutes.

Add the mushrooms and the sorrel to the pan, mix and cook for 2–3 minutes.

Beat the cream with the egg yolks and the salt and pepper; pour this into the sauteuse and remove immediately from the heat. Stir gently until the sauce has covered all the elements. Correct the seasoning.

Bring immediately to the table in a handsome serving dish.

Note: this can be accompanied by some Creole rice or, better still, gnocchi. Make them yourself so that you can fashion them to be the same size and shape as the stones, so as to flummox your guests a little.

Plovers' eggs à la Du Barry

If you can lay your hands on some plovers' eggs you will find this recipe delicious. Hard boil a dozen plovers' eggs. Take out the yolks and reserve them. Stuff the whites with a mixture of foie gras, truffles and ten of the yolks that you kept back. Arrange them in a saucepan with bacon, a bouquet garni, Madeira and a little meat juice and season them with salt, pepper and nutmeg. Take some artichoke hearts, dig them out so as to form a deep bowl and fill them with a chicken forcemeat. Put them in an oven-dish lined with bacon and moisten it with a little consommé. Cover them and poach them in the oven. Once the stuffing is poached, arrange the hearts on a dish and place the stuffed eggs on them. Add some cock's stones. Sauce them with some game stock and a little demi-glace.

They say that no virtue can resist the virtues of plovers' eggs. See if that is true.

Curnonsky and André Saint-Georges, La Table et l'amour

---

* The collecting of plovers' eggs is now illegal in Britain. Those who want eggs from the wild have transferred their affections to gulls' eggs, which are available for a very short season at a very high price. *Translator.*

Batalia omelette

Use if you can cock's odds and ends [i.e. the stones and the combs
– the French word here is *béatilles* which, as noted in the lexicon
above s.v. Batalia or Battalia pie, page **68**, was the word used by the
seventeenth-century English author Robert May (*Translator*)] and,
having chopped them up, quickly fry them with the spices that suit
them best: nutmeg and ginger.

Take some very fresh eggs and leave out half the whites. Beat them.
When this is done, add the *béatilles* and cook your omelette in the
usual fashion, thick and but still creamy. Casanova liked this omelette
a good deal. He used to add a truffle, which proves that he had good
taste from time to time.

Curnonsky and André Saint-Georges, La Table et l'amour

Pâté à la financière

[Line a terrine] with a pastry case for a pâté and fill it with flour or
stewing meat. When [baked in the oven and] your meat has cooked
and takes on a good colour, removed the meat or flour [if you filled
the case instead with flour] as well as any [superfluous] crumb [from
the inside of the crust. Fill it with a good *financière*.

As you know, your *financière* is made as follows, from cock's combs
cooked in a blanc along with cock's stones; strain them when you want
to use them, together with the stones. Put the appropriate quantity of
reduced velouté in a pan if you want a white ragout. If you want a
brown one, used a reduction of espagnol adding a little consommé. If
your sauce is too thick, simmer the cock's combs for a quarter of an
hour; a moment before serving, add the the stones, a few mushrooms
that you have cooked, artichoke hearts and truffles, according to taste.

Alexandre Dumas, Le Grand dictionnaire de cuisine

Léontine potatoes (stuffed with a *salpicon* of cock's stones)

Léontine potatoes are potatoes that have been richly filled and finished
under the grill. Take some nice Dutch potatoes, peel them, wash them,
dry them and cook them in the oven.

Cut them three quarters of the way up in order to form a lid;
empty them, leaving only a few millimetres of pulp, then fill the voids
with a *salpicon* of cock's stones, chicken breasts, sweetbreads, smoked
tongue and *sauce suprême* dressed 'in mourning' by adding a great
many mashed truffles. Put back the lids, place the potatoes in an oven

dish and scatter them with grated cheese. Put them in the oven to finish off.

Léontine potatoes are an excellent hot hors d'oeuvre, and can also be served as a vegetable *entremets*.

Ali-Bab, Gastronomie pratique

Batalia soup

For two people, you need 300 grams of offal, poultry's for preference. After you have cut them into the smallest of pieces, put them in a casserole containing at least a litre of water, with a chopped onion, a clove of garlic, a turnip and a bunch carrot finely diced, a small stick of celery, a finely chopped small truffle, a good pinch of salt, a turn of pepper and a hint of thyme.

Stew these for as long as necessary – the time will vary according to which sorts of offal and which vegetables you have put in to cook – then, without draining, serve it up after adding a beaten egg if you wish to follow the old Dutch custom, or a small glass of good Cognac if you want to do as our forefathers did.

Both solutions work well. They will pep you up. The recipe comes from the old man Brantôme. * Thanks be to him.

Curnonsky and André Saint-Georges, La Table et l'amour

A ragout of *béatilles*

Soak and blanch 250 g of lamb's sweetbreads and cook them gently in butter. In a blanc cook 125 g of cock's combs that have been scalded to remove the skin and properly soaked in cold water, together with 25 g of cock's stones (simply cooked in a tenth of a litre of Madeira and a spoonful of butter). On a high heat, sauté 250 g of trimmed and sliced chicken livers seasoned with salt and pepper. Cook in some butter 250 g of button mushrooms that you have previously trimmed and washed. Put into a pan the sweetbreads, the livers, the cock's combs, the stones and the mushrooms. Add 125 g truffles cut into thick strips. Moisten the whole with 150 ml Madeira. Cover and stew.

Prepare a white sauce with a very strong chicken stock, in other words a velouté, and add to it half its volume in fresh cream. Reduce by half, perfume it with a little Madeira, add butter and strain. Pour this sauce over the ragout.

Prosper Montagné, Larousse gastronomique

---

* Pierre de Bourdeille, seigneur (and abbé) de Brantôme (*c.* 1540–1614) was an historian, soldier and biographer. His *Memoirs* first appeared in 1665 and are particularly good fun for his descriptions of high-jinks and frolics with and among *les dames galantes* at the court of France. *Translator.*

A ragout of cock's combs and cock's stones à la Périgord

Cut about thirty pieces of truffle into olive shapes and simmer them in Champagne; to this add a Champagne sauce. When it is sufficiently reduced, mix in around thirty large cock's stones, bring just to the boil and serve your ragout in the proper fashion.

Antonin Carême, L'Art de la cuisine française au XIXe siècle, volume 3 (The Art of French Cookery in the 19th Century, 1847)

A ragout of cock's combs and cock's stones à la Périgueux

Boil a good garnish of cock's combs in half a glass of Madeira, then add a *sauce Périgueux;** let it bubble a few times then add the stones, serving your ragout in the proper manner, placing some nice looking cock's combs here and there on top.

Antonin Carême, L'Art de la cuisine française au XIXe siècle, volume 3

A ragout of cock's combs and cock's stones à la Toulouse

Bring to the boil two large ragout spoons of *sauce allemande†* to which you must add two handfuls of medium-sized mushrooms with their reduced cooking stock, a bit of chicken glaze, some butter, a pinch of grated nutmeg and dozen double cock's combs.§ Reduce the sauce properly and mix in twenty-four fat cock's stones: allow it to bubble several times and serve your ragout according to the rule.

Antonin Carême, L'Art de la cuisine française au XIXe siècle, volume 3

A ragout of cock's combs and cock's stones à la Toulouse, sauce suprême

Trim two large truffles and slice them thinly then simmer them in chicken consommé; them mix in two spoonfuls of *sauce suprême*, some cock's combs, some mushrooms and their reduced cooking stock, and a pinch of grated nutmeg; reduce it properly; add some large cock's stones to the ragout and a little fresh butter; serve.

Antonin Carême, L'Art de la cuisine française au XIXe siècle, volume 3

---

* A *sauce Périgueux* is a simple truffle sauce with a demi-glace. *Translator.*

† A *sauce allemande* is a simple, but rich velouté. *Translator.*

§ Double cock's combs are from certain breeds of poultry, e.g. Polonaise or Crèvecoeur, and are horned in shape. *Translator.*

OBSERVATION

You could also serve ragouts of cock's stones with peas, à la macédoine, with fat asparagus tips, with asparagus tips with peas and French beans; the same method would be employed in just using cock's combs in these diverse garnishes. You may also make these ragouts using new-season's cucumbers.
Antonin Carême, L'Art de la cuisine française au XIXe siècle, *volume 3*

Risotto Milanese (recipe from 1936)

Serves four:
  175 g rice
  1 litre stock
  125 egg dumplings made from chicken, cock's combs and cock's stones
  125 g roast veal and chicken breast or, better still,
    sweetbreads and ham
  125 g mushrooms
  1 truffle of 20 – 25 g
  3 spoonfuls of tomato purée, fresh or tinned
  110 g grated Gruyère
  15 g Parmesan
  30 g butter

Sift the rice before you wash it, put it on the heat in some boiling stock. Cook without stirring on the lowest flame until the stock has been completely absorbed by the rice, add salt and pepper to taste. Now mix the rice with the tomato purée, butter, egg dumplings, then the cock's combs and stones, the veal and the chicken or the sweetbreads and ham, the mushrooms and the truffle, all cut into dice; the last thing you add is the cheese. Put the preparation in a terrine dish and place in a bain-marie in the oven and allow it to melt in the oven for fifteen or twenty minutes. Serve in the terrine.

Madame Scheffer and Mademoiselle François, Recettes de cuisine pratique
(Practical Cookery Recipes, 1936)

Risotto with cock's stones and white truffles

At the outset, risotto was a bourgeois dish of northern Italy, Lombardy in particular: rice traditionally being cultivated in the Po valley. For a good decade it has been fashionable in France and has muscled into the restaurant scene in a way that I need hardly describe. Several books have been written about it. Some authors have used Escoffier to justify the view that you should not add stock little by little to the dish as it cooks but, on the contrary, cover the rice from the start with the all the liquid and then not stir it during the cooking.*

I have some sympathy with the advocates of this method, especially those restaurants dealing with large quantities, for it is certainly more practical; but, having lived in Italy nearly four years (and in Lombardy moreover), I can guarantee that this 'lazy method' is not approved by Italian home-cooks. It is hard to know at the start what quantity of stock is going to be required; it will vary according to the rice's absorbency, even when large quantities are used. And if you do add all the stock at the beginning, there are two major drawbacks, especially if you are cooking small amounts for family consumption (4–6 people): either the liquid will not be absorbed by the end of the cooking and you will have something sloppy known as *risotto all'onda* (wave risotto) and a texture not suitable for all garnishes; or you will need to prolong the cooking until the rice is completely soft, running the risk of it no longer being *al dente*, even overcooked. It is therefore the traditional method – that which ensures the maximum softness and richness of the rice – that I recommend here, but you will need to be patient and add the stock ladle by ladle.

Serves four to six:

500 g cock's stones	8 tbsp olive oil
4 grey shallots	400 g Arborio or Vialone rice
1 ½ litres (more or less) of very	50 g butter
good de-greased chicken	100 g freshly grated Parmesan
stock (if possible home-made)	1 fresh white truffle
400 ml dry white wine	fine sea salt, freshly ground
2 g saffron threads	white pepper

Peel the cock's stones, peel and chop the shallots.

Heat the stock, pour 500 ml into a separate pan, adding half the white wine and poach the stones at a simmer for 5 minutes. Take off the heat and reserve.

---

* Nor is Escoffier alone. This method is also counselled in French cookery schools, where between the wars risotto used to be part of the classic canon of 'bourgeois home cooking'. It was, however, just an adaptation of the authentic Italian regional dish, and 'Piedmontese' rice – as they called the round grains – was relatively difficult to obtain, as it was rarely sold by grocers and could only be found in grain merchants. Now, the common or garden long grain rice of the period (Carolina rice) did not suit al dente cooking, which is a prerequisite for risotto (see recipe). It is noteworthy that in the original edition of *Larousse gastronomique* (1938), Prosper Montagné himself stipulates the traditional method: 'Stir 100 g of chopped up onions in butter, without allowing them to colour and add to the onion 500 g of Piedmontese rice. Cook slowly in a corner of the hob, stirring so that every grain is well impregnated with butter. Pour in pot-au-feu stock, or white fond, to cover the rice to double its height, adding more liquid five or six times, but not adding any until the previous dose has been fully absorbed by the rice. Cook the risotto covered for 18 to 20 minutes. Add, once it is cooked, two spoonfuls of butter and 75 g of grated Parmesan. Note: risotto can be complimented with diverse things such as ham cut in cubes and turned in butter, mussels, peas (which can be cooked in the rice), black truffles cut in cubes and turned in hot butter, or white truffles, which should be added to the risotto at the last moment.'

Stir the saffron into the rest of the stock and let it infuse until you need it. Pour the oil into the thick-bottomed pan and sweat the chopped shallots but do not let them brown. When the shallots have melted, add the rice (it should not be washed, if you insist you may rub it in a clean teacloth) and stir it about in such a way that every grain is covered by the oil. Continue until the grains become translucent, but without letting them colour or fry, as they must not become crunchy. Immediately, pour in the rest of the white wine, stir and allow the rice to steep for one or two minutes before adding a ladleful of stock (about 250 ml), mix with a spatula and allow to cook on a very low heat until the rice has absorbed the stock. As soon as the rice begins to soften on the surface, add another ladleful, stir and continue until the rice is *al dente* which will be between 17 and 20 minutes depending on the quality of the rice. Towards the end of the cooking, add the stock in smaller amounts, in order to avoid making the mass too liquid: it must retain its creamy consistency.

Remove from the heat straight away.

Off the heat, stir in the butter, season and adjust the seasoning and stir.

Drain the stones and, after cutting them in 4 or 8 pieces lengthways, in cubes or in strips, add them carefully to the mixture, together with the grated Parmesan. You can toss them in butter first.

Turn out into a very hot bowl and grate the white truffle over the surface of the risotto. Serve at once.

You may mix the cock's stones with cock's combs. This is a tasty variation.

Rich rice with a *salpicon* of chicken livers, cock's stones and cock's combs, mushrooms and black truffles

Rich rice is excellent in itself, but may be served with a garnish of white truffles, fresh morels, stuffed tomatoes, grilled mushrooms, etc. It is very good served with roast quails and it is perfect with a *salpicon* of chicken livers, cock's combs and cock's stones, mushrooms and black truffles. It is also a fine garnish for veal kidneys and chicken livers.

For 6 people, take: 1125 g of good beef or veal stock – 250 g rice – 125 g butter – 125 g bone marrow – 50 g grated Gruyère (optional) – 2 medium shallots – 1 medium-sized onion – salt and pepper

Chop the shallots and the onion.
    Wash the rice, soak it in cold water for an hour, drain it and dry it in a kitchen cloth.
    Put the butter, bone marrow, shallots and onion into a pan and let them cook without browning. Pass them though a sieve then add rice

and mix well. Spread them out over the bottom of the pan, moisten them with a few spoonfuls of stock and heat them, uncovered.

As soon as the stock has been absorbed, shake the pan in such a way as to detach the grains of rice from the bottom of the pan, add more stock and repeat the process until all the liquid has been absorbed.

Season the dish while it is cooking, but taste all the while as the seasoning will depend on the stock you have used.

At the last moment, add the grated cheese, stir well and serve.

The rice should be soft and the grains whole, not broken.'

Ali-Bab, Gastronomie pratique

Cock's stones in Marsala

Slowly cook 36 good cock's stones in butter. Put them together with half a Madeira-glass of good Marsala into a sauteuse together with a ladleful of demi-glace, as much veal glaze and a claret-glass of double cream. Add in 36 good slices of raw truffles and leave on the heat until the sauce is of a consistency to coat the stones and truffles. Put it into a silver timbale and serve at once on hot coals.

Fernand Fleuret, 'Septième journée, les hors d'oeuvres chauds', in L'Héptaméron des gourmets, *Paris 1919.*

Cock's stones *au vin*, as a canapé

Obviously, a proper *coq au vin* must be made with a real farmyard cockerel and not an old chicken, and logically the bird is still endowed with its natural attributes, which will become apparent when you are chopping it into pieces. You must not take away that delicious morsel. Leave the testicles attached to flesh and cook the bird as is your wont. At the moment of serving, carefully cut off the testes and offer them as the dish of honour to a chosen guest so that he (or she) eats them reverently with crushed salt or crushed pepper.

It goes without saying that the stones are just as delicious if the bird has been cooked in vin gris, vin jaune, beer or cider.

Preserved cock's stones

Cock's stones, we all recognize, are used in any number of garnishes to emphasize the delicacy and refinement of the dish. They may be preserved in the following manner:

General method: Soak the testes and then blanch them; drain them and put them in small jars, fill up with a strong, clear jelly [reduced stock], let them cool, cover with a centimetre of fat, and when that has set firm, seal hermetically.'

Joseph Favre, Dictionnaire universel de cuisine

Cock's stones and chicken livers in aspic

Prepare a good aspic with a calf's shin and foot, chicken giblets and vegetables. Clarify it well.

Put a layer of this jelly into a mould and then a layer of cock's stones, chicken livers and sweetbreads prepared earlier in a strong liquor, and with the addition of some smoked tongue. Cover with a reduced and well-seasoned *chaud-froid* sauce. Alternate the layers until the mould is full. Let it set on ice.

Remove from its mould at the moment of service.

This is an excellent luncheon hors d'oeuvre. It is clear that chicken livers may be replaced by small scoops of foie gras.

Ali-Bab, Gastronomie pratique

Stuffed cock's stones as hot hors d'oeuvre, garnishes, etc.

Choose some good poached cock's stones; split them in two lengthways and trim them so that they stay upright.

Stuff them with a cornet filled with a purée of foie gras, ham, chicken breast or truffles together with an equal measure of butter. Season well.

Paint them with a brush dipped in a *blanc*, or *sauce rose*, according to circumstances, them arrange them in a shallow timbale and cover with soft jelly.

The cock's stones can be put into petit-four moulds, enrobed in jelly and used as a border for cold fowl.

Auguste Escoffier, Le Guide culinaire

Cock's stones as garnishes

Wash repeatedly 125 g of white, firm cock's stones. Put them in a little saucepan with a tenth of a litre of water, a pinch of salt, 25 g of butter and a few drops of lemon juice.

Turn up the heat, but at the first sign of boiling, place the pan in the corner of the hob and let it cook under a cover for ten to twelve minutes, making sure that it does not boil.

Prosper Montagné, Larousse gastronomique

Cock's stones, *sauce râpure*

Marie Rouanet asks the question à propos of this recipe that I wanted to pose as an opening to this chapter: 'Could one offer a woman anything more succulent?'

If you go to a country where birds are still caponized, try to procure some testicles, and if that is not possible, get them from a bullock. You will find cock's combs and wattles if you ask a poultry breeder to keep enough heads for you to mix in with your real or false sweetbreads. You will need to sauté them quickly in some fat, and scatter them with *râpure* which is another word for breadcrumbs, together with garlic, parsley and a dash of vinaigrette.

Marie Rouanet, Petit traité romanesque de cuisine

Salad of spinach leaves with cock's stones and quail's eggs

Serves four:

24 trimmed cock's stones	50 g pine kernels
100 ml dry white wine	3 tbsp vegetable oil
24 quail's eggs	1 tbsp olive oil
a large handful of young spinach leaves	1 tbsp sherry vinegar
	1 tsp balsamic vinegar
8 dried tomatoes '*sott'olio*'	fine sea salt and freshly
40 g fresh Parmesan	ground pepper

Pour the white wine into a saucepan and bring to the boil. Poach the stones in this for 5 minutes shaking the pan two or three times, then take it off the heat and let them cool in the liquor.

Cook the quail's eggs until they are soft, rinse them immediately in cold water and shell them.

Sort and wash the spinach and spin it dry. Pat dry the tomatoes, cut them into strips. Cut or grate the Parmesan into thin shavings. Brown the pine kernels for a few minutes in a non-stick pan.

Make vinaigrette with the two different oils and two different vinegars in a bowl. Add salt and pepper and beat to a fine emulsion.

Put the spinach shoots and tomatoes into the salad bowl and mix well.

Share the salad out between four plates, and evenly distribute the cock's stones and the quail's eggs, scatter a few Parmesan shavings and pine kernels.

Serve straight away. You may use rocket instead of spinach.

Salpicon of chicken livers, cock's combs, cock's stones and truffles

> For six people, take 400 g chicken livers – 250 g consommé – 150 g button mushrooms – 125 g Madeira – 125 g cock's combs – 100 g cock's stones – 100 g butter – at least 75 g black Périgord truffles – 50 g chicken or meat stock – 20 g flour – lemon juice – salt and pepper.
>
> Blanch the stones and cock's combs in almost boiling consommé for 3 minutes and the chicken livers for 5; remove them from the stock and keep them hot; reserve the consommé.
>   Make a roux from the butter and the flour. Moisten it with the consommé and Madeira and let it cook gently for three-quarters of an hour. Skim the sauce during the cooking and season it with salt and pepper, but after tasting, as all depends on the seasoning of the stock you have used. Sharpen it if necessary with lemon juice.
>   A quarter of an hour before the finish, peel the truffles and cut them in slices, peel the mushrooms and dip them the lemon juice; and put them into the sauce; at the last moment add the meat juice, livers, stones and cock's combs and mix well. Raise the heat then serve on a dish of rich rice.
>
> *Ali-Bab,* Gastronomie pratique

Sauce suprême with a *salpicon* of cock's combs and cock's stones

> For the *sauce suprême,* see the recipe for chicken bouchées stuffed with cock's stones [p. 124] or the recipe for rich vol-au-vent [p. 143].
>   When you have done this, enrich the sauce with a *salpicon* of cock's combs and testes (see the previous recipe).
>
> *Ali-Bab,* Gastronomie pratique

Cock's stones *en gelée* on croûtons

For six people, take: 250 g cock's stones – 150 g whipped cream – 125 g well-seasoned, concentrated veal stock – 100 g cooked goose foie gras – 12 small slices of white bread (English-style) – as many truffles as you like – Madeira – butter – salt, pepper, paprika and four-spice mix.

Cook the truffles in the Madeira and the cock's stones in the hot but not boiling veal stock. As soon as they are firm, take them off the heat and keep them hot.
Fry the bread in butter, let it cool.
Purée the cock's stones and the foie gras, add the whipped cream, work them both together over ice so as to make them perfectly homogeneous, season to taste. Spead the mix on the croûtons and decorate them with slices of truffle. Then cover with the cooled veal stock: allow it to get really cold when it will form a jelly.
Serve as an hors d'oeuvre, covered with a napkin.

Ali-Bab, Gastronomie pratique

Batalia pie (*Tourte aux béatilles*)

'Carême remarked in his treatise *Entrées chaudes de pâtisserie*: "The pie as an entrée is no longer luxurious enough to appear on our opulent tables because it looks too vulgar; even the bourgeoisie disdains it, and only eats hot pâtés and vol-au-vent, whereas in the past the families of rich merchants were delighted to eat a modest pie as their entrée. But in those days, tradesmen did not put on the airs and graces of gastronomes. *O tempora, o mores!*... Our great chefs in former times served this pie at the table of princes..." Since Carême wrote these words about the decline of pies in his lifetime, this excellent hot pastry entrée has come back into fashion and now, not only do the "tradesmen" alluded to by Carême revel in them, but even more refined gastronomes.' Prosper Montagné wrote this in the first edition of his *Larousse gastronomique* of 1938!

To make a batalia pie for eight people roll out two circles of puff pastry of 400 g each, half a centimetre thick. On one of these spread a thick layer of *ragout de béatilles* (see recipe) or one of the other recipes for cock's stones that are suggested as garnish for *bouchées* or vol-au-vent. Depending on which recipe you choose, bind it with a little *sauce velouté*, *suprême* or *financière* and cover it with the second round of pastry. Make sure the two rounds are well joined with water or egg white. Draw a rose on the top or make a border of leaves. Gild it with an egg, place it on a slightly moist baking tray in the centre of the a pre-heated oven (210°C, Gas 7) and cook for around 30 minutes. Reduce the temperature to 180°C half way through the cooking.
Serve at once.

A turban of chicken garnished with a *salpicon* of cock's stones

For six people you will need: 600 g strong veal or chicken stock – 250 g the palest veal fillet, without skin or nerves – 250 g ox suet, firm and trimmed – 250 g button mushrooms – 150 g thick cream – 135 g butter – 6 g salt – 1 g pepper – 20 g four-spice mix – 24 the whitest cock's stones – 18 live crayfish – 2 fresh whole eggs – 2 fresh egg yolks – a good, tender, plump chicken – plenty of truffles – some puff pastry leaves – lemon juice – salt and pepper.

Make 30 *quenelles de godiveau à la crème* (oblong meat dumplings) out of the veal fillet, suet, the double cream, 6 g of salt, the gram of pepper, the four-spice mix and the 2 whole eggs.

Cook the truffles for 20 minutes in the veal and chicken stock into which you have poured the Madeira, port or sherry.

Cook the crayfish in a *court bouillon*; peel them, put the tails to one side and make a crayfish butter with the rest and 60 g of butter.

Grease the chicken with 25 g of butter; roast it but do not completely cook it. During the cooking, baste it with veal and chicken stock.

Finally, finish off the cooking of the chicken in the *jus*, in an open pan. Skim any fat off the *jus*.

Put the mushrooms in a pan with the rest of the butter, lemon juice and salt and cook them for a quarter of an hour.

Poach the *quenelles de godiveau* in the chicken *jus* for as long as it takes to cook them, then the cock's stones for just a few moments. Strain the juice and then concentrate it.

Put the mushrooms, *quenelles de godiveau*, cock's stones, crayfish tails together in a small pan. Keep them hot.

Take 150 g of concentrated cooking juices, bind it with the egg yolks, finish the sauce off with the crayfish butter. Taste and adjust the seasoning.

Cut up the chicken, arrange the pieces in a turban on a dish, glaze them with a little reduced stock; place the *salpicon* at the centre of the turban and cover it with the crayfish butter sauce: garnish the peripheries of the turban with little puff pastry leaves lightly browned in the oven and alternating half truffles.

Serve, sending the rest of the cooking juices round in a sauceboat.

It is a lovely and beautiful dish.

Ali-Bab, Gastronomie pratique

Rich vol-au-vent*

One of the best possible fillings for a vol-au-vent consists of a *salpicon* of *quenelles de godiveau* with truffles, sheep's or calf's brains, calf's or lamb's sweetbreads, cock's combs and cock's stones, mushrooms and truffles, all bound together by a *sauce suprême*.

For eight people you will need:
1°) For the pastry: 600 g flour – 600 g butter – about 300 g butter – 10 g salt – two fresh egg yolks.
2°) For the filling: 150 g cock's combs and stones – 125 g turned mushrooms – 25 g butter – 40 little *quenelles de godiveau* with truffles or chicken quenelles – 3 lamb's brains – one nice veal sweetbread – truffles and lemon juice.
3.°) For the sauce: 200 g Madeira – 150 g chicken glaze – 125 g thick cream – 30 g butter – 30 g flour – a litre of concentrated veal stock – 3 fresh egg yolks – mushroom essence – truffle essence – pepper.

Make some puff pastry using the elements listed in the first paragraph, turning it and rolling it out 8 times; then, using the pastry, prepare a vol-au-vent case and cook it in a hot oven.

Trim the sweetbread and put it into soak in cold water before cooking it in some of the veal stock.

Clean the truffles.

Cook the brains in salted water to which you have added herbs and vinegar. Cook the mushrooms in butter and lemon juice and the truffles in the Madeira.

Poach the quenelles in boiling salted water or without fat in the oven.

Blanch the cock's combs and cock's stones.

Keep all these ingredients hot.

Meanwhile, make the *sauce suprême*: put the Madeira left over from cooking the truffles together with the liquor from the mushrooms together in a pan and add pepper to taste and reduce by half. Work the flour into the butter, let it brown before adding the remaining veal stock, the cooking juices from the sweetbread and the Madeira reduction. Concentrate the sauce and skim it during the cooking, before adding the chicken glaze in the end. Reduce it further until it is thick enough to coat a spoon. Take it off the heat and perfume it with the mushroom and truffle essences (according to taste). Strain it through muslin, and keep it hot in a bain-marie.

---

* The name of the dish is *Vol-au-vent au gras*. Much of French cuisine was divided between *gras* and *maigre* dishes, where the *maigre* indicated that it might be consumed during Lent and on fast days, while the *gras* were rich, filled with meat and other morsels. *Translator.*

Cut the brains into slices, cut the sweetbread into dice and finely chop the truffles.

Put the sauce together with the truffles, mushrooms, brains, sweetbreads, quenelles, cock's combs and cock's stones and continue cooking for a few minutes more, before binding it all with a liaison of egg yolks and cream.

Heat the vol-au-vent for 5 minutes in an open oven, fill it with the *salpicon* and serve.

Ali-Bab, Gastronomie pratique

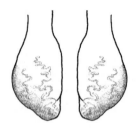

Just this once... we end up with bollocks!

Cocktail

Huevo de chivo (Kid's bollock)

In Latin America, *huevo de chivo* is a cocktail which gets its name from the simple fact that there is a maraschino cherry in the bottom of the glass!

LA RUEDA DE MATE (THE MATÉ CIRCLE)

In Argentina, maté drinkers (it is called 'yerba mate' in Argentinian Spanish) generally take this tea-like infusion from a calabash that might be made of metal, wood, or even the skin of a bull's testicle.

Maté is meant to have properties that are at once stimulating and mildly narcotic, and it is almost always drunk in a group, according the ritual known as 'la rueda de mate' or the maté circle. It may only be drunk directly from the bowl, with the help of a straw or bombilla.

The recipe as a testicle-tease

Eggs in the manner of donkey's bollocks

These donkey-bollock eggs, so dear to Rabelais, are nothing more or less than *oeufs en meurette* [poached eggs in a red wine sauce]. You'll recall that the donkey's virility has always intrigued us, no doubt because of the more than ample proportions of its sexual organs, the penis above all. In essence, the donkey is the most generously endowed (from the point of view of length to weight) of any land animal (an average erectile size of 70 cms as opposed to a 'mere' metre for an elephant, the biggest beast of all, at 5–6 tons). Hence the popular idiom, 'hung like a donkey'. It was this that must have inspired Frédéric Dard* (also a man with

---

* The reader will encounter Frédéric Dard (San-Antonio) many times in the pages which follow. His surname means 'dart' or 'sting'. He was in truth a very popular French thriller writer (1921–2000) whose 173 novels under the pseudonym San-Antonio are masterpieces of creative language and comedy. *Translator.*

an evocative name) to call his account of the sex-life of San-Antonio's assistant Alexandre-Benoît Bérurier – a man with a redoubtable reputation as a sexual animal – *Si Queue-d'Âne m'était conté* (If I Had Been Told About Donkey Pricks [but in his punning way, *queue d'âne* is also the child's game of pin the tail on the donkey], 1976)! For centuries the ass was anathema to the Catholic Church, together with his stablemate the ox (although he had been castrated), despite the fact the donkey warmed the infant Jesus with his breath in the cradle and that it was on a donkey that Christ entered Jerusalem – the Christophorean animal *par excellence*. The word *viédase* (which is composed of two elements, *vié* [from the Late Latin *victis* which became *vit* in French, i.e. penis] and *ase* or *aze*, i.e. ass or donkey, therefore meaning literally donkey-prick, but usually in the figurative sense of fool or dolt) is often used by Rabelais. In the south of France today, harking back to its literal meaning, it is their word for aubergine. By extension, the donkey's penis or *viédase* symbolizes the face of sin in Romanesque sculpture.

For this recipe it is fun to choose very large eggs (over 73 grams as opposed to 60 grams for a medium egg). It can also be made with duck eggs (which are a lot bigger but less refined, the white having a rubbery texture). I would rule against using ostrich eggs to create the illusion of elephant's balls.

Serves two (two pairs of balls):

2 shallots	100 g cured belly pork
80 g butter	(not too salty)
1 bottle of robust and	100 g button mushrooms
tannic red wine	4 small slices of slightly stale
1 bouquet garni (sprig of	brown bread
thyme, bay leaf, small stick	2 cloves garlic
of celery, 3 or 4 sprigs of	4 very large eggs
flat-leaf parsley)	salt, freshly ground pepper

Peel and chop the shallots finely, put them in a saucepan or little frying-pan and sweat them in 20 g of butter until they have melted but not browned. Moisten them with a third of the wine, add the bouquet-garni and let it reduce to the consistency of a glaze (almost syrupy).

Meanwhile, put the belly pork in a saucepan filled with cold water and blanch it by simmering for 5 minutes. Drain it, dry it and cut it into very small, matchstick-like pieces. Peel the mushrooms, halve or quarter them if they are large or of middling dimensions.

Melt 20 g of butter in a sauteuse, and start by warming up the lardoons, then add the mushrooms and cook for 5 five minutes, stirring often. Remove from the pan and reserve.

Rub the bread hard with the garlic until you have a little hollow in the crumb. Pour the rest of the wine into a saucepan and boil for a few minutes to remove the alcohol.

Strain the shallot sauce through a chinois, pressing hard to get out all the liquid. Put it in a pan and add the bacon, mushrooms, and seasoning. Stir, and put on a low flame just to keep it warm.

At the same time, fry the bread slices on both sides in the rest of the butter until them are nicely golden. Pat dry.

Finally, while you are doing this, poach the eggs in the wine for a maximum of 3 minutes.

To serve, put two slices of bread in two well-heated shallow bowls (or two little pans). Take out the eggs with a slotted spoon and place a pair of balls (two eggs) on each plate, one on each canapé. Top it with the mushroom and bacon sauce. Serve piping hot.

The recipe which deceives

Salep or A blancmange of powdered testicles or Rose-scented sperm (or with orange flowers)

A salep is a powder of boiled orchid roots that have been dried in the sun. What then, is the connection to testicles? Well, the orchid derives its name from the Greek *orkidion* (little testicle), which in turn originates in *orkhis* (testicle), because it looks like a bulb. This is why its name in botanical Latin is *Orchis mascula* or male testicle. You could, on the other hand, see an analogy between the two functions of that seminal organ and the pretty, immodest flower (which looks like a vulva) which secretes a mass of liquid in its petals which comes out in the form of little horns.

Salep is highly prized in the Middle East where it is used to make a dish which, from its milky whiteness and its thick, viscous texture, resembles sperm. It is in fact a sort of blancmange. In Turkey they make a drink and an ice which they have christened 'of foxes testicles'. It is made from powdered wild orchids. Salep is reputedly aphrodisiac. To top it all, in ancient Greece it was called *satyrion* – which gives you an idea of the effects it was supposed to produce – and it was used to make stimulating draughts.

Satyrion was used to make an aphrodisiac concoction in Petronius' *Satyricon* which the maid Psyche feeds to Encolpius:

> The maid, who was called Psyche, carefully spread a carpet across the flagstones and set about fondling my privates, which were as dead as

a thousand stiffs. Ascyltus had covered his head with his cloak, as he had learned that it was unwise to poke your nose on other men's business.

The maid produced two thongs from her dress, and with one she bound my feet, and with the other my hands.

[...at this point the maid must have offered Encolpius a draught]

As the conversation was petering out, Ascyltus said, 'And I, don't I deserve a drink?'

The maid was betrayed by my smile. She clapped her hands and said, 'I gave it to you, young man, and you yourself drank all the medicine.'

'Is that so?' said Quartilla. 'Encolpius has really drunk all the satyrion?' And her body trembled with a gracious laugh.

Serves six: 500 ml milk
1 sachet (56 g) or two level tbsp salep (powdered orchid root)
1 tbsp rosewater or orange-flower water (optional)

To serve: 1 tsp of powdered cinnamon,
1 tbsp dried flower petals
1 tbsp shelled pistachios or blanched almonds.

Stir the salep into the milk, pour it into a saucepan and bring it to the boil on a very gentle heat, stirring with a spatula until it thickens.

Take it off the flame and at this point you may choose to perfume it with some rosewater or orange-flower water. Stir it in well.

Pour it into a pretty shallow bowl, ice-cream bowls or ramekin dishes.

You can sprinkle some powdered cinnamon or scatter some flower petals, pistachios or crushed almonds on top. Serve cool or at room temperature.

Note: you may obtain salep, rosewater and dried flower petals in oriental grocers' shops.

AN ACCOUNT OF SALEP BY ALEXANDRE DUMAS

This name is of Persian origin, and is given to the dried bulbs of the orchids that grow in great number in Persia and all over Asia Minor. These bulbs were well known to the ancients, and both Pliny and Theoprastus make mention of them in their writings. The Greeks and the Romans knew them above all for their aphrodisiac qualities, which were only due, however, to the different spices they added, such as ginger, amber, musk, cloves, etc. It seems that a man can derive sufficient nourishment for a day with an ounce of this substance and as much animal fat dissolved in water, and Orientals provide themselves with salep for their travels.

To make salep, Orientals harvest the orchid bulbs when they begin to flower; they then strip them of their bark and toss them in cold water, where they remain for several hours. Next they cook them in boiling water and thread them with horsehair, or better still cotton and let them dry in the air. The bulbs become almost translucent, very hard and look much like tragacanth gum. They can be stored indefinitely providing you avoid humidity. Sometimes, instead of hanging them up to dry, they are left out on a bolting cloth. When they want to make jellies they reduce them to powder, moistening them first with a little water, without which pulverization would be impeded by the extreme hardness of the material. A small quantity is dissolved in boiling water which, perfumed and sugared, rapidly turns into a transparent jelly as it cools.

The salep jelly you find sold in shops is as often as not mixed with flour, but it is easy to spot the fraud if you dissolve 2.15 g salep in 225 g distilled water adding to the resulting liquid 1.9 g magnesium calcite: at the end of a few hours the mixture will take on a well-pronounced jellied consistency which will not be the case if the salep has been falsified.

Geoffroi says that if you evaporate the water in which you have cooked the salep on clay plates, there will remain a viscous extract the odour of which is comparable to that of a flowery meadow when the wind sweeps off it. Its aroma is also like that of sweet clover when the flower begins to blow.

Alexandre Dumas, Le Grand dictionnaire de cuisine

The recipe as a bollocks

Swiss balls or Belgian buns?

The name gives nothing away, but the recipe for Swiss balls is in fact a Belgian one which, it appears, comes from Hainault. They are round doughnuts the form of which evokes 'things', hence the name, but that doesn't explain why they should be Swiss. They look a little like the French 'pets de nonne' (nuns' farts),* another baffling name, except that they are cooked in water and not in fat. These

---

* Pets de nonne are the same as the gougère that is an inevitable compliment to a wine tasting in Burgundy. They are light, hollow buns flavoured with Gruyère cheese, which must explain the reference to farts. Translator.

doughnuts (they come in a number of different forms) are also called *couques* and some people maintain that the word is no more than a euphemism for balls, just like that other Belgian dish, *choesels* (see lexicon, page 61). Others refute this attribution, noting that *couques* describe a multitude of cakes in Belgium, but is rarely extended to doughnuts.* Fairground doughnuts are usually called *smoutebolle* (balls cooked in lard) or *oliebolle* (balls cooked in oil), *croustillons* when they are hollow, and *beignets* when they are filled. *Couques* are more like enriched breads† and *couques au beurre* are little *pains au chocolat* shaped like croissants (let's not forget we are in Belgium).§ When it comes to *couques à la crème*, they come as figures-of-eight, the fat bits being covered with cream. Well I never, isn't that odd! – in figures-of-eight and covered with cream, and they have nothing to do with bollocks? (For further elucidation, see the lexicon, s.v. 8 (eight), on page 177.) Whichever derivation is correct, why don't we impose universal accord by rechristening these doughnuts *couqu'ougnettes* (see the lexicon again, s.v. Sweets, *coucougnettes*, p. 212)?#

For about ten brace of balls:

500 g flour	2 whole eggs
40 g fresh baker's yeast	400 ml milk
1 level tsp fine salt	30 g of butter
2 tbsp granulated sugar	melted butter and brown
	sugar, to serve

Crumble the yeast into the warm milk. The milk should not be too hot, as it will kill the yeast, or too cold, which would stop it from working.

Mix together the flour, the salt and the sugar in a mixing bowl. Break in the whole eggs, then work with a wooden spoon.

Once the yeast has dissolved in the milk, work it into the mixture as well as the softened butter. Mix with a wooden spoon at first then knead for 10 minutes. Let it rise for 2 hours in a draught-free place.

When the dough has risen, cover your hands with flour and break off pieces before fashioning them in the form of bollocks.

---

* The name of this recipe in French is '*Couilles Suisses et Couques Belges*'. *Couques* is of the same origin as the German *Kuchen* and the English cake. They are not to be confused with 'Belgian buns' in English, which are similar to Chelsea buns: a glazed version of the spiral the Germans call a *Schnecke* (which exists in many forms) or snail and the French know as a *pain aux raisins*. Both the denominations 'Belgian' and 'Chelsea' have become rare these days. The spiral bun is now referred to by the adjective 'Danish' transmogrified into a noun. *Translator*.

† I.e. of the family of *croissants*, *pains au chocolat*, etc. *Translator*.

§ From the time of Baudelaire and before, the French have enjoyed poking fun at the Belgians. *Translator*.

Coucougnettes are a sweetmeat made of crushed cane-sugar almonds mixed with grilled almonds caramelized with a touch of ginger *eau-de-vie* and a dash of Armagnac. The shape is suggestive. *Translator*

Bring two large saucepans filled with salted water to the boil. Throw 6–8 balls into each. Turn them, without pricking them, for a minute. Let them cook for 3–4 minutes until they are brown and have risen nicely.

Remove with a slotted spoon, scatter them with brown sugar and coat them with melted butter. Serve hot.

Note: the water should carry on simmering during the cooking of the balls.

Magic recipes

Tristan and Isolde's love potion (with cock's stones)

Just at the moment of completing this book, a correspondent sent me this recipe which might be worth printing. It is meant to be authentic. I am happy to accept it, but I cannot insist you believe it. If you manage to make it, send me a sample so that I can smell it, so that I can taste it and so that I might experience once more the charms of Abisag. *

You will need 2 litres of old burgundy in which you must infuse 300 g of finely chopped truffles while the moon is waxing.

After 3 whole days, cook 12 crayfish in a stock seasoned with pepper, cumin, aniseed, thyme, bay, red chillies and a stick of celery. Let it boil for 20 minutes and then pound all the elements of your preparation to make a thin purée. Put this in a bain-marie and let it concentrate slowly for 24 hours. Strain it through a cloth and put it in a non-metallic bowl. Take the chopped-up testicles of a two-year-old white cockerel and marinate them [in the same bowl] for 3 hours. Strain the liquor off and mix it with the burgundy. Let your mixture marinate overnight in a big glass bottle perfectly stoppered and sealed with wax. Filter the wine then macerate a little bouquet of freshly gathered mandragora flowers in it for around 75 minutes.

A liqueur glass for the woman of your dreams and a liqueur glass for yourself, and you will see what you will see. They say the love that Tristan bore Isolde was thanks to this philtre…

Curnonsky and André Saint-Georges, La Table et l'amour, nouveau traité des excitants modernes

---

* Allusion to the beautiful young virgin who was sought all over Israel to become the maid to the old King David with a view to 'rekindling' his flame. Despite her beauty, Abisag the Sunamite did not manage to reawaken the ardours of the impotent old king. He did not succumb to her charms and he never slept with her (First Book of Kings).

A means of increasing genital ardour (using the testicles of a billy-goat or a ram)

Drinking sugared milk in which one has boiled a billy-goat's testicles or those of a ram produces vigour.

Vatsyayana, Kama Sutra *(Part Seven: Aphrodisiacs)*

A marvellous recipe for rendering the member proud and increasing virile power (with cock's stones)

The sheik Suyûti gives a marvellous recipe which he had from the sultan of Tlemcen who had personally tried it out and deflowered forty virgins in one night. You take the testicles of three male chickens (or eight, or fourteen). You add to these green ginger, nutmeg, perfumed walnuts, chilli essence, tubipora [a coral], a clove, cinnamon, dried earth from India, some palm seeds of the type known as 'intelligence grains', an ounce of Hyderabad salt and a quarter of an ounce of saffron.

Pound, blend and knead with a good honey, previously skimmed. Put it all in a glass jar. Close it hermetically with a bit of the clay of wisdom. Let the mixture simmer three nights and three days near a fire until it thickens. Let it cool down. Roll it into balls the size of a chickpea and take the equivalent of a lentil every time you want to make love. The member rises in erection and there is no means of softening it besides drinking a little vinegar.

Abdelwahab Bouhdiba, quoting Cheikh Jalaeddîne al-Suyûtî, Kitâb al rah'ma, *in* La Sexualité en Islam *(Sexuality in Islam, 1975).*

A love potion (with a hare's balls)

Draw some blood, preferably on a Friday in springtime and put it into the oven to dry in a little pot together with the two testicles of a hare and the liver of a dove. Pound it all up to make a fine powder. Make the person whom you want to love you swallow it.

Jacques Durand, ed., Almanach des pays d'Oc *(The Languedoc Almanac, 1985)*

A potion to heighten virility according to Nicolas Flamel (using the left testicle of a white billy-goat)

This formula was worked out by Nicolas Flamel (1330–1418), a famous medieval alchemist:

Take a burdock seed, pound it in a mortar and add the testicle of a three-year-old white billy-goat and a pinch of powder originating from the hair of a completely white dog that you will have cut off on the first day of the new moon and burned on the seventh. You will put the whole to brew in a half-filled bottle of brandy which you will leave uncorked for twenty-one days, so that it might receive the influence of the stars. On the twenty-first day, which will be precisely the first day of the next moon, you will cook it up until the mix is reduced to the state of a very thick porridge; then add in four drops of crocodile spermatozoa and you will then carefully strain the mixture through a stocking. Having collected the liquid that flows through, there is nothing left to do but to rub the natural parts of a man and it will perform wonders immediately.

quoted in Marcel Rouet, Le Paradis sexuel et les aphrodisiaques *(Sexual Heaven and Aphrodisiacs, 1971)*

The twin balls of satyrion

Satyrion is also called *orchis* or *serapias*. It was a herb with the leaves of a leek, a tall stem and a purple flower. Its root consisted of two tubers that looked for all the world like a pair of testicles. The larger of the two, which was the harder, provoked a carnal appetite; the smaller, which was the softer, drunk in goats' milk, would blunt the arrow of love. It was important, therefore, not to confuse them when when you used them.

Curnonsky and André Saint-Georges, La Table et l'amour, nouveau traité des excitants modernes

A pommade to fortify sexual appetites

Greater sexual prowess is ensured by the following potion: you take a little lichwort [or pellitory-of-the-wall, *Parietaria officinalis*] called *Quoun toûs*, a little ginger and you reduce them to a fine powder; you mix them with a lily pommade and anoint the intimate part and the two testicles. If you do this, oh reader, you will be strong at the hour of coupling, your seed will increase in quantity, your conduits will widen and all the phenomena of which we have spoken will be experienced with greater intensity.

Mohammad al-Nafzâwî, La Prairie parfumée où s'ébattent les plaisirs *(The Perfumed Meadow where Pleasures Frolic, 1976)*

An unguent to increase vigour in copulation

To obtain the proper unguent, you will need to start by mixing lavender, Spanish pellitory [or Spanish camomile, Anacyclus pyrethrum] Roman nettles [Urtica pilulifera, larger and stronger than the common nettle] staphysagria [delphinium] with a small amount of narcissus extract. Once you have made a mixture, you will need to daub the stomach, lower abdomen, hips, genitals and the soles of the feet with it. This potion presents great advantages when it comes to vigorous coition.

Ahmed ibn Souleimân, Le Bréviaire arabe de l'amour (The Arabic Handbook of Love, 1998)

From bollock to lips (with a horse's testicle)

If you dip lac into the sweat of a testicle from a white horse, until it is saturated, then apply it to a red lip, that lip becomes white.

Vatsyayana, Kama Sutra (Part Seven:Aphrodisiacs)

Of the virtues of ox or cow dung in curing tumours of the testicle

I have made frequent experiments and the same dung is marvellous for tumours of the testicle. I took fresh cow dung and fried it in a pan with camomile flowers, roses and mellitory. This I applied to my testicles, which were cured on the second day; you might have said that they had never had a problem.

Le Grand et le Petit Albert, Les admirables secrets d'Albert le Grand (Third Book:'The Virtues and Properties of Many Sorts of Dung'), first published from 1668

CASTOREUM*

The beaver produced this substance; we once thought it his testicles because of the form it takes in the glandular pocket that holds the secretion.

It is hardly used in pharmacy these days, although, employed in tiny quantities, it allowed American Indians to achieve — or so it seems — astonishing records when it came to bouts of sex. And it is for that memory, and for the desire to be complete, that I speak of it at all.

Curnonsky and André Saint-Georges, La Table et l'amour, nouveau traité des excitants modernes

* Aromatic secretion from the anal region of a beaver, used in pharmaceuticals and scents.

A Lexicon of Human Testicular Terms

> *They don't melt in the hand or the mouth, you can only feel them rolling under*
> *their wrapping of slightly flabby flesh. They are very touching! Without them men*
> *would not be men. Of course, you can see the same, even more impressive ones, on*
> *bulls and billy goats, but those on a human are a lot more mysterious.*
> *Fellacia Dessert, 'Les boules de chair' (Balls of Flesh), in* La Première gorgé de
> sperme, c'est quand'même autre chose *(The First Mouthful of Sperm: It's*
> *Altogether Different, 1998)*

Man being a mammal, it is not totally unreasonable to think that his testicles would also be edible, even if only among tribes of cannibals. Whatever the case, they are certainly dishy… and there is no shortage of terms of endearment to designate the 'appendices to the subject'. In a word, having made an inventory of the anatomical or culinary terms used for comestible testicles (see the section on cookery), this is now the pendant (if you'll pardon the expression): a list of everyday words to denote a man's testicles. The list is in no way exhaustive.

---

* When it comes to the chosen quotations, I could have made thousands of others, drawn from literature, songs, cinema or the language of the streets to evoke the 'thing' or rather the things. If at the end of my readings and re-readings I have chosen some rather than others it is for two reasons (that is normal, I hear you say, the subject calls for binary numbers) : either they evoke a reflection as a result of the word itself, or because they illustrate the gamut of languages or literary genres in which the word is used.

A testicle is the first draft of a coracle.

David Mitchell (BBC Radio 4, July 2011)

Translator's note

The translation of a dictionary or glossary from one language to another is always a teasing problem. A word may have a use or meaning in French that is absolutely not mirrored in English. And although Mme Vié is generous with her references to English terms and expressions, there are some that she may not have thought worth bringing to the notice of her French readers. To naturalize this section, therefore, I have usually included the French headword(s) after my translation and I have added certain headings that are peculiar to the English-speaking world.

Accessories (French: *accessoires* n.f.): a nickname for testicles, implying a secondary role to the penis. It also stresses their character as added instruments. See also Accessory Store, under Back of the shop.

> ... apart from his socks full of holes, Béru was naked, as naked as a piglet on a plate. To cover his modesty he had only his pubes. These were certainly long, certainly curly, but for all that they were not enough to camouflage the robust accessories with which nature had endowed him! And these were jiving to the beat of his fury! Alarm bells, going full throttle; lashing their proud possessor, whipping him.
>
> *San-Antonio (Frédéric Dard),* Bérurier contre San-Antonio *(Bérurier versus San-Antonio, 1967)*

> 'Blast, it's a Charolais,' said Béru. 'Pretty breed. Was it yourself who gave him that perm, Alfred? Oh but sorry! You have bitten off the boy's accessories? Oy, Mister Felix, you've got a rival.'
>
> *San-Antonio,* Les Vacances de Bérurier ou La Croisière du 'Mer d'alors' *(Bérurier's Holidays or the Cruise of the 'Mer d' alors', 1967)*

Acolytes (French: *acolytes* n.m.): at first, acolytes were the servants of the priest at the altar, but the word has degenerated to mean boon companions or accomplices. And when it is used to denote testicles you can imagine the sort of religious service that is implied. Sometimes they say more precisely 'the two acolytes'.

Adam's apples: Of course, everyone knows that in the singular an Adam's apple is the protuberance formed by thyroid cartilage in the front of the neck, and it owes its name to the fact that it is more obvious on a man than a woman. I like to imagine, however, that in the plural, these little apples that belong to man alone are perhaps the fruits that tempted Eve in Garden of Eden.

Advantages (French: *avantages* n.f.): natural, of course. In the plural the word is metaphor for all the sexual bits one might choose to glorify on a man or a woman: breasts, buttocks, cunts and notably the sexual organs of a man.

Agates (English): an old term for testicles.

Anorchia: congenital absence of testicles. A rare condition: a survey of two million men carried out in 1938 revealed only 52 cases. Anorchism is the absence of one or both testicles.

Appendices (French: *appendices* n.m.): a word deriving from the Latin *appendix* signifying 'hanging from' and which means in French a prolongation of a main part. In the proper sense it is used to qualify all sorts of prolongations and expansion: nasal appendix (nose), caudal appendix (tail), ileocaecal appendix (bowels), or even in the figurative sense of an appendix to a book. It is similarly used by botanists in referring to parts of flowers, and by entomologists when talking of bits of insects. It is therefore easy to understand that, by extension, that the word appendix can mean a man's organ, penis alone when in the singular and the whole shooting-match when used in the plural.

Apples (English): see the entry under Fruit.

Attributes (French: *attributes* n.m.): virile, it goes without saying. They are sometimes called 'natural attributes' (see below s.v. eggs). Term applied to the trinity of male genital organs.

> 'It was bigger than me', she admitted. 'It was quite stupefying to find myself all of a sudden in presence of your attributes and it shocked me. It was a positive sort of shock. All of a sudden, I felt myself freed from the spell. How do you explain that?'
> *San-Antonio,* La Queue en trompette *(Turned-up Dick, 1997)*

> If the subject finds himself touched in his animal soul alone, he becomes inverted in a feminine way. He will be happy to comport himself as women do. His exterior virile attributes, however, will remain those of a normal man for all that.
> *Ahmad al-Tifachi,* Les Délices des coeurs, ou ce que l'on ne trouve en aucun livre *(The Delights of the Heart, or What You Will Never Find in a Book, 1981.*

Avocado (Nahuatl): the origins of our avocado pear lie in the Aztec word for testicle.

Back of the shop/Shop/Outbuildings/Shop window/Accessory store (French: *arrière-boutique* n.f.; *boutique* n.f.; *dépendances* n.f.; *devanture* n.f.; *magasin des accessoires* n.m.; Persian: *bazaar*): in popular speech, the front of the shop means the 'flies' or zip, and it is easy to imagine that the testicles lie at the back. For certain authors, however, it also evokes the anus.

Boutique (shop) denotes the sexual organs of a man or a woman and is used above all in the expression 'open up' or 'shut the shop'. The flies or zip represent the shutters.

The Persian *bazaar* also means a public or covered market in Arab countries and North Africa. In Europe the word means a shop which sells all sorts of merchandise (*Petit Larousse*). By extension, it is a nickname for the whole panoply of male genital organs, as in the expressions 'show me your bazaar' or conversely 'hide your bazaar', because they suggest the idea of unwrapping and rewrapping, an act performed in markets. It is the oriental equivalent of the accessory (see above) shop or store. You can also go over the top and talk of the 'big bazaar.'

It is easy to see why *dépendances* (outbuildings) might mean testicles.

The shop window (*devanture*) is a metaphor evoking the make genital collection and is even stronger than the word *boutique*. It is used in the expression '*y a du monde à la devanture*' (there is a crowd in the window) just as they say '*y a du monde au balcon*' (there is a crowd on the balcony) for a woman's breasts.

Bags (Irish English) (French: *poches* n.f.; *sac* n.m.; *sac à avoine* n.m.; *sac à grains de semence* n.m.; *sac à provisions* n.m.; *sac de nuit* n.m.; *sacoches* n.f.; *poche* n.f.; German: *Hodensack* n.m., i.e. scrotum; Spanish: *talega* n.f.): A synonym for 'purse': a metonymic metaphor denoting the two testicles nestling in the scrotum. Purse is also the etymological origin of the word cullion.

In French there are a number of variants: *sac à avoine* (bag of oats – oats being a French synonym for sperm, cf. sowing your wild oats in English), *sac à graines de semence* (bag of seeds: '*j'ai pris un coup de pied dans les sacs à semence*' – I was kicked in the seed bags), *sac à provisions* (shopping bag) or *sac de nuit* ([over] night bag.

> After him, as part of a group,
> Came a very honest young swain,
> With his night bag all cock a hoop.
> **Paul Scarron (1610–1660),** Nouvelles tragi-comiques *(New Tragi-comedies)*

Sacoches is a diminutive form, as in 'bicycle bags' (*sacoches à vélo*).

The scrotum is called *la poche* in Quebec. It is similar to bag, money-bag, etc.

In James Joyce's *Ulysses*, Molly Bloom creates the metaphor of 'bags full' in her monologue when she admires the statues of women and compares their beauty to that of men.

> curious the way its made 2 the same in case of twins theyre supposed to represent the beauty placed up there like those statues in the museum one of them pretending to hide it with her hand are they so beautiful of course compared with what a man looks like with his two bags full and

his other thing hanging down out of him or sticking up at you like a
hatrack no wonder they hide it with a cabbageleaf...

James Joyce, Ulysses, 1922

The Spanish for a bag is *talega* and it is used for the scrotum as well as what
goes in it. It is also amusing to note that *taleguilla* (the diminutive of *talega*) is
the name given to the torero's shorts.

Ballasts (French borrowing from English): a term applied occasionally to testicles, the metaphor suggesting their function. Borrowed from English, the word
designates the bladders which by virtue of being filled or emptied of water allow
the submarine to dive or return to the surface or a merchant ship to adjust the
balance of its cargo. Ballasts are filled or emptied on a boat in order to find a
better balance (*Petit Larousse*).

> My life is getting back to normal. Bothered by some strange game that
> Salami dragged in, I avoid going out. Fed up with twosomes, I manoeuvre
> to fight single-handed with a lance (poor Henri II) and empty my ballast
> in order to reach the surface. Which I did.
>
> San-Antonio, La Queue en trompette

Ball bearings (French: *roulements à billes* n.m.): a metaphoric nickname for balls.

Ball-less (English): see anorchid.

Ballocks (French: *basses-nobles* n.f.; *balloches* n.f.; *basteaux* n.m.; *batoches* n.f.):
a dated form of bollocks. You also see the adjective ballocky. The French slang
word *balloches* or *baloches* would seem to be related. You might be led to believe,
however, that it is a hold-all word formed from *balles* (for obvious reasons – see
below) and *valoches* (*valises* – suitcases), both because of weight and balance. In
fact, the word seems to be derived from *baler* in the sense of balance, oscillate, be
in movement, swing or, by a degeneration of the Picard verb *ballocher,* oscillate in
hanging (*Dictionnaire de l'argot français et de ses origines*, Larousse 2002).

Another French slang expression for testicles is *basses-nobles* (n.f.). In his
delicious work *Le Livre des darons sacrés or La Bible en argot* (Paris 1974), Pierre
Devaux makes it clear from his glossary: 'same sense as *balloches*, but with more
dignity.'

In modern French slang there is also *basteaux* (n.m.), which may be written
bastaux. A *gonzesse à basteaux* means a bird with balls, i.e. an effeminate
homosexual (Pierre Guiraud, *Dictionnaire érotique*, Paris 1978).

Batoches is a probable corruption of *basteaux* and *bastos* (s.v. bullets).

Balloons (French: *montgolfières* n.f.): a superlative metaphor. The French word is
for the brothers Montgolfier, who made the first balloon flight in 1783.

Ballop (English): scrotum.

Balls (French: *balles* n.f.; *ballustrines* n.f.; *boboles* n.f.; *bouboules* n.f.; *boules de gomme, – de naphtaline, – de pétanque* n.f.; *éteufs* n.m.; *boulettes* n.f.): slang word for testicles in English of great antiquity. *OED* records its first use in 1250. It is used in expressions such as he has a lot of balls, or the American, break somebody's balls, or to have the balls to do something, and finally, to have blue balls, meaning that the person's balls are about to break from lack of use. You will also find the word ball in the adjective ballsy meaning someone who has them.

Since the late nineteenth century, it also has the negative sense of balls meaning rubbish, nonsense. To make a balls of something, to make a balls up, means to do something badly, do a bad job. To have someone by the balls, means to have someone in your power.

To break someone's balls (to berate someone) is American, coming probably from the Italian *rompere le palle*. To bust or break your balls can mean to perform a very hard and nasty labour.

In French, *balles* is slang for testicles by metaphor. They maybe qualified according to type: ping-pong or tennis as a superlative metaphor. There is none the less a pejorative connotation in the French expression *ça vaut peau de balles* (it's only worth the skin of a grain of corn), a worthless wrapping.

Balles are closely related to *boules*, although the latter are bigger – more like the balls used to play pétanque. It is a popular metaphor for testicles. In popular speech, the evocative expression *avoir des boules* means being so angry that your testicles rise to your throat, the confusion between amygdales and testicles being therefore deliberate. The word *glandes* can be used in the same context.

> We arrested the tourist in the landau that the witnesses had seen throw the bomb. He had reason to protest, did Monsieur Van Moulinha: they had kicked the shit out his his shins and beaten his gums with a bat. It's stupid, as he was on honeymoon and the military knee that hit him in the bollocks [*roustons*] transformed his balls [*boules*] into finials on a newel post.
> *San-Antonio,* Des Gonzesses comme s'il en pleuvait *(It Was Raining Chicks, 1984)*

> And it took your breath away! When it came to tempt you, like it was served on a plate, on top of two lovely appetizing balls [*boules*], a terrifying and marvellous banana! Confess it, there are moments when you give up fighting the desire to eat it all up, down to the last mouthful of whipped cream.
> *Fellacia Dessert, 'Banana Slip', in* La première gorgée de sperme, c'est quand'même autre chose *(The First Mouthful of Sperm is Altogether Something Else, 1998)*

Boules de gomme (gum balls), is used above all in the expression *faire boule de gomme*, which means to lick or suck testicles in the course of a sexual encounter, it is an allusion to the sweets.

Boules de naphtaline (mothballs) is a favourite expression of the famous French detective San-Antonio when he wishes to indicate that he has not 'emptied his balls' (or disgorged his amygdales) for some time. How delicately he expresses these 'things'!

> As she seemed to like that and the body language gave it away, I showed off my wares to the full. As I have said anyway, it had been a few days since I had presented my credentials to a woman and I was beginning to find my mothballs encrusted with beasties.
>
> San-Antonio, Du Poulet au menu *(Chicken on the Menu, 1971.)*

Pétanque balls (*boules de pétanque*) are a superlative version of *boules*, referring to the magnificent size of the testicles in question, but also to the terms used in the game: draw, point, bugger up, etc. (see also *Lyonnaises*).

Éteufs is an obsolete term for testicles. It is probably Frankish in origin, it appeared in the thirteenth century in different forms and versions include *estuef*, *estue*, *estuet* and *esteuf* (in François Villon), then *éteuf*. The word denotes a little ball which was used for playing real tennis. Since the early twentieth century it also designates the ball of tow (now, of course, plastic) on the end of a fencing foil.

> 'Oh Madam,' he said, 'you're playing *that* sort of tennis (*vous jouez donc de ces esteufs-là*).'
>
> Gédéon Tallemant des Réaux (1619–1692), Historiettes *(Little Histories)*

Boulettes (meat balls) is also a diminutive of *boules*, but see also kefta. *Caillettes* or faggots is another epithet of the same sort. They are little meatballs with greens that are made all along the River Saône from the Dombes to Lyon, and also in the Rhône Valley between Valence and Montélimar. Those of the Vivarais and the Dauphiné are particularly appreciated. They are about the size of a pétanque ball and owe their name to the fact that they *caillent* (harden) as they cool. For more elucidation, see the etymological explanation under the entry for *kall*. As an affectionate metaphor, they are applied to testicles. In his *Dictionnaire érotique*, Pierre Guiraud claims that it is a zoological metaphor and that in the sixteenth century the word *caillettes* denoted the sack that contained a sheep's testicles.

Ballustrines (occasionally *balustrines*) is another word given to testicles, a sort of portmanteau word formed from *balles* and *lustrer* (to polish), indicating clearly enough that testicles enjoy a vocation to be lit up, polished or stroked.

Boboles is a term for testicles formed perhaps by amalgamating *balles* and *boules*. *Bouboules* is a affectionate diminutive of boules.

Ball bag (English): scrotum.

Basket (US English): among American homosexuals: the scrotum – especially perceived through tight clothes. Can also be applied to the testicles. Lunch basket is a similar expression, see lunch box.

Baubles (English): a dated term for testicles.

Bells (French: *cloches* n.f.; *cloches de Notre-Dame* n.f.; *cliquailles* n.f.; *clochettes* n.f.; *grelots* n.m.; *sonnailles* n.f.; *sonnettes* n.f.): *cloches* (bells) is a nickname for testicles. *Cloches de Notre-Dame* is a facetious one, notably used by the singer Pierre Perret. [Pierre Perret (b. 1934) is a French singer and composer famous for his creative use of the French language and argot.]

> His balls swung like the bells of Notre-Dame and had just collided with Culculine's nose.
>
> *Guillaume Apollinaire,* Les Onze Mille Verges ou les Amours d'un hospodar

Clochettes (little bells) is another nickname for testicles:

> 'I couldn't be wrong about things like that, San-A. He's like some sort of wrinkly tramp. I swear that if he has committed that terrible thing, I'll cut off his jingle-bells (*clochettes*) with an embroideress's scissors.'
>
> *San-Antonio,* Un éléphant, ça trompe *(An Elephant, it Fools you, 1975)*

The word *cliquailles* plays on the swinging and the jingling or ring-ringing of balls or bells (*cliquetis*).

Grelots are little dog-bells and by extension the penis is the clapper that you need to shake to make them ring. The Quebecois version is *gerlots* which is half way to *verlan*, the French slang that reads (and speaks) words backwards.

> As plump as a tumulus
> In a field of yellow corn
> An *andouillette* – a phallus
> Proudly got up at dawn
> With his little angel airs
> Troyes' civic 'majesté'
> Put his bells [*grelots*] away in pairs
> So's not to scare his prey
>
> Posing as a *torero*
> Dreaming of *pasos* true
> And heading for the Hérault
> Questing pastures new.
>
> *Philippe Roman,* Le Péché original de notre cuisine, Mets et Mots *(The Original Sin of our Cuisine, Words and Dishes, 1996)*

> She wrote: 'It's winter. Let me be your blanket. You need to be warm, properly warm. Come, I'll give you my little duvet of white chick feathers to keep your bells [*grelots*] hot.'
>
> *Louis Calaferte,* La Mécanique des femmes *(How Women Work, 1992)*

The discussion was frantic. A full colonel must have said something not to the taste of his general, because the latter gave him a kick in the bells [*grelots*].

San-Antonio, Béru-Béru (1970)

Sonnailles suggests both the swinging and the ringing of bells; *sonnettes* is similar:

> And at her feet two pretty bells
> Pretty and lovely as well.
>
> Jannet, Ancien Théâtre français, *quoted by Louis de Landes (Auguste Scheler) in* Glossaire érotique de la langue française *(1861)*

'Also a whore has gentle words, smiles, kisses and glances in her armoury. But this is none of that. She has in her hands rubies and in her stock of weapons pearls, diamonds, emeralds and all the harmony of the world.'

'How is that?'

'How? What? There is no one who does not touch heaven with his fingertip when his lady love, whom he loves so dearly, at the moment when she slides her tongue between his lips, takes his thing in hand, grasping it two or three times between her fingers in order to make it stand to and as soon as it is standing stiff, gives it a little shake, then leaves it in suspense. After resting thus for a little while, she takes his little bells in the palm of her hands and tickles them voluptuously; then she slaps your buttocks, scratches among the pubic hairs and begins to tease you anew, so well that the cucumber, now in a good humour, looks like someone who would like to vomit but cannot. Our swain, subject to her stroking, puts on the airs of an abbot, and would not exchange his blessing for that of an itchy pig; when he sees himself ridden by she whom he thought he would ride himself, he falls into a swoon like a man on the brink of death.'

Aretino, Dialogues, The Education of Pippa (1537)

Belly (French: *bas-ventre* n.m.): euphemism for the bit below the belt and covering the genital regions of men and women.

> having finished [reciting] his verses, he covered me with the most indecent kisses then came and sat on my bed and, using all his force, undressed me despite all my resistance. Attaching himself to my belly, he kneaded me for ages, but it was in vain.
>
> Petronius, Satyricon

Bermuda Triangle (French: *triangle des Bermudes* n.m.): a metaphor for the genital area. It is generally applied to women (in Sweden, for example). The Bermuda Triangle is that part of the Atlantic where many boats have mysteriously disappeared. Certain authors none the less use it to signify male organs:

> I would also like to listen to myself, and do that which spontaneously
> springs to mind as it passes through my Bermuda Triangle.
>
> San-Antonio, Bacchanale chez la mère Tatzi *(Bacchanal at Mother Tatzi's,*
> *1985.)*

Between the legs (French: *entrejambe* n.f.): *entrejambe* is a euphemism to
denote the lower abdomen with all its sexual paraphernalia, either in a woman or
a man, but more usually a man. It is used in a figurative sense to mean a degree
of courage. You say, for example '*il en a dans l'entrejambe*' (he's got something
between his legs).

> She meted out the customary care to her husband's mouth, to the bit
> between his legs, his household and his wealth.
>
> Pascal Quignard *(1990)*

Big guns (French: *artillerie* n.f.; *batterie* n.f.; *matériel* n.m.): names for the trinity
of male sexual organs, particularly in the expressions, bring out his artillery, a
three-piece battery or, more rarely, kitchen equipment (*batterie de cuisine*).

> I folded the photo in two and put it in my pocket. This meant Raymond's
> mug pitched up against the three-piece battery of his fellow centaur.
>
> San-Antonio, Les Vacances de Bérurier ou La Croisière du 'Mer d'alors'

The genital collection as a whole is indicated by *matériel* as in, *fais voir ton matériel*
(show us your equipment). *Matos* is a variant. It is used for the equipment carried
by musicians.

Billiards (French: *bistouilles* n.f.): the French word *bistouilles* signifies the testicles
and is probably a fusion of the two words *bistouquette* (billiard cue and, by
extension, penis) and *couilles* (balls).

Bits and Bobs/things/stuff (French: *affaires* n.f.): it goes without saying that
these are 'personal', i.e. the penis and testicles. You will also encounter 'little
things'. It is a term most frequently used in the West Indies (Martinique) to
designate male organs in a sugary sort of way, notably in expressions like 'put
away your stuff', 'hide your bits and bobs', etc. It might be worth mentioning
that the Arab word *soualah* (see below), means the same.

Bladders (French: *vessies* n.f.): hardly used any more, the French word *vessies* (cf.
the English vesica and vesicle) refers rather to the bladders of a fish.

> Men swim better than women because they have two bladders below their
> belly that sustain them in water.
>
> Tabarin (c. 1584–1633), Works, *quoted by Louis de Landes (Auguste*
> *Scheler) in* Glossaire érotique de la langue française *(1861)*

Bollocks (English): slang nickname for testicles in Great Britain, it was in standard use from early medieval times until the seventeenth century. The Sex Pistols named one of their albums *Never Mind the Bollocks*. Generally also used to mean nonsense or rubbish, a mess or confusion: don't talk bollocks, what a bollocks, it's bollocks. To drop a bollock means to make a howler. You can also work your bollocks off (work very hard) and receive or administer a bollocking: a severe rebuke.

The bollock cod is the scrotum.

[Also used in Ireland, where the [dog's] bollocks means the *ne plus ultra* or the best, and where a bollocks, ballocks or bollix (note the use of the indefinite article as opposed to the definite) means a very nasty person / a cunt.]

Box (English): a hard triangle worn in the game of cricket to protect the genitals, a successor therefore to the cod piece. By extension, a metonym for the testicles themselves. Sometimes used for the vagina.

Brontë Sisters (French): one of a number of epithets for testicles given by the diabolic verve of Frédéric Dard (who spells it in different ways). We should stress that there were in reality three Brontë Sisters:

> There's a person who knows how to do it and to empty the Brontë Sisters* without making a fuss, or at least, very little.
>
> * OK There were three, but they are only lent out to the rich.'
> **San-Antonio, Fais-moi des choses** *(Do Things to Me, 1969)*

> The Mammoth* is fascinated by testicles. 'Say,' he whispered, 'with fire-shovels† like that I wouldn't like her to cause me grief! They're enough to tear the skin off the Brontë Sisters.'
>
> * Bérurier. † In the language of Bérurier, these are fingernails.
> **San-Antonio, A prendre ou à lecher** *(To Take or to Lick, 1980)*

> 'A strange stratagem which makes me really worried, I prefer to say that straight out before you apply a soldering iron to the Brontë Sisters to get an answer out of me.'
> **San-Antonio, Bouge ton pied que je voie la mer** *(Shift Yourself so I Can See the Sea, 1982)*

Bullets (English; Provençal, Spanish, Portuguese: *balas* n.f.): testicles in several southern European languages. In French there is also *bastos* meaning rifle bullets. It is in the same vein as prunes, sugared almonds etc.

In English, it is dated. Pistol tells Falstaff in *Henry IV Part 2*, 'I will discharge upon her, Sir John, with two bullets.'

Bunch (English; French: *grappe* n.f.): suggests the whole collection.

Buttons (English): the testes of an animal (*OED*).

Cakes, pastries and ices of all sorts (French: *bouchée double* n.f.; *bugnes* n.f.; *bougnes* n.f.; *cornet à deux boules* n.m.): *Double bouchée* [*de la reine*] is a little name from my personal repertoire.

Bugnes is a gourmand metaphor, *bugnes* being big doughnuts. It is a term employed notably by the French playwright Antonin Artaud (1896–1948).

Bougnes derives from *bugnes* and is found in the expression that describes some designs of underpants that show off the lunch-box, *remonte-bougnes*.

Chouquettes (puff pastry balls sprinkled with sugar) is a fantasy term and a gourmand metaphor.

Un cornet à deux boules is an ice-cream cornet with two scoops, a metaphor that describes a penis garnished with two balls (of ice-cream).

Croquembouches (literally 'crunch in the mouth') are little bits of choux pastry shaped like balls, which are used as a basis for nibbles (garnished with some sort of cheese for example), or a cake of the Saint-Honoré sort when they are filled with cream. By extension, they are sometimes used as a metaphor for testicles as they are also filled with cream.

Croquignolles is another pet name for testicles evoking the fact that they are cute (*croquinoglet*) and of course *à croquer*: good enough to eat! In origin, *croquignolles* were a cake and the most famous were Parisian *croquignolles* which might imply that there is no one so well endowed as a Parisian.

Profiteroles need no introduction: little choux-pastry balls covered with diverse sauces after they are cooked. The best known are *profiteroles* with chocolate. By extension it is a nickname for testicles; there is an analogous form and maybe a gourmand suggestion too because those who eat them 'profit' by the experience. Sometimes written *profiterolles*.

Charms (French: *appas* n.m.; *câlines* n.f.): *appas* derives from the verb *appâter* which refers to the physical charms of a woman, mostly the breasts. But some authors use it also to evoke male organs.

> Awoken by the din, a lady of the night
> Said 'what d'you think you're doing, beasts, that's not right!'
> There are many men today who are utterly perverse
> And insist on balling Cupid in reverse
> And so many men robbed of their virile charms
> That those who have them still should let them come to harm.
> **Georges Brassens, 'Le Mécreant', 1960**

Câlines (meaning cuddles) is an affectionate little name for testicles, similar to *douillettes* (meaning cosy) suggesting that they should be cupped and cuddled.

Chaser (English): a monorchid ram (*OED*, noting a usage of 1818).

Chilly bits (*frileuses* n.f.): *les frileuses* suggests that testicles are sensitive to cold as that is the meaning of the adjective *frileux, frileuse*.

Clappers (English): an allusion to bells.

Clogs (English): an ancient English term for testicles.

Cloots: balls in Flemish.

Cobblers (French: *Antilles* n.f.): here we have two sorts of rhyming slang. The English is clearer, cobblers derives from cobblers' awls, i.e. balls. The first recorded use of 'cobblers' for balls is 1934, but it remains popular as a dismissive term for rubbish: what a load of cobblers! The French seems more speculative. Pierre Guiraud in his *Dictionnaire érotique* (Erotic Dictionary, 1976) suggests that the use of Antilles to indicate testicles is because it rhymes [just, but it seems stretching it] with the French verb *enter*. This means either to cobble something together or to graft (a tree).

Cobbs (English dialect): testicles (mid-nineteenth century).

Cocos: testicles in French Creole.

Cod, codling (English): one of the oldest names for the scrotum, dating from the eleventh century. *SOED* derives it from Old Norse, and in Nordic languages it signifies a pillow or cushion, a usage replicated in parts of England where it also means a pod (as in peas), a bag or a wallet. The codpiece is the 'bagged appendage to the front of a man's breeches'.

Coglioni: balls in Italian.

Coille: ball in old French.

Cojones: balls in Spanish (Castilian). Introduced into English by Ernest Hemingway in 1934 in his novel *Death in the Afternoon*.

> The late David Balls was one of the first men involved in the promotion of Spanish wines in Britain. He used to explain to bemused Spanish winemakers that his name meant '*cojones*'. In the London trade he was invariably known as 'C.O.Jones'. *Translator.*

Colehole (French: *soute à charbon* n.f.): the full Monty.

Colei: balls in Latin, the plural of *coleus*, leather bag.

Colhoes: balls in Portuguese.

Collé-jumelles (French Creole): means twin fruits in the same wrapping, sometimes referred to as *philippines* (q.v. under Members of the family). It can be used to designate two testicles together in the same scrotum.

Collones: balls in Catalan.

Colocynth (French: *coloquintes* n.f.): nickname given to testicles in the region of Mascara in Algeria. They also say *les fruits de coloquintes* (Mark Chebel, *Encyclopédie de l'amour en Islam*, vol II, Paris 1995).

Conkers (English): horse chestnuts, used in a boys' game of that name and deriving from 'conquer'. Their shape is suggestive of testicles.

Containers / phials / test tubes (French: *burettes* n.f.; *carafon d'orgeat* n.m.; *contenants* n.m.; *flacons d'eau de vit* n.m.; *mignonettes* n.f.; *pépites* n.f.): *contenants* or containers is a metonymic that recalls the ambigious function of testicles, as is also suggested by the etymology of the most widespread terms such as cullions and purses. The word containers itself has been borrowed by the French from the English to give a more modern turn to the word *contenants*. It is similar to *jerrycans*, q.v.

> When desire is intact, the things that are responsible for the paucity of sperm are fivefold: the weakness of the sperm 'containers', which neither ensure the flow of sperm, not the mastery of it; a liver in a poor state which no longer purifies the blood as it should do, and, as a result, binds the vital instinct; the ingestion of a large quantity of food, especially those – humorally speaking, either hot or cold – which harden the veins and cause problems to the circulation of the blood in the genital regions; old age, when sperm becomes considerably more rare; and finally, intercourse without any medical precautions which, in the course of time, can only diminish sperm.
>
> Ahmed ibn Souleimân, Le Bréviaire arabe de l'amour

Phials (Fr. *burettes*) are a metonymic name for testicles emphasizing their role as containers.

> 'Up your bums you old goats! Are you complaining my friend: I have leaches sucking at my phials. My bollocks must look like chandeliers.'
>
> San-Antonio, Béru-Béru

A *carafon d'orgeat* (bottle of barley water) is another domesticity for testicles, the *orgeat* (barley water) playing the part of sperm. It is used notably in the expression 'emptying his little bottle of almond milk'. That is, he's ejaculating.

It would be hard to imagine a better image of testicles that *flacons d'eau de vit* (little bottles of penis essence: a *flacon* usually describes a perfume bottle; *vit* is the slang French for penis; it's a pun on little bottles of eau de vie).

Mignonettes are also miniatures of spirits, and it is another genteel expression meaning testicles. The suggestion is that they are cute (*mignon*), and like little sample bottles.

Test-tubes (*pépites*) are also used, as in the expression 'test-tubes of joy' – *pépites de joie.*

Pot au lait (milk churns) is a metonymic for testicles which was used by Rabelais as early as the sixteenth century.

Coucous: nickname for balls in Cantonese.

Counterweight / counterbalance (French: *contrepoids* n.m.): a metaphor for testicles. San-Antonio claims that the *contrepoids à bascule* (see-saw) means a woman's buttocks.

> 'You want to take her in your arms, close your eyes, and run her nose all over your body, then do the same with her lips, and then her see-saw.'
> **San-Antonio, Béru et ses femmes *(Béru and his Women, 1967)***

> 'Anyhow, as regards my counterweighted nutcracker, that solves nothing. Oh! What a pillock, that bloke from the CRS !'
> **San-Antonio, Un éléphant, ça trompe**

Crystals: an Anglo-American term. In the same vein as 'family jewels' but relating to the testicles alone. [Possibly it comes from Cockney rhyming slang: 'crystal balls'. It is very rare.]

Cup-and-ball (French: *bilboquet* n.m.): *bilboquet* or the game of cup-and-ball is sometimes used to indicate the male genital apparatus even if only one ball is used in the game. Maybe homage is paid to monorchids. Napoleon I, it seems, was thus. You also hear the phrase *bilboquet à moustaches* (where *moustaches* refers to the pubic hair).

Cullions (French: *couilles* n.f.): in France, the word *couilles* is the one most popularly used to denote testicles. It comes from the classical Latin *coleus*, meaning a leather bag, and the word also spawned the diminutive *couillon*.

> My grandfather's balls
> Are hanging on the stairs
> And their desiccation calls
> To my grandmother's despair
>
> **Popular song**

> The rector of Camaret
> Has pendulous bollocks
> The rector of Camaret
> Has pendulous bollocks
> And when he sits down on them

They get lodged in his bum
Up springs his cock!
His cock!

'Le curé de Camaret' (bawdy song)

Who sent me this fucking saveloy?
He's got nothing in his balls, the boy.

'La Patrouille' (bawdy song)

Double ball, twin ball, ball progenitor, you are never so dear to me as
when you get on well with that prick above and the hand that strokes you.

Marquis de Sade, quoted by Richard Ramsey in Le Dictionnaire érotique

My cock has a great calibre, but it is a slut from balls to the breech.

Paul Verlaine, quoted by Richard Ramsey in Le Dictionnaire érotique

My cock it reddened to a happy scarlet
In the springtime of my days
And my balls swung this way and that like ripe fruits
Looking for a basket.

Guillaume Apollinaire, Les Onze Mille Verges ou Les Amours d'un hospodar

Seated on the edge of the copper bed, he caught his breath. He examined
his feet, his toes rough and thin, the bones in his legs, his vanished calves.
He saw his two bony knees like wooden knots, the soft, flabby skin on his
thighs, the half swollen sheath of his penis between his legs and his balls
blown up to half their size again like thrushes' eggs. And he cried for his pains.

Pascal Quignard, Albucius *(1990)*

Shelling peas, she plunged her hands voluptuously into the bowl where
they were piling up. 'I have them in my fingers, its cold and gentle. I
think that they are a pile of little balls and that makes me excited.'

Louis Calaferte, La Mécanique des femmes

Hard, round balls swung to the same regular beat as the enormous cock
went in and out, methodically, as if it was a question of breaking down a
door with the help of a ram.

Alina Reyes, Derrière la porte *(Behind the Door, 1994)*

God wants us to be free.
   Your soul and your balls have nothing in common and have no possible
connection.
   You may darken your life by practising evil on others – but in no case
by the use of your balls.
   If you feel uneasy metaphysically, think about metaphysics – not about
your balls.
   What happens to your balls is a matter for the doctor, not the priest.

Louis Calaferte, L'Homme vivant *(Man Alive, 1994)*

I have remade my vision. In my new eyes there are no more Palestinian men, Israeli men, American men, Frenchmen, Algerian men or Moroccan men. The only sort of man I recognize from now on is one with balls. He is a destroyer. His penis is an umbilical cord which connects him to the universe. Full stop, that's all.

Azouz Begag, Le Marteau pique-coeur *(The Hammer that Pricks the Heart, 2004)*

It seems, you spineless gits, that I have just put two and two together and made five (which is not as bad as having five balls).

San-Antonio, Béru-Béru

To put it concisely: I have functioned. That's all: functioned. Did the Lord God want any more of me? If he's playing the big cat watching the mouse from up high, he could give the artist due praise; I have played my part in the logic of things after all, his things and my own. I am not frightened to say this: I have done him proud, perfectly proud. With my guts, my fists and my balls, from the moment he gave them to me.

San-Antonio, Si Queue d'Ane m'était conté ou La Vie sexuelle de Bérurier

I was right to be completely pissed, I remembered in most cases feet came in pairs, like ears, balls and coppers on the beat.

San-Antonio, Dégustez, gourmandes *(Taste this, Greedy Girls, 1985)*

So, if I have understood Freud correctly, um, the world has two problems: arses and money.

As we know that everyone has an arse, let's talk about money!

No, because the arse, we are not allowed, are we? Oh dear! It's dirty, isn't it? First of all, it's dirty and it's coarse! An arse is coarse! Yuck! Pricks and balls, yuck! It's dirty and it's coarse! It's not allowed, right!'

A bird, with her eyes alone she rips off your shirt...Ho, ho, ho, and then you can touch her there!

You are there, stuck in your pants 'cross your balls from Playtex'. Do you see? You can't move, and it's building up, no? It's mounting...

Coluche [French comedian, 1944–1986], sketch: J'ai tout lu Freud *(I've read all of Freud, 1980)*

Couillettes means balls of a small calibre, the balls of a young boy, or simply a term of endearment.

The first girl to give me an erection was a pretty peasant who carried me to vespers with her hand laid on my naked buttocks. She tickled my ball-ettes and, when she felt me stiffen, she kissed me on the mouth with virginal enthusiasm.

Nicolas-Edme Restif de la Bretonne (French writer, 1734–1806)

The old word *couiller* used to denote a scrotum:

In front just let me welcome you
And they have cut my scrotum too.
Quoted in Glossaire érotique de la langue française

In the old days *couillons* meant testicles just like the word *couilles* but then in the sixteenth century it became singular, figurative and pejorative and meant 'naïve, idiotic, imbecilic', and this sense succeeded in supplanting the original. Even so, in the seventeenth and eighteenth centuries, some writers – notably erotic ones – continued to use it in the original way.

And he proclaimed with a double carillon of cullions.

I answered that I had more cullions than I had lucre.

François Rabelais

Here is the greatest treason
Of the vile cullions that I hate,
When their master is in prison
These ingrates dance at the gate.
Le Cabinet satyrique *(The Satirical Cabinet, verses published in 1660)*

My cullions, when my penis stirs,
Grows to the size of mule's tool,
Delight my lady's fingers
More than rosaries as a rule.
Théophile de Viau *(1590–1626)*

My cullions are swollen from fucking you so much.
Théophile de Viau *(1590–1626)*

Ah, Eugénie, if only you knew what a mischievous climax you get when a big cock fills your backside; when pushed in as far as the cullions and it shudders with ardour; when pulled out as far as the prepuce, it digs back in to the pubic hairs.
Marquis de Sade, La Philosophie dans le boudoir ou Les Instituteurs immoraux *(Philosophy in the Boudoir or Immoral Teachers, 1795)*

The Tartar, excited by the spectacle that he had just witnessed and in which he had been the protagonist, did not hold back for long the sperm that was bubbling in his cullions.
Guillaume Apollinaire, Les Onze Mille Verges ou Les Amours d'un hospodar

The Acadian Canadian word *les chenolles* may be related to *couilles.*
The English version of the word is cullions. It is now largely archaic. In the *Pardoner's Tale*, Chaucer writes 'I wolde I hadde thy coillons…' It was also used (like *couillon*) to denote a base, despicable or vile fellow.
Some varieties of orchids were called cullion' – dog's cullions, sweet cullions, soldier's cullions; and the tuberous roots of the same plant were called cullions.

Cushions (*coussinettes* n.f.; *douillettes* n.f.): *coussinettes* are little cushions and the word evokes the soft and juicy side of the testes, their supple texture.

Douillettes is an early word for testicles that also suggests softness, tenderness, fragility, sensitivity and juiciness. It was used in the Paris market, Les Halles. [The adjective *douillet, -ette,* means soft or downy, and of a person, one who fears pain or needs molly-coddling; the noun *douillette* is used for a quilted coat or wrap.]

Deputies (French: *adjoints* n.m.): a nickname for testicles which shows that the testicles are meant to accompany the penis. It is mostly used in the expression, the two deputies (*les deux adjoints*).

Didumos, didymoi: testicle in Greek, from the word for twins. It surfaces in English as didymis (*c.* 1400). This is the origin of the word epididymis, the long strip that runs alongside the testicle and contains the twisty canal which carries the spermatozoa.

Distaffs (French: *quenouilles* n.f.): a malapropism that has come to denote testicles, probably as a result of deliberate confusion between the expressions *tomber en quenouille* (to fall under the subjugation of a woman) and *partir en couille* (to do sod all).

> And you are going to do it? By my distaffs, yes! Really too cowardly!
> San-Antonio, Béru-Béru

Dismissaries (English): testicles. Now archaic.

Dolls (French: *poupettes* n.f.): *les poupettes* is an affectionate diminutive suggesting cute little dolls.

Dolly Sisters: a French nickname for testicles, an allusion to the famous American singers of the twenties. Cf. Bronte Sisters, q.v.

Dongers (French: *carillon* n.m.): a peal of bells – *carillon* – is a facetious name for testicles, in the same vein as *cloches* (bells) and *clochettes* (dongers, clappers). It is to be noted, however, that the word *carilloner* means 'to make love to a woman, joyously swinging his clapper in her clock' (quoted by Richard Ramsey in *Le Dictionnaire érotique*). See also cullion, *couillon*.

> He is always naked. 'His *carillons* are joyless', that's what I see through the crack in the door.
> San-Antonio, San-Antonio chez les gones *(San-Antonio with the Kids, 1962)*

Doodahs (English): embarrassed euphemism that can mean just about any sexual bit you do not care to name.

Eggs (German: *Eier* n.n.; Italian: *ovette* n.f.; Spanish: *huevos* n.m.; Arabic: *baïdh*): eggs are a metaphorical nickname for testicles in German, Spanish, Italian and other countries (particularly in the Mediterranean basin and above all in Arabic, a language in which the word *baïdh* signifies both eggs and testicles in literary Arabic). It is also interesting to note that the word *ovule* literally means little egg. The analogy of form between eggs and testicles has led the Arabs to baptize the virile member the dove (*el-hamama*).

It is called *el-hamama*, the dove, after it has been swollen and the moment when it returns to a state of repose. It looks like a white dove sitting on its eggs.

Sheikh Nefzaoui, Le Jardin perfumé. Manuel d'érotologie arabe *(The Perfumed Garden. A Manual of Arabian Erotology, 2002 edition)*

And all the women giggled when they saw it, and sullied him with saucy jokes. One said to him, 'Monkey! You could masturbate by yourself and copulate with the air!' And another had it, 'Look! You are hardly as big as the *zebb* of our lovely master! And your two humps are just about the size of his eggs!'

21st Night from Boulak's Egyptian edition of The Thousand And One Nights

Then she got up and went to place a red copper pan on the fire into which she put oil and soft cheese; and she waited until the cheese had melted and the oil had begun to boil before she returned to me, still lying spread out on the floor and held down by female slaves. She came to me, knelt, and undid my undergarment; during this handling a succession of shivers of shame and terror racked me: I could guess what was going to happen. Having now exposed my belly, she seized my eggs and attached a waxed string to the very root; then she handed the two ends of the string to her slaves and ordered them to pull hard, while she herself, with a razor in her hand, with one blow lopped off my manhood, which she especially prized.

126th Night from Boulak's Egyptian edition of The Thousand And One Nights

When people come together
May the words be refined,
May foot be entangled with foot,
May saliva cover the inside,
May penises collide with eggs,
May lances begin to jig,
Then the generous be patient and abandon all fear,
Submit, be obedient and make no rebuke,
People then peacefully disperse,
Taking with them the best of prizes,

The heart and breast are cured,
The soul's heat is calmed,
All desire ebbs,
All will to flee the lover is killed forever,
The strings are placed at both ends,
And the union is tied never to be undone.

Abou Hayan al Tawhîdî, Kitab al imtâ' wal mu-ânassa, *cited by Abdelwahab
Bouhdiba in* La Sexualité en Islam

From what we have said so far, let us examine the different possible cases.
Let us take first that of a newborn male who finds himself feminized by
the weakness of the masculine principle that presided over his conception.
It will be observed in this example that the member, the two eggs that
hang below and the different aspects of masculinity are hard to make out,
have hardly emerged, are weak in consistency, of small size and lacking
in any vigour. Besides this, they are often attached too high and are
lost in the folds of the abdomen, as if the crack were ready to swallow
a virility that was too modest. (All the same, a woman's instruments of
reproduction find themselves naturally placed inside the belly and not
outside, sunk in the depths of an intimate crack.) From now on it may be
explained that the boy who finds himself in that state will feel very itchy.
This excites the liquid which will tend to flow in excess. And more and
more, sensations will reach the back region, in a direct prolongation of the
excited area, and not the region in the middle which is the natural place
where the eggs should be active. It will be seen, that these eggs are rarely
of large dimensions. On the contrary, they are more often small, retracted
high up and placed to the right. Eggs are even the exception in feminized
individuals whose baton [*baguette* or French stick] is also in keeping.

One possible treatment consists of strengthening the baton and the two
eggs by pulling them gently down. The patient would be well-advised to
avail himself of the services of a hot-blooded young serving-girl with a
perfect face, whose ardour would recommended itself adding its virtues
to the massage in question. Between the sessions, the precaution should
be taken to anoint the belly and the complete equipment with Egyptian
willow grease which has been marinated with white horehound, musk or
a little Persian asafoetida. He should make sure that the baton is rubbed
with it and should not hesitate to allow some of the mixture to enter
the channel. He will let the ungents work for a while before sitting in a
properly hot bath, which will allow him once again to massage the baton
and the eggs. Once a week, he will have recourse to a distillation of pine
resin mixed with hot water, and will dip the regions requiring treatment
in it: it is one of the most effective substances that I know for effecting
this sort of cure. If he feels the onset of excitement in the course of the
treatment, if the eggs begin to drop, if the baton wakes up at the same

time as he feels desire, it is a sign that the treatment employed was the right one.

Ahmad al-Tifachi, Les Délices des coeurs, ou ce que l'on ne trouve en aucun livre

Easter eggs: is an ironic epithet for testicles:

I am quite beside myself I am so sorry, it is gnawing away at the pit of my stomach and it is going down further, into the Easter eggs, whence it is giving me writer's cramp.

San-Antonio, Plein les moustaches *(Hit About the Head, 1985)*

Eight (French: *huit*): significant because of the conformation of the two balls joined at the waist. The figure eight symbolizes Justice (because of the two scales). In esoteric language, it means cosmic balance as well because it is supposed to have magic properties as the first cubic number ($2 \times 2 \times 2 = 8$). The Pythagoreans made it the symbol of love, prudence and reflection, whereas for Christians, it heralds the beatitude of the future in another world (The Eighth Day). Finally, lain on its side, it represents the infinite in mathematics. Already rich in meaning, therefore, the figure eight has, however, found a new job: essentially, it has been adopted on the Internet as a graphic symbol of a pair of balls when it comes to describing natural prowess in a discussion group. As regards the penis – which is called the prick in this case – it is described by the sign = which is then multiplied as many times as possibly to signify length: === for example. Finally, the prepuce itself is represented by a D, from which, for the male trilogy, gives the following complete formula: 8===D! Little pricks will be therefore 8=D; normal ones: 8==D; a good-sized prick: 8===D, without going into the prodigies! In the end it is quite poetic...

Equipment / tools / instruments / machines (French: *équipement* n.m.; *attirail* n.m.; *chasse mouches* n.f.; *chibres* n. f.; *couvert trois pièces* n.m.; *instruments* n.m.): *attirail* signifies the collection of objects destined to perform a particular task, like, for example, the plumber's tools or the burglar's equipment. By an ironic twist, it is also applied to male sexual organs. It is related to the words accessories and panoply (qq.v.).

Equipment comes closer to 'material' or 'supplies'. It is said of a well-endowed man that he is well equipped.

Instruments implies the collection, like tools, accessories, etc.

Now, do we need to know if the reverend father was well known for plying his instruments like this?

Les Cent Nouvelles nouvelles, *15th century (translated as One Hundred Merrie and Delightsome Stories, 1899)*

Tools (*outils*) is used above all in the expression *déballer ses outils* (taking out his tools). It is also said that a man who is well endowed is *bien outillé* (well-equipped). [In English 'a tool' tends to mean the penis alone.]

Fly-swatters (*chasse-mouches*) are usually encountered in the expression to have a nice fly-swatter which, for a man, means having a good sexual organ.

The argot word *chibre* means a penis in the singular and testicles in the plural. [Its etymology is uncertain, but one explanation is it comes from the German verb *schieben* to push or shove.]

Un couvert trois pièces (a table-setting of three pieces) is the equivalent of three pieces of cutlery or a knife, fork and plate. The metaphor encompasses the penis and the testicles.

In the nineteenth century the Parisian *grisettes* referred to the equipment of their lovers as 'machines'. *Grisettes* – from the grey cloth that clad the humble girl workers – is also a euphemism.

Family silver / jewels / jewellery box / crown jewels / precious stones / jewellery drawer (French: *argenterie* n.f.; *bijoux de la famille* n.m.; *coffret à bijouterie* n.m.; *joyaux* n.m.; *joyaux de la couronne* n.m.; *précieuses* n.f.; *tiroir à bijoux* n.m.; English US: family jewels; diamonds): denotes the whole shebang, testicles and penis. It is employed notably in the expression 'to shine the silver'. Naturally the expression stresses the fact of having something precious. In Belgium, the expression 'family jewels' has a culinary sense (see p. 61).

> You'll see how he leaves you in peace, the stomach, when you have properly satisfied the neighbour in the flat downstairs. A jockey's diet for the bread box and a Carthusian regime for the family jewels will take you straight to the tomb!
> San-Antonio, Bravo, docteur Béru *(1968)*

> The customer made a face. To make up his mind, Rita naughtily slipped her hand into his jewellery box.
> San-Antonio, Béru et ses dames *(Béru and his Women, 1967)*

Jewels (*joyaux*) is an epithet that stresses the full trinity. Let's emphasize that the etymology of *joyau* derives from *joie* (joy). A variant is 'jewels in the crown':

> I can see between the fringe of my long, enchanting eyelashes (a woman said that to me once) the half-caste face of one of the guards. My immobility gave him courage. He lent over. Bad luck for him! I planted my boot in his jewels with such gigantic force that this gent will not be in a condition to procreate until further notice.
> San-Antonio, Bérurier contre San-Antonio

Diamonds is an Anglo-American term in the same vein as the family jewels, but denotes the testicles alone.

Precious stones (*précieuses*) are a metonym (where one thing means something else related by metaphor or fact) for testicles. In French, the adjective has been converted into a noun. Molière was right [in his play *Les Précieuses ridicules* translated as 'The Pretentious Young Ladies']: certain precious things (*précieuses*) are silly (*ridicules*).

> He felt the weight of my two plates of meat in his precious stones and even though he looked as if he was built like the Eiffel Tower, it had an effect, I swear.
>
> San-Antonio, Des clientes pour la morgue *(Lady Clients for the Morgue, 1954)*

> Old soak, that's it: he's gaga, his head's gone soft... his grey matter is short of phosphorous; his prostate is waiting to pounce; his liver has been half-eaten by moths; he has beetles in his precious stones, and the beginnings of an ulcer are tormenting him; the last gasps of bronchitis are sitting on his lungs and for all that, in extreme cases, he is with you and always very dignified, with his gummy eyes, his threadbare moustache and his gladrags that stink like a badly kept tomb...
>
> San-Antonio, Du poulet au menu

> But this is some sort of sickness of yours? I need to ask the barber. Did you grope her Fredo? Are you wanking or what? It wouldn't be that your nerves are gnawing at your meatballs? Or, perhaps, that they installed you with batteries, rather too technical, instead of your waltzers, my poor mate! You've got CO_2 in your jewellery draw! Take some bromide instead of your pre-prandial! Or change your lover, old mate! Share your happiness with lots of broads.
>
> San-Antonio, Béru-Béru

Favourites (French: *favourites* n.f.): a little epithet for testicles which their owner generally uses when talking of his own, suggesting as well that he awards them a privileged place, in his ego at least, and that he is prone to whispering sweet nothings to them.

Flings (French: *amourettes* n.f.): in French culinary language, *amourette* means bone marrow, but it is also improperly used for fries (see above, passim). The confusion is doubtless engendered by the fact it contains the word *amour* (love). By extension it has come to mean a man's testicles as well as those of a lamb.

> Count yourself lucky, mate, and don't come breaking my balls about my natural instincts.
>
> San-Antonio, Bouge ton pied que je vois la mer,

Friends/companions (*compagnons* n.m.; *colocataires* n.f.): companions in the sense that they accompany the penis. It is used above all in the expression 'the two companions' and is similar to acolytes and deputies (qq.v.) or valets (see under servants).

The master who castrated me tore off my two companions so gently that
I felt almost nothing.

P. Delarivey (French dramatist, 1541–1619)

Compères or chums generally go around in pairs like acolytes, deputies and
companions, hence the binary metaphor. It is a bit juicier if you write it *com-paire*.

Colocataires (joint-tenants) describes the testicles' relationship to the
penis, suggesting that they lodge in the same apartment. It is also used in the
expression, my downstairs neighbour and his joint-tenants (*le voisin de dessous et
ses colocataires*) which describes what happens below the belt.

Frivolities (English; French: *frivoles* n.f.; *frivolités* n.f.): is a culinary term (see p. 62)
but in old-fashioned speech it can mean a man's testicles as well as an animal's.

> 'What happened to you?' I asked him. He stuck his hand down his
> trousers and announced that he had to sit down on an anthill. These
> women are beginning to wear out his waltzers, and he can't stand the pace,
> the old toe-rag. 'Go to the bog,' I told him. 'You're drunk mate, you're
> wearing your trousers back to front. Go through the shithouse door like
> that and the draught will blow the cobwebs off your frivolities.'

San-Antonio, Bravo, Docteur Béru *(1968)*

Fruit (fresh and dried) (French: *beloces* n.f.; *belaux* n.m.; *blatses* n.f.; *abricots*
n.m.; *brugnons* n.m.; *figues* n.f.; *guigne* n.f.; *litchis* n.m.; *olives* n.f.; *pastèques* n.f.;
pêches n.f.; *prunes* n.f.; *reinettes* n.f.; English (US?): plums): *beloces* are wild plums,
and by extension, a nickname for testicles. You also hear *blosses* or *bloces*. *Belaux* is
an antiquated term (16th century), which derives from *beloces*. *Blatses* is a dialect
name for plums, and is also used for testicles.

Berries is a nickname for testicles used particularly in the United States.

In the singular, an apricot (*abricot*) evokes a woman's vulva, notably for
the cleft in the middle, but in the plural is sometimes used as a metaphor for
testicles.

Peaches (*pêches*) is a metonymic metaphor that refers both to the form and
velvet texture of the scrotum and its contents.

Brugnons or nectarines is another metaphor:

> The daughter of an alderman
> She went and lost her trousers when
> While picking by the great ravines
> An aubergine and two nectarines,
> Her trousers held oh, her trousers held, oh they had to go…
> The alderman he need not know,
> Such things are beyond his brief…

Georgius (French singer and comedian Georges Guibourg, 1891–1970), 'La
vraie Gigouillette'

Figs may have a certain similarity of form, but they rarely see their name conveyed by transference onto testicles, in the West at least, doubtless because a singular fig is used more to describe a female sexual organ – the vulva. In Italy, however, it is synonymous with arsehole and constitutes the supreme insult, generally accompanied by an evocative gesture with the hand (the thumb placed between the ring finger and the index) which is rightly known as doing the fig. It is, on the other hand, used in the expression *avoir des figues molles* (to have flabby figs) to refer to someone who does not feel sexual desire. But in Arab countries, the fig (*tîn, karmous/kartous* in North Africa) is an evocation of the testicles: 'from its appearance, its colour and from the sugar that oozes out of the fleshy part, the fig conjures up quite precise erotic pictures. Dried figs play a part in the *baraka* (blessing) at the moment when, in Kabylia [in northern Algeria], figs are given the same name as testicles: *tibekhsisin.*' (Malek Chebel, *Encyclopédie de l'amour en Islam*). The same author also draws the analogy between the fig and the purse (or scrotum): fleshy outside and hugely complicated within... an association of form and content.

Another fruit that falls into this category is cherries (*guignes* in French, geans in English). The French insist on the variety with the long stem and soft flesh.

Little pears (*petites poires*) are suggested by their testicular form. It goes without saying that the pears in question are to cure thirst.

Lychees also come in for the treatment as a fruit analogous to bollocks. It was used by the French television presenter Jean-Pierre Foucault talking to Christophe Dechavanne on 29 March 2005, on the programme 'Who Wants to Be a Millionaire?'

There is something pejorative in the word *mirabelles* (little yellow plums), presumably because of their small size.

Olives are yet another metaphor. In the publicity campaign organized every year by the city of Nîmes – which calls itself the City of the Olive Tree – for the Mediterranean Olive Festival, one of the two posters for the first festival in 1999 showed a monochrome sketch of a bull seen from behind and his slabs were symbolized by two good olives: one green and the other black. It was a successful design by the Gardois Jean-Pierre Desclozeaux.

Reinettes are a variety of apples the skin of which has a tendency to wrinkle though they are as juicy as you could want. By extension, they are used as a metaphor for testicles. It is possible to go up a notch by saying *reines des reinettes* (queen reinettes – which means the very best of the said apples). Apples denoted testicles in Victorian and Edwardian English slang.

Reine-claudes is the French for greengages and a metonym for testicles.

Olives de Poissy is another figurative term for testicles. The joke is in the place-name Poissy, far beyond the olive-belt, thus they can't be real olives. [It is now a suburb of Paris, but once was the site of a convent. The high-jinks and frolics of its nuns were made much of by anticlerical writers and pornographers. Balzac has a story about the nuns of Poissy in his *Contes drolatiques* the second paragraph of which goes: 'If you ask one of them what the olives of Poissy are, they will answer you gravely that it is a periphrase relating to truffles, and that the way to serve them, of which one formerly spoke, when joking with these virtuous maidens, meant a peculiar kind of sauce. That's the way the scribblers hit on truth once in a hundred times.' Perhaps the usage derives from this.]

In the film *Remember the Titans* directed by Boaz Yakin in 2001, coach Herman Booze (Denzel Washington) promises players at the Titans American football team of T.C. Williams High School in Alexandria, Virginia a boot in the watermelons if they don't obey orders at the summer training camp at Gettysburg. He was appointed trainer in 1971, in a period of heightened racial turbulence. It is, of course, a superlative metaphor. It is to be noted that the diverse forms of marrows, gourds, cucumbers and courgettes with lubricious forms, indeed the whole family of cucurbits, lends itself very easily to salacious metaphors, just as much for the penis as the testicles.

There is a suggestion that plums (*prunes*) might be comprehensible in English. In popular French, the singular form (*prune*) can mean a punch or a cross-examination. In the plural it can mean testicles, metaphorically, as in the expression *les prunes de monsieur* (the gent's plums) or even *la liqueur de prunes de monsieur* (the gent's plum brandy) which is sperm (quoted in Perret, *Le Nouveau Petit Perret illustré*). Other varieties of plum (see above) are also used for testicles in French.

> Us? I can see clearly that your precious stones are out of kilter. I'm going to tell you something: I would rather die than go home without my shiver-making machines. No Bérurier has ever landed up with his plums in a jewellery box.
>
> San-Antonio, Bérurier au sérail *(Bérurier in the Harem, 1969)*

Currents (*raisins de Corinthe*) was a metaphor used by the comic actor and singer Christophe Alévêque to mean testicles during *On a tout essayé* (We've tried everything) a television programme presented by Laurent Ruquier in 2004. Indeed, despite their small dimensions, raisins do suggest quite well the worn-out and wrinkled aspect of testes in their scrotum.

Games (French: *virolets* n.m.): the French have the expression *les deux virolets* which means testicles. It alludes to a child's game, perhaps played with rings (*viroles*), although the word *virolet* itself indicates (in childish worlds) a toy windmill.

Genital apparatus (French: *appareil genital* n.m.): designates the ensemble of organs of reproduction (penis and testicles), although it is sometimes used for just the testicles, because they enshrine the reproductive process. Sometimes the expression for the collection of genital organs is rendered as 'sexual apparatus'.

Genitals (English; French: *génitailles* n.f.; *génitoires* n.f.; *genitores* n.f.; *germinales* n.f.; Latin: *genitalia*): [Scientific blanket term taking in all organs of reproduction, male or female.] The Latin word *genitalia* refers to the genitals in general, see also *arma virilia*, *colei*, *pudenda* and *vilia membra*. The French word *génitoires* alludes to their reproductive functions.

> A king in the Greek histories
> Knowing of kin plotting treason,
> Wanted to re-impose reason
> By snipping their genitories.
>
> Le Cabinet satyrique.

She was telling the truth, Berthe, just now when she congratulated him on his powerful constitution. He fools everyone this dwarf! I have never seen girls like Sheila before! Felix is a little monkey when you see him from the side, but with the genitories of an elephant. He's not a man, he's a petrol pump!

San-Antonio, Les Vacances de Bérurier ou La Croisière du 'Mer d'alors'

And then, after being shaken to the bottom of my genitories, we were swallowed up, she and I, by a sleep that was so dense and so deep, so total, that it came bloody close to annihilation.

San-Antonio, Des Gonzesses comme s'il en pleuvait.

Similar is the word *genitores*:

> There's a nation of Moors
> Whose men have genitors
> As long as a carter's.
>
> Octave Mirbeau, Farces et moralités.

Génitailles was coined by the French novelist Alicia Reyes from *génitoires* and the argot suffix *-aille* which ensures that the word has a devaluing or pejorative sense. In fact it manages to give the language a medieval connotation:

> I offered my hand, placing that great hot kernel in my palm which stood up like a prow under his pantaloons. In my fingers I could feel the extreme fullness of his *génitailles* and his broadsword so stiff that losing heart I could think of nothing more from then on than letting him grind my bum.
>
> Alicia Reyes, Derrière la porte (Behind the Door, 1994)

Germinales stresses the reproductive role of testicles.

Genitor/Genitory (English): is now obscure. Sometimes rendered as 'membris genytores'.

Gesticules: another neologism by Frédéric Dard facetiously used to denote testicles in one of his San-Antonio books and, inevitably, it is placed in the mouth of the ineffable Bérurier:

She looked at me, with a worried look which worried me. At that moment, I started thinking again of the lady notary at Saint-Locdu-le-Vieux. She looked so much like her you could have noshed my *gesticules*.

San-Antonio, Si Queue d'Ane m'était conté ou La Vie sexuelle de Bérurier

Glands (French: *glandes* n.f.): testicles are reproductive glands, gonads, or seminal glands, also called genitals. In the language of the French streets, the word *glandes* is used as a synonym for *boules* (q.v.) particularly in expressions like *avoir des glandes* (have some balls) or *foutre les glandes* (piss off someone):

> While he's waiting, a reasonably civilized negro, as I think of myself in my happier moments, needs to conquer his place in the shade, not just with his brains, but above all with his genital glands, sir. If good marriages are off the menu for the time being, we can certainly hope for happy adultery.
>
> *San-Antonio*, Les Vacances de Bérurier ou La Croisière du 'Mer d'alors'

> I ploughed.
> I stuffed them. All.
> And I had a few leftovers to finish off. In the evening, I looked at a communion photo of some unknown grandma and her randy look went straight to my glands despite the fact that she had popped her clogs before the war of 1870.
>
> *San-Antonio*, Si Queue d'Ane m'était conté ou La Vie sexuelle de Bérurier

A variation is *glandes brimbalantes* or *brinquelablantes*, or swinging glands [*brimbalant* in French is a part of the verb *brimbaler*, meaning to dangle, to shift yourself from foot to foot, or to oscillate, a synonym of which last is *branler*, which also means to masturbate] an evocative name for testicles due once again to the sparkling imagination of Frédéric Dard, better known as San-Antonio:

> I had just one advantage for myself, when I got pissed that time. Every time I get properly arse-holed I go on the bonk. It excites the swinging glands (or clanking glands if you prefer a 'k').
>
> *San-Antonio*, Dégustez, gourmandes

Glandules (English): sometimes testicles.

Globes (French: *globes* n.m.): mostly used for women's breasts, but sometimes testicles as well. When this happens it is almost always accompanied by the adjective *petits* (small):

> Two little globes down below,
> To strengthen the mystery

Counter-balance the blows,
And make for less austerity.'

Le Cabinet satyrique

Gonads (French: *gonades* n.f; *animelles* n.f.): is one of the most usual terms to designate the testicles. It comes from the Greek *gonê* meaning seed. The gonads are the sexual glands that make gametes and secrete hormones. The testicle being the male gonad and the ovary the female. All the same, the word testicle was used indifferently to denote both male and female gonads, the term ovary only appearing in the seventeenth century, formed from the Latin word for egg.

> To tell the truth, we only write for the pleasure of having at least embraced a destiny; but give us the chance to express the beating of our hearts, the cadences of our lungs, the spasms of our gonads, the movements of our legs, under the sole control (and not much of that thank goodness) of the will and we would happily abandon the motions of our pens which on some nights write nonsense of the sort, *Breton Breton petit patapon* [a nonsense refrain to children's songs].
>
> Dominique Noguez, Dandys de l'an 2000

Animelles is a butcher's word for animals' testicles in French and by extension, used for men too.

Also gonadal, gonadial, gonadic, gonadectomy, gonaduct.

Goods (French: *marchandises* n.f.): in the singular *marchandise* means the collection as in the expression *remballe ta marchandise* (put away your goods). It is rarer in the plural, when it means testicles.

> And the adolescent arose from out of the whiteness of the young girl and assumed his original of bearded billygoat with horns, cloven hooves, brobdingnagian goods (*marchandises énormes*) and all that that entailed. And nothing remained of the coupling, the encounter, save a few bloodstains on the ceremonial towel.
>
> A Thousand and One Nights *(the story of the billygoat with the king's daughter)*

Goolies (English of Hindustani origin): a gooly comes from the Hindustani for a bullet or a ball. It is a popular slang word for testicles: 'Ow'd yer like a kick in the goolies?'

Gourd(s) (French: *gourde(s)* n.f.): the whole panoply of penis and testicles. Gourds are used in the plural to mean testicles. For me, I'd say 'A good man is made from gourds and a bludgeon.' [This is a play on words: the gourds of course are the bollocks; the bludgeon is, in French, *le gourdin*. So the whole apothegm is '*gourdes et gourdin font l'homme de bien*'.]

When my hand grasps the neck of his gourd brimming with milk, he closes his eyes like the pigeons he smothers.

Marcel Jouhandeau (French writer, 1888–1979)

Grenades (French: *grenades* n.f.): a nickname suggesting a goodly size. They are never quite so effective until the pins have been pulled. Grenades can evoke a lot of sexual activity.

Hangers (English): self-explanatory term, now uncommon. In Mallory's *Morte D'Arthur*, faced with the prospect of sex with Morgan Lefay, Alisaunder says 'O Jesu, defend me. I had liefer cut away my hangers than I would do her such pleasure.'

Hind legs (French: *pattes de derrière* n.f.): one of the sauciest of the imaginative expressions that dripped from the fecund pen of San-Antonio:

The lord of Saint Locdu's pointer was standing up on its hind legs.

San-Antonio, **Princesse patte-en-l'air** *(Princess Legs-in-the-air, 1990)*

[The lord of Saint Locdu was the Rabelaisian character created by San-Antonio.]

Histories (French: *histoires* n.f.): a general euphemism for male sexual organs (like thing, thingie, or tool). It can refer to women as well.

Mademoiselle, oh great misfortune! The evil fellows have torn off his histories.

Béroalde de Verville (French novelist and poet, 1566–1626)

Honey pots (French: *bouteilles à miel* n.f.): a name suggesting testicles by dint of its contents:

'Conette! Massage, massage my master's balls! Massage the honey pot of his love-staff.'

Nicolas-Edme Restif de la Bretonne (French writer, 1734–1836)

[Jackson Pollocks]: Cockney rhyming slag: the testicles being referred to as Jacksons.

Jelly-bags (English): rare. [It can also mean breast implants.]

Jerrycans (English): metonymic metaphor for testicles, stressing their role as containers. It will be agreed that masculine vanity is sometimes vastly exaggerated when one knows that the jerrycan is a can containing around 20 litres of fluid! Jerry cans are naturally filled with super. [The German *Wehrmachtskanister* was called a 'jerry can' because Germans had been called 'Jerries' since the First

World War. Its removable spout was called a 'donkey dick.' The term is not to be confused with 'jerry bags': used for the women of the Channel Islands who slept with Germans during the Occupation.]

Jingle Balls (English): a parody of 'jingle bells', from the seasonal song. A rare instance of an English nickname evoking ringing bells.

Jock (English): male genitals, hence 'jockstrap.'

Kall (Breton): testicles in Breton, deriving from the Gaelic *caill* (testicle) which evolved into *caljo* (stone) in Gaulish [spoken in Celtic Gaul until approximately the second century AD] and which stems from *callum* (*callus*) in Latin. This root from the Celtic has given us the word *caillou* (stone), and a number of place names such as Chelles in Seine-et-Marne or Caille in the Alpes-Maritimes, referring to a particularly rocky subsoil. French also takes the words *caillot* (clot of blood), *caillé* (curds), *caillebotte* (mass of coagulated milk) and even *caillette* (faggot) from it, all words that mean a little hard thing. Otherwise, the French word *cail* (now obsolete), meant among other things the starter for cheese-making. Not everyone agrees with this etymology, some people insist that the route passes from the Latin *coagulum* (coagulate) from *co-* (with) and *agere* (act), therefore 'bring together, put together' and by extension 'solidify, condense, set with rennet' which seems to be a more baroque explanation. Moreover, if the verb *cailler* means 'to be cold, to chill' in a figurative sense, is this not because cold hardens like a stone? It is more amusing to note that the word *kall* has given the French the expression *à califourchon* (astride or straddling): i.e. a bollock at each end of a fork created by the spreading of the legs.

Kanakas (Australian English from Hawaiian): the original word means 'human', but one suspects that it is also a variant on the cockney knackers (q.v.).

Karamazov sisters (French: *soeurs Karamazov* n.f.): as everyone knows, there were brothers in the Dostoyevsky novel of that name! It is one of myriad examples of the inventive language of Frédéric Dard, in the detective stories written under his pen-name of San-Antonio:

> In revenge, the lover (in quotation marks) gave me a kick in the Karamazov sisters.
>   San-Antonio, Fais-moi des choses (Do Things to Me, 1969)

Kefta (Arabic): meatballs in Arabic. You can also say *kafta* or *kofta*. By extension it is an epithet occasionally conferred on testicles. The usage is not common among Arabs themselves. It is used in expressions like 'a merguez and two *koftas*' meaning male attributes in a rather prosaic way.

Khassiya, khassyâne (Arabic): in Arabic the word means a pair and, by extension, testicles. This is the derivation of *khassî*, which means a neutered animal (Malek Chebel, *Encyclopédie de l'amour en Islam*)

Kiwis (French: *kiwis* n.m.): a nickname for testicles, for each party's similarity to the other. The genus *Actinidia* (kiwi fruit or Chinese gooseberry) originates in China and the metaphorical exchange goes two ways: one sobriquet of the kiwi fruit is 'Mao's bollocks'.

Knackers (English): of obscure origin (possibly from knack meaning a trinket). Knackers has been synonymous with testicles since the mid-nineteenth century. It is still popular today. Graham Greene writes, in *Travels with my Aunt*, 'I may regret him for a while tonight. His knackers were superb.'

A knacker is otherwise a gypsy, particularly in Ireland, or a debilitated horse or a dealer in such animals or in debilitated goods of any sort. Castanets are also knackers. Could there be a connection between the idea of testes as clappers, bells, etc. and the short, sharp clack of the castanet?

Knappes (English): an ancient term for testicles.

Knots (French: *burnes* n.f.): the French *burne* is a term for testicles which comes from the language of Picardy in northern France called Rouchi, or Chti or Chtimi (it is an old *langue d'oïl* as opposed to *langue d'oc*). It means 'a knot, an excrescence on a gnarled old tree' (*Dictionnaire de l'argot et ses origines*, Larousse 2002). Other writers insist that it is a variant of *prunes* or plums.

> To make a compote of knots [i.e. mash up the balls], there are those who use split cane and those who bring out the mouli-légumes like Grandma used to.
>
> **San-Antonio**, Béru-Béru.

> To finish, as far as I see it, is to start again at the beginning – to go back to those happy times when I was swinging about in the old man's balls [knots].

> I see the different seasons all over again. There was summer and then autumn and also the moments when I chilled my knots in the snow or when the peach trees were covered in pink blossoms that drove the bees wild.

> I don't want to break out the beer just for Bérurier, that would put me in a tight spot. For all that Dad, I have to say it was great watching him screw. Bugger me, one would feel pretty proud to have knots like them. Like fists boy! Like fists, and hairy, god's brothel! Hairy!
>
> **San-Antonio**, Si Queue d'âne m'était conté ou La Vie sexuelle de
> Bérurier

Another variant on *burnes* is *burnicherie*. It brings to mind the word *boucherie* (butcher's shop) and evokes a shop well-stocked with merchandise of what appears to be of a very special sort.

Burnailles is a neologism created by Frédéric Dard from *burnes*. According to the principles of French slang, it is enough to add the suffix *-aille* to a word to render it dismissive or pejorative. In the same vein he invented the verb *déburner*, to debollock.

> Bertha, I can't see any other solution than a quick hump, just to decant my knackers so to speak.
>
> *San-Antonio,* Fais-moi des choses

Lights (French: *lampions* n.m.): *les lampions* is slang for eyes, except that in the writings of Frédéric Dard it has been rerouted by Bérurier to mean testicles. In an unlikely bout of wrestling, he says:

> Have you got a pin so I can bust his balls [*lampions*]?
>
> *San-Antonio,* Bérurier au sérail

Little ones (French: *petites* n.f.): affectionate term, similar to the word *fillettes* (little girls, s.v. members of the family).

> Would the chief inspector of my two dear little girls be having a piss, by any chance?
>
> *San-Antonio,* Béru-Béru

Living, alive (Algerian French: *vivantes* n.f.): a pretty epithet for testicles used by the inhabitants of the region of Tlemcen in Algeria, and revealed by Malek Chebel in his fascinating book *Encyclopédie de l'amour en Islam*.

Love apples (English) (French: *pommes d'amour* n.f.): the metaphor seems obvious and harks back to the original thought that the tomato was an aphrodisiac. In French the *pomme d'amour* is nowadays more likely used to designate the toffee apples found at funfairs.

> I kneeled in the grass and looked at his sleeping body. It was tender and muscle-bound, and there was an endearing basket of fruit on offer below the belt, with a ravishing banana laid out across two round love apples that looked good enough to eat.
>
> *Alina Reyes,* Derrière la porte

Love nuts (American English): for nuts, q.v. Love nuts is an Americanism describing when a man's passion goes unrequited, synonymous with blue balls.

Lovers (French: *aimants* n.m.): in French, an obsolete term for sexual organs, masculine and feminine, stressing the fact that they attract one another like lovers and are made to come together.

Low Countries (French: Pays-Bas n.m.): a metaphor for the sexual bits.

> Oh let me behold your little foot, Jeanette!
> Oh let me see your pretty calves naked, please!
> – 'No, Lucas my good friend, please!
> – That's the way that your willy might get
> – No, Lucas my good friend, please!
> It's the road to the Low Countries!
>
> *Refrain from an eighteenth-century Angevin song, quoted in Curnonsky and*
> *André Saint-Georges,* La Table et l'amour

Luggage / kit (French: *baggage* n.f.; *fourniment* n.m.): invokes an image more of the trinity of genital organs whereas *valises* (suitcases – see below) designates testicles alone.

> In the course of that first interview, no effort was too great to obtain his consent, no compliment too flattering that I could offer to put him in a good mood. Once the drink had had its effect on him, he was voluble in the pleasure he took in hearing us sing and the excitement that he derived from our frenzy caused him instantly to abandon his habitual reserve. The morose aspect of his physiognomy had vanished. His young servants, knowing my scheme, left the room and us alone. It was then that I extended my hand towards his luggage, anxious to grab them and not doubting (to my misfortune, as I had deluded myself) that I was going to be doing business with something of large dimensions, powerful in the extreme and ready for majestic development.
>
> *Ahmad al-Tifachi,* Les Délices des coeurs

> Even a prudent traveller can lose his luggage. Except one…
>
> *Japanese proverb*

Le fourniment invokes the soldier's kitbag, and by extension the panoply of male genital organs, notably in the expression, 'the whole kit.' [In English 'get your kit out' or 'put your kit away' would have a similar meaning.]

Lunch box (English): the panoply as perceived through the trousers. Generally used in expressions to express admiration: 'Cor! He's got a big lunch box!'

Lyonnaises (French: *lyonnaises* n.f.): the largest size of ball in French bowls or the Marseilles game of pétanque; hence a term of admiration.

Mallets (French: *mailleaux* n.m.): testicles, from the old form of *maillet*: a double-headed hammer made of wood.

> And the mallets, didn't I say
> Which are attached to his arse.
>
> *Anciens fabliaux (Middle Ages)*

Marbles (French: *billes* n.m.): *bille* has several meanings. First and foremost it is a ball: as in the French for ball-bearings and ballpoint pens. Then it is the marble in the child's game of marbles. In popular slang it often refers to the eyes, but also the testicles, which have an analogous form. [In English slang, to lose one's marbles, is to lose your wits or mind.]

Marjolles (French n.f.): this is an obscure and obsolete word for testicles dating from the seventeenth century. The allusion is in fact to the caruncle or wattle of the turkey – obscure indeed. Pierre Guiraud's *Dictionnaire érotique* defines the word *marjoler* as meaning to caress.

Marshmallows (French *Chamallows* n.m.): the sweetmeat the Anglophone world calls marshmallow is *guimauve* in French. This is commercialized in France by the Haribo Company as Chamallow. It is also a tender epithet describing the testicles because of the supple, lissome texture of these toothsome round sweeties.

Marsupium (English from Greek): means little bag, hence scrotum.

Meat (Arabic: *klaoui*; French: *paupiettes* n.f.; *rognons* n.m.; *cochonailles* n.f.): *claouis* is a slang term which seems to have found its way into argot from African troops fighting in the French army, and comes from a Gallic rendering of the Algerian Arabic *klaoui* (*kelàoui* or *klawi*). In Arabic, the word means 'kidney' and it was sometimes an epithet for testicles because of the similarity of form. Occasionally found written as *glaouis* even though this means pasha in Morocco.

> The Nobel Prize committee would be stunned if they set eyes on my central heating! Say, you might see a jar of San-Antonio in the Museum of Mankind stuck between the brains of Methuselah and the *claouis* of Father Dupanloup.
>
> *San-Antonio,* Du Poulet au menu,

Meatballs (see *kefta*) are another popular metaphor. The word *paupiettes* comes from the Old French *poupe* which means 'meaty part'. A *paupiette* is meat rolled and stuffed: a gourmand metaphor that will be appreciated.

Cochonailles is a plate of sliced pork sausages and ham. It also means testicles, a nothing, a typical French sot.

Rognons (kidneys) is another slang word for testicles, a euphemistic transfer to the human male of a word that relates to animals (human kidneys are *reins* in French). The term *rognons blancs* is used in cooking to mean testicles.

> 'I came to give you a kiss.'
> And I kissed her all over, for I have to say that, seen from that angle, she surely does ruffle the kidneys
>
> *San-Antonio,* San-Antonio chez les gones

In France, among the young, the word *steaks* (i.e. beefsteaks) has become a synonym for *couilles,* as in *j'm'en bats les steaks* (I don't give a damn / a monkey's / a fuck).

Medakir (Arabic): meaning 'organs' of virility, that which makes you a man.

Members of the family: twins / couples / two little orphans / little girls / sisters / brothers / tomboys / kids / flirts (French: *binos* n.m.; *couples,* n.f.; *deux orphelines* n.f.; *fillettes* n.f.; *frangines* n.f.; *frérots* n.m.; *gamines* n.f.; *gosses* n.f.; *grisettes* n.f.; *jumelles* n.f.; *philippines* n.f. ; *siamoises* n.f.; Greek: *didumos*; English US: twins): *binos*, from the Latin for two, is used in a trivial sense to denote testicles:

> You have no siblings
> Good god! What lovely twins (*beaux binos*).
> L' Ancien théâtre français, *edited by Pierre Jannet (1820–1870)*

In the French word *couples* the stress is on twinship. It is used in the feminine, and is a synonym for 'pair'.

Les deux orphelines (the two orphan girls) is a nickname for testicles that comes from Pierre Perret's '*le petit chose et les deux orphelines*' (the little thing and the two orphan girls):

> Perhaps we'll finally know
> Who is the sacred monster who wields all this power so
> And with no more ado she unveils
> The little thing and the two orphan girls.
> Pierre Perret, *song* Le Zizi (The Willy, 1974)

Les fillettes (the little girls) is an affectionate term which dates from before the war and is little used now. The speaker is generally referring to his own 'little girls.'

The slang *frangines* means sisters and it is one of the many epithets for testicles that tells us that they go two by two, even as sisters.

> He went to work on her triple A snatch. She wasn't used to being mounted so hard and that was why she used her knee to administer a crushing blow to his sisters.
> San-Antonio, *Les Gonzesses comme s'il en pleuvait*

Frérots (little brothers) is also used to suggest our bollocks' fraternity, twinship even. It is in the same vein as sisters, twins, twin brothers, twin sisters…

Gamines (tomboys) is an affectionate term used generally to designate the speaker's own: *mes petites gamines*.

Another affectionate nickname is *gosses* (kids) used in the expression *mes petites gosses*, which is similar to *petites* (little girls) or *fillettes*. It is used a lot in Quebec. In this expression the word *gosse* is in fact a slip of the tongue from *cosse* (*gousse* – a clove – in the sense of a clove of garlic), a vegetable wrapping which contains grains, seeds, and is therefore a metonymic metaphor.

Jumelles are female twins.

An excellent investigation, Chief Inspector of my twin girls.'
San-Antonio, Un éléphant ça trompe

Philippines is another nickname that suggests twinhood: *philippines* being twin almonds. The name is a deformation of the German *Vielliebchen*: an affectionate game played when two people are challenged to eat the same fruit.

'As long as we get there on time' said Béru, 'or that they have only removed half of his phillipines. That's better than nothing. It marks a man.'
San-Antonio, Bérurier au sérail

Petites soeurs des pauvres (little sisters of the poor, i.e. Sisters of Mercy) is one of the many mysterious epithets which have come straight out of the imagination of Frédéric Dard, via his Police Commissioner San-Antonio and his side-kick Alexandre-Benoît Bérurier.

At the same time, Le Vaillant planted a magisterial kick in the meatballs (*claouis*) of the second copper who was following the reconstruction with all the interest you could wish for. The other dropped everything to clutch his little sisters of the poor.
San-Antonio, Des gonzesses comme s'il en pleuvait

Siamoises are Siamese girl twins. This is another neologism of Frédéric Dard:

And by the way, if it is just M'sieur Felix, it would be impossible to recognize him as you can't see the head, only the arse (*dargibus*), the Siamese twins and perpetual motion.'
San-Antonio, Les vacances de Bérurier ou La Croisière du 'Mer d'alors'

She objected by hitting him in the Siamese twins with a copper coal shovel.
San-Antonio, Un éléphant, ça trompe

He was surrounded by an assembly of girls, saffron-scented nymphs; laughing, trilling and over-excited. Which one of them was going to stroke his dingledangle, praise his Siamese twins (that's the *mot juste* here), touch his most sensitive places with her finger tips?
San-Antonio, A Prendre ou à lecher *(To Take or to Lick, 1980)*

The French word *grisettes* is no longer used much. In the original sense it was a young working-class girl of easy virtue, so-called because of the cheap grey garments she usually wore.

Merry-makers (French: *enjoliveurs* n.m.; *joies de ce monde* n.f.; *joyeuses* n.f.; *luronnes* n.f.; *valseuses* n.f.): *enjoliveurs* (literally, the verb *enjoliver* means to make more cheerful by means of ornament, to embellish) is a piquant term to denote testicles.

> You need to see him playing with the ball before his last (he is convinced) service. He bounces it several times on the ground, wipes it on his white shorts, and then weighs it in his hand, like your girl weighs your merry-makers (*enjoliveurs*) after use to show her admiration and gratitude.
>
> *San-Antonio,* Les vacances de Bérurier ou La Croisière du 'Mer d'alors'

Joies de ce monde (joys of this world) is an evocation of the pleasures the testes might engender (in the real and figurative senses). It is worth noting that the noun *joie* derives from the verb *jouir* which may mean to achieve a sexual climax.

Another popular facetious French term is *joyeuses* (joyfuls). It is used especially in detective novels, but also in cooking. It is a metonymic use of an adjective taken from a verb that goes back to the noun *joie*, see above. *Joyeuses* are perhaps a memory of that happily carnal usage that has been often bastardized today.

> 'With a man like me,' said Bérurier, 'who never hesitates when it comes to singing his own praises, with a man like me, honey, its is better to fondle the joyfuls than to break them.'
>
> *San-Antonio,* Bérurier contre San-Antonio

> 'Ah! That's funny! Ah! That makes me laugh! I can't take it! I feel I am going to meet my maker! I can't breathe! Look, I'm crying! It's too much! It's tickling my guts! It's twisting my joyfuls!'
>
> *San-Antonio,* Béru et ses dames

> 'For what it's worth, my joyfuls are as wrinkled as a strawberry under the chin of Henri II's queen [Marie de' Medici].
>
> *San-Antonio,* Béru-Béru

Valseuses (waltzers) is a metaphor that alludes to bollocks' swinging movement on the march. It had fallen out of use until it was revived by Bertrand Blier in his film *Les Valseuses* of 1972.

> Keep an eye on your trousers, boys! What are you complaining about, old mucker. I have leaches sucking my phials and my waltzers must look like a crystal candelabra.
>
> *San-Antonio,* Béru-Béru

Luronnes suggests good health and merriment. The word *luron* means a merry chap, and *luronne* a cheerful woman, a good sport. There might, however, be some connection to *larrons* (thieves, q.v.).

Money-bags (French: *aumônière* n.f.): a nickname for testicles using a metonymic metaphor that alludes to the leather or cloth bags that used to be carried on the belt. The French word *aumonière* comes from *aumône*, the alms given to the poor which, like the English, derives from the Latin *alemosina*, which in turn comes from the Greek *eleêmosunê* (compassion) which runs together the words *eleêmon* (sympathetic) and *eleos* (pity); and it is true, in fact, that some money-bags inspire pity.

'I'm off!' added the courageous lad added as he launched himself. Blimey O'Riley! Just watching him made you realize that if Man didn't descend from the apes, at lthe east his ancestors were firemen. For God's sake, he clamped himself to the giant tree-trunk as if he were a caterpillar. You'd say his limbs had suckers, the way he stuck to it. If any of you lads think of imitating him, you'll be covered in grazes and break your balls (*aumonières*).

San-Antonio, Béru-Béru

There I was, with an accidental nudge of the elbow (or my tits, who knows?), I pressed the horn. Oh not hard, not for long, just a little beep and nothing more. No sooner done, mate, than I felt a ghastly pain in the balls. I nearly puked in agony. I put my hand down to feel, and you know what I found? The woman driving the taxi's ugly little mutt had just clenched his teeth round one of my money-bags and was growling full throttle. It was horrible, no other word for it. The old woman thought it was me, expressing my pleasure. With dewy eyes she sighed,
'It's good no? It's good, isn't it big boy?'
It would have been good if I had had the hound by the bollocks!
San-Antonio, Si Queue d'âne m'était conté ou La Vie sexuelle de Bérurier

Morels (French: *morilles* n.f.): this is an epithet conferred when the testicles in question are particularly wrinkled. For example: 'his balls are as wrinkled as dried morels'. By extension, the word morels is applied to the balls themselves.

Mud (Russian): testicle.

Musical instruments (French: *castagnettes* n.f.; *cymbales* n.f.; *fifre à pedales* n.m.; *maracas* n.m.): castanets are a metaphor for testicles. They are one of a series of figurative uses based on musical instruments that are used in pairs.

She is big, blonde and impeccably made. She plays the part of a devoted daughter. It would be fun to break her into the mysteries of the retractable lanyard* and swinging castanets.
San-Antonio, San-Antonio chez les gones

*The lanyard in question is of course the penis. San-Antonio calls it the *Scoubidou*, a reference to the French children's activity of knotting plaits or lanyards out of coloured plastic fibres. It was a fad in France from the late 1950s. *Translator.*

' – here's justice Augustus', rhymed Béru kneeing him sharply in the castanets.

San-Antonio, Béru et ces dames

Cymbals is another binary musical metaphor: there are always two. As there are maracas.

Un fifre à pédales (a fife with pedals) is a French argot expression to denote the full house, the testicles being the pedals and the fife the penis. Variants include a 'fife with whiskers' and a 'fife with bells.'

Nadgers (English): a cross between nads and tadgers. It was first used on the popular 'Goon Show' in 1956, and is thought to be a combination of 'knacker' and 'todger'.

Nads (US English): a contraction of gonads, and may be applied to male or female organs as was once the case in French.

Neer (English – regional and Scottish): now obscure, it is related to the German *Niere* (kidney).

Nether regions (French: *bas morceaux* n.m.): a popular expression to denote the bits below the belt. It also enters into French slang in the form *bas morcifs*.

> Béru was kinglike when he walked up to the second scumbag. He was wearing a handsome meditative expression – much like a housewife choosing aubergines in the market – when he decided to administer a blow with his knee to the nether regions.
>
> San-Antonio, Béru et ses dames

> You can't stop yourself from being cocky when you are lugging around at least a pound and a half of nether regions between your legs.
>
> San-Antonio, Tarte aux poils sur commande (Pussy to order, 1989)

Nibbles (French: *amuse-bouche* n.f.): it's not hard to figure out what sort of feast we're talking about here, to what these are the gourmand preliminaries. You must be careful, however, not to bare your teeth.

Noodles (French: *nouilles* n.f.): a play on the French word *couilles* (balls) and more genteel. It had its five minutes of glory in the sixties, notably in boys' colleges and religious lycées.

Nothings (French: *riens* n.f.): in the twelfth century *rien* (nothing) was a feminine noun which, used in the plural, denoted in a roundabout way the bits labelled 'immodest' on a man. Paradoxically, the critic Pascal Quignard explains that the word itself derives from the Latin *rem* (accusative of *res*) which means 'thing' (see Mythology) and he quotes:

Everyone who names them
Calls them Lord knows what,
Logs, harness, things (*riens*), jugs or pricks (*pines*).
**Pascal Quignard, Petits traités, 'Le mot de l'objet', (Little Treatises, 'The
name of things', 1990)**

Nutmegs (English): a word that has now fallen from grace.

Nuts (US English; French: *amygdales sud* n.f.; *cacahuètes* n.f.; *marrons* n.m.; *nios*
n.m.; *noisettes* n.f.; *noix* n.m.): the word nuts for testicles is a universal usage in
current English, although it was first recorded (in the singular) as referring to
the *glans penis*. *Amygdales* is the French word for tonsils. It derives from the Latin
amygdala, almond. The French for almond, *amande*, is a corruption of that Latin.
Amygdales sud for balls (literally, southern tonsils) is another term that owes its
origin to the characterful language of the French crime writer Frédéric Dard
(San-Antonio). He also writes about *amygdales de dessous* (tonsils down below)
and sometimes just a single-barrelled *amygdales*.

> In stuffing Lola I was committing a crime of *lèse-majesté*. I should be
> sentenced to impalement and loss of my southerly tonsils (*amygdales sud*).
> **San-Antonio, Bérurier au sérail**

> I found the hostesses so sexy I could have died and I thought my nuts
> (*amygdales sud*) would explode if I didn't manage to put at least one of
> them into orbit.
> **San-Antonio, Dégustez gourmandes**

Walnuts (*noix*) are a popular designation for testicles, above all in expressions
such as 'of my walnuts' or 'crack my walnuts' (*casser mes noix*). They are slightly
emollient versions of break or crush my balls (*couilles*).

> As I am not a cheap novelist and only capable of selling you funny little
> tales, I need to perfect your education by telling you that coconuts are as
> important in Thailand as my walnuts are to my whole persona.
> **San-Antonio, A Prendre ou à lecher**

Nios is a slang inversion, partial *verlan*, of the word *noix* or walnuts. [*Verlan*
is a latterday development of French *argot* or slang where words in common use
are inverted or jumbled, e.g. *café* becomes *féca*. Its origins lie in the immigrant
communities of the outer suburbs of larger cities, particularly among the young,
but it has been adopted more widely both as a gesture of solidarity with these
new French citizens, and as a generational marker.]

> Listen, product of my two *nios*, it's not the moment to overstep the mark,
> I swear to you!
> **San-Antonio, Du Poulet au menu**

Hazelnuts (*noisettes*) are another nut-based metaphor for the bollocks:

They asked Abou Nouwâs:
'Why did you give two dirhams [unit of currency] to that young boy,
and only one to the eunuch?'
'Because the young boy has two hazelnuts in the middle of the field
where he grazes his ewes.'
Ahmad Al-Tifachi, Les Délices des coeurs ou ce que l'on ne trouve en
aucun livre

Another common sobriquet is *marrons* (chestnuts). Some authors talk of
marrons glacés (candied chestnuts):

– Pillock! Everyone knows what bollocks are, good God, because everyone
has them, even Lisé's old Miraut [a dog], and they know too that they
look like chestnuts without their shells, but what a pillock! Pillock!...'
Louis Pergaud, La Guerre des boutons

A final nutty epithet for testicles is *cacahuètes* (peanuts), though there is an
implicit derision in the usage, given the size of the nut in question.

Nux vomica (Poison nut; French: *noix vomique* n.f.): another slang term for the
testicle, this time alluding to the fruit of the strychnine tree. It is used by Pierre
Devaux in *Le Livre des darons sacrés ou La Bible en argot* (The Book of the Holy
Fathers, or The Bible in Slang, 1974).

Oïdia (Greek): this is from the ancient Greek for egg (*ôon*). It designates testicles
both by euphemism and metaphor, notably in medical terminology – when
visiting the doctor, for example – in the way that a 'learned word' seems less
incongruous than one in common use which might be vulgar. It will be noted
that *oïdia* is the plural of *oïdium*, the name of the famous wine blight.

Orchis (Greek): plant of the orchidaceous family, like the orchid. *Orkhis* and
orkidion mean testicle and little testicle respectively in ancient Greek, an
etymology which is down to the evident resemblance to the bulb of the flower
which, paradoxically, looks like a woman's vulva when it is open. [Taking a
different route, the Greek stem moves into rhythm and dance and is the source
of the word 'orchestra'.]
    In his *Encyclopédie de l'amour en Islam*, Malek Chebel informs us that the
Arabs use the orchid as a love potion and an aphrodisiac, and he quotes a legend
recorded by Mathéa Gaudry which would lead us to believe that the orchid was
much feared because 'one of its roots, the living one, is used as an aphrodisiac; the
other as an anti-aphrodisiac' (see also the recipe for salep and the paragraph on
the twin balls of satyrion on pages 147 and 153 above). By some sort of boomerang
effect, testicles are sometimes called orchis in a deliberate desire to use a precious
'cultural' term. It should be noted that orchitis means an inflammation of the

testicles; that monorchid describes someone who possesses just one testicle, and that cryptorchidism describes testicles that have not dropped and which are still hidden inside the belly.

In English, the orchid was once called the 'ballocke flower', the cuckoo orchis was 'fooles ballockes', the *orchis spiralis* 'sweete ballocks', and great orchis 'hares ballocks.' An orchidologist is an expert on orchids, not testicles and orchidophile means a lover of flowers, not of balls.

Orchic means pertaining to the testicles.

Organs (genital, reproductive or sexual): here we have an euphemistic contraction meaning all the organs, bringing together, for example, the penis and testicles and much else besides. It is also significant to note that certain classical Christian authors (Seneca and Saint Augustine, for example) call them 'shameful organs', while certain sixteenth-century Arabic erotic writers (such as Ahmed ibn Souleimân) prefer the term 'essential organs' (see Mythology).

> Learn that God, in his munificence, wanted the races to survive, and granted these races reproductive organs. He inserted into these organs an instinctive force without which there would be no enjoyment in procuring pleasure. He made it fun to use one's sexual attributes.
>
> *Ahmed ibn Souleimân,* Le Bréviaire arabe de l'amour

> Mademoiselle, as soon as I saw you I felt my genital organs unfold towards your sovereign beauty and I found myself more heated than if I had drunk a glass of arak.
>
> *Guillaume Apollinaire,* Les Cent Mille Verges

Ountayân (Arabic: testicles): 'The word has the privilege of sharing the same linguistic root as "girl" and "feminine sex" (*ounta*). However, the meaning of words – dictated by men of course – has privileged male sexual organs at the expense of those of women. These are deprecated, both in practice and linguistically. The tendency in favour of the male in Islamic culture reflects social arrangements, as well as religious and political power structures.' Malek Chebel, *Encyclopédie de l'amour en Islam.*

Ovette (Italian: n.f.): 'little eggs' and therefore testicles.

Packet (French: *paquet* n.m.; *paquet d'amour* n.m.; *paquet de la mariée* n.m.; *ballottins, ballotins* n.m.; *ballots* n.m.; *balluchons, baluchons* n.m.; *petits paquets* n.m.; Spanish: *paquete* n.m.): packet is an evocative epithet for the trinity of male genital organs, and sometimes just the testicles. The French comedian Jean-Marie Bigard had himself photographed wearing just a pair of underpants, with his protuberances in exaggerated stark relief (from all the evidence, the garments were stuffed with two tennis balls) and, as a caption (this was also the title of the show), he wrote '*Bigard met le paquet*' ['Bigard pulls out all the stops']. There is a double-entendre here: the phrase *mettre le paquet* means to pull out all stops, or to do everything possible.] The allusion was flagrant. This sense of packet is very popular in Quebec.

> He is male anyway: I have held his packet.
>
> P. Delarivey *(French dramatist, 1541–1619)*

Paquet d'amour (love packet) is an affectionate variant on the last.

Paquet de la mariée (the bride's packet) is similar to the English 'wedding tackle'. It means the whole shebang and has for variants *paquet de l'épousée* (married woman's packet) or *paquet de ménage* (household packet).

Petits paquets (little packets) is a genteel term for the testicles of young boys, the penis being called *kiki* or *zizi*. It was a fashionable expression in the fifties and sixties, but it is no longer used today.

The Spanish *paquete* is like the French little packets, used in the past when speaking to children, just as the words thingies or willy are used in England.

The French word *ballots* means bundles. In this sense, it is a diminutive of the word *balles* which means (in some instances) bale, as in bale of straw. There is a culinary side to *ballot*, in the word *ballottine* which is a wrapped meat loaf or galantine (e.g. *ballottine* of duck). The word *ballottin* also means a bundle, although when spelled *ballotin* it can mean a box of chocolates. In English, the origin of the term ballot is this same bundle business. *Ballotin* is of course a nice metonymic metaphor for testicles, for boxes of candies are supposed to contain delicacies, which gives the game away.

Balluchon and *baluchon* are variant spellings of another word meaning bundle (often particularly a bundle of clothes).

The German word *Schachtel* (packet, as in cigarette packet) does not mean testicles. It refers to a woman who has seen better days – an 'old bag.'

Pairs: in French 'having a nice pair' would refer to testicles: i.e. the man is well-endowed. In Britain it is more likely to be applied to a woman's breasts.

> I think it was a flash of vanity, le Gros. The laurels of victory have gone to his head. Going to have to give him a peerage, send him straight up to the House of Lords, or maybe it's more pairs than peers; English peers and pairs of balls (it's often much of a muchness).
>
> San-Antonio, Béru et ses dames

Palle (Italian: n.f.): balls in Italian.

Panoply (French: *panoplie* n.f.): refers to the whole collection of male genital organs: penis and testicles. The panoply can belong to the perfect philanderer or the plumber-cum-pipefitter, according to the imaginative power of the author.

'Come-on San-A,' I rallied myself, 'unpack that panoply of the perfect philanderer and show what you can do in the minimum of time with the maximum of audacity.'

San-Antonio, Bravo, Docteur Béru

Parts / private parts (French: *parties* n.f.): a euphemistic contraction meaning testicles when used in the plural: 'give him a kick in the [privates]'. It can be had on its own or served with several side-dishes: genital parts, virile parts, sexual parts, natural parts, intimate parts, casual parts, carnal parts, immodest parts, shameful parts or parts of shame, as in the Bible (Deuteronomy 25 11–12), the Koran (XXXIII, 35) and classical Christian authors such as Tertullian, Seneca, Saint Augustine, or even dishonest parts, as in Father Gury's *Théologie morale* (Moral Theology). For his part, in his translation of the *Thousand And One Nights*, Joseph-Charles Mardrus uses the term honourable parts. They correspond to what Arabs call the blind part (*al-'aoura*) because shame effectively prevents you from seeing them. The expression refers above all to a woman's belly (Malek Chebel, *Encyclopédie de l'amour en Islam*). When it comes to San-Antonio, with his usual verve he doesn't hold back:

A useful man belongs to no party, but he is a man of parts. And big ones!

San-Antonio, Dégustez, gourmandes

I can't just say hello to her. I devour her, taste her. I anticipate, I prolong, I do it again, I interfere, I presume, I transcend, show captivating parts (*parties prenantes*), foretell the future, have the shakes, see double! My brain twitches, my balls (*glandes*) throb, just as they should.

San-Antonio, Bacchanale chez la mère Tatzi

Parts of shame (English): a literal translation of the Latin *pudenda*, and usually applied to the female parts.

Patrimony (French: *patrimoine* n.f.): the ensemble of genitalia, with a strong stress on value.

Pelotas (Spanish: *pelotas* n.f. French: *pelotes* n.f.; *pelotons* n.m.): in Spanish, *pelota* is not only the Basque national ball game (like Eton fives) but an expression meaning both testicle and stark naked. It is also used in the expression *tocar las pelotas* (touch the balls), to mean something that annoys someone; to touch someone's balls is to annoy them.

The French *pelote* means a ball of wool or thread. *Peloton* is a diminutive of that. Its use as a name of sexual parts appears to have started with Rabelais. There is not really any connection to the other meaning of *peloton*, which is a group or crowd of people, an army squad, or the main group of runners or riders in a race.

Pendant (English): an old word for a testicle. Not used much today.

Pieces (French: *pièces* n.f.): used principally in the phrase *exhiber ses pièces* (show off his pieces).

Pillock (English): pillock can mean a small pill, hence perhaps testicle. The word also means a fool or, applied to a youth, a nice young chap. It is a variant of pillicock and they have a common root in the northern dialect word pill, which means penis.

Pills (English): first recorded in 1608 and still occasionally used today. The form is clue enough to the transfer of meaning.

Pious odds and ends (French: *béatilles* n.f.): the literal translation of the French *béatilles* (the collective noun for smaller, more delicate offal, see above for a longer discussion, p. 60). In general its use is entirely gastronomic.

Pleasures / charms (French: *agrément* n.m.): this means of course natural pleasures and denotes the whole collection of male organs.

Plums (US English): testicles.

Plum scapular (French: *scapulaire à quetsches* n.m.): the scapular is the hood worn by pilgrims. You need an unbridled imagination and the creative language of a Frédéric Dard to create this hapax suggesting the scrotum garnished with testicles. The plums in questions are *quetsches*, popular in Central Europe. In German they are called *Zwetschgen'* which is surely the origin of the French word. Dard is talking of eunuchs in this passage.

> The fellows I'm talking about, even though they have been deprived of their plum scapulars, they don't look like little girls.
>
> *San-Antonio*, Bérurier au sérail

Poachers' pockets (French: *gibecières* n.f.): a metonymic metaphor for testicles.

Pompoms or pompons (French: *pompons* n.m.; *pomponnettes* n.f.): an out-of-date metaphor for testicles:

> I've seen the big willie of a verger-ette, rogue, rogue
> Who rang the Angelus, hands behind his back, rogue, rogue
> And of a nautical Breton
> Who had lost both his pompoms.
>
> Pierre Perret, song Le Zizi (The Willy, 1974)

The diminutive *pomponnettes* has also had its day. In cooking, *pomponnettes* are sorts of rissoles made in the form of miniscule purses (*Larousse gastronomique* 1938).

I felt nostalgic in the *pomponnettes.*

San-Antonio, Dégustez, gourmandes

Pouch (English): scrotum, as in purse.

Prides (English US?): Some aver that Shakespeare was referring to the sexual parts
in these lines from Sonnet CLI:

> But rising at thy name, doth point out thee
> As his triumphant prize. Proud of this pride,
> He is contented thy poor drudge to be,
> To stand in thy affairs, fall by thy side…

Princesses (French: *princesses* n.f.): a rather precious term for testicles, and one
that stresses their preciousness:

> The matador persisted. Without letting go of his adversary, Béru kicked
> him in his suit of lights (*traje de luces*). He might have the nicest little pair
> (*princesses*), Alfonso, but he still was still kicked in the plums (*quetsches*).
>
> *San-Antonio ,* Les Vacances de Bérurier ou La Croisière du 'Mer
> d'Alors'

Privates (English): the whole paraphernalia. From 'private parts'. Another form is
privy parts / privy member, privy stones or privies.

Pudenda : the Latin gerund which means 'that which should cause me shame' –
i.e. the sexual bits – which should be prudishly covered.

Purple bits (French: *purpurines* n.f.): a nickname for testicles, a metaphor that
recalls the colour of certain plums.

Purses (French: *bourses* n.m.; German: *Beutel* n.m.): The word comes from the
Latin *bursa.* Purse signifies the whole bag of flesh in the form of a purse (scrotum)
and the glands therein, rather than the glands themselves. It is a metonymic
metaphor referring to the form of the scrotum sack. In Latin, the word *coleus*
means a leather bag, and from this derive the French words *couille* and *couillon.*
You will appreciate its true value in Frédéric Dard's very juicy 'untied purses',
which mean purses in action.

> He produced a wallet which lit up Rita's goggles. Her paws were boiling
> hot. I came to the conclusion that she was more likely to stroke the skin
> of his wallet than fondle his purse.
>
> *San-Antonio,* Béru et ses dames

Good old Béru, just like his handsome boss he's led by his tail. Flesh
dominates, flesh barks, flesh consumes! Fuck! Béru. Fuck! old cock. Empty

those magnificent untied purses. Do the job one more time. Intercourse
makes life the richer: it helps you get on in life. Every time you shoot off
a barrel it adds to your balance in life; it justifies your existence.

San-Antonio, Bouge ton pied que je vois la mer

Praise be to the one who gives us the gift of pleasure in nibbling and
sucking our lips, of placing chest on chest, thigh on thigh and of placing
our purses on the threshold to the gate of clemency!*

Cheikh Jalaleddîne al-Suyûtî, Kitâb al îdhâh'fi 'ilmil nikâh

* 'The tone is intentionally irreverent and the text begins with a pure and simple
pastiche of the traditional Friday sermon in rhyming prose. That is extraordinary
from a pious fakir and respected exegist of the Koran,' says Abdelwahab Bouhdiba
in his essay *La Sexualtié en Islam* (1975).

In English, purse has been used to denote a scrotum since the mid-thirteenth
century, but it is obscure today. It is sometimes called the nether purse or the
bollock purse.

I hauve wedded fyuve. Of whiche I haue pyked out the beste, Both of
here nether purse and of here cheste.

Chaucer, Wife of Bath's Tale

The German *Beutel* means a purse, and its most famous testicular application
is the *Bocksbeutel* or 'goat's scrotum': the suggestively shaped bottle used for wine
in Franconia and two communes in neighbouring Baden.

Quails (French: *cailles* n.f.): Curnonsky says somewhere:

What a pretty endearment! When a lover, addressing his belle, says my
little quail, maybe it is because he would like to eat her...

I should like to parody this:

What a pretty endearment! When a lover speaks of the appetizing bulges
of her beau as 'my little quails', maybe she would like to eat them...

There are those who would be frightened by this. On the other hand there are
men for whom the expression 'eat me' forms part of their erotic vocabulary, but I
grant you, this is not quite 'eat them'. Even if...

Cailles d'amour (love quails) is a darling little epithet for testicles, suggesting
that they (the quails) are tucked up in their nest.

Rags / tatters / cloth (French: *agobilles* n.f.; *brimborions* n.m.; *dandrilles* n.f.; *floches*
n.f.; *friponnes* n.f.; *guenilles* n.f.; *ripons* n.m.; *roupettes* n.f.): *agobilles* is an example
of French slang. In this instance it hails from Metz in Lorraine, where the patois
is influence by proximity to Germany. In origin it means worthless things (see
Dictionnaire de l'argot français et de ses origines, Larousse).

Brimborions (meaning bagatelle, piece of fluff) is another term for testicles suggesting worthlessness; yet it may be used intentionally to have quite the opposite implication and to signify their value.

Dandrilles is an name for testicles, evoking a little bit of soft fabric-like rags and tatters. Similarly *guenilles* means a worthless bit of cloth.

> He will certainly pack him off
> Dragging his tatters (*dandrilles*), by God.
> **Étienne Jodelle (1532–1573, French playwright)**

Floches (flock) is an adjective that San-Antonio made into a noun. In normal life it refers mainly to fabrics (flock-silk – cf. flock wallpapers) but doubtless because the wrinkled skin of testicles is reminiscent of these fabrics, it is pressed into creative service:

> What do you want me to do with the skin of my *floches*, make an umbrella out of it?
> **San-Antonio, Fais-moi des choses**

Friponnes is a well-brought-up term for testicles, slightly debonair. The word comes from the Old French *frepe* which itself comes from the Low Latin *faluppa* which means something without value.

Ripons are the wood shavings left on the floor by the cabinetmaker. It is then another worthless thing like a rag. *Ripons* sounds suspiciously like *friponnes*.

Roupettes is an epithet conferred on testicles towards the end of the eighteenth century (1795). It could be a contraction of *roubignole* (q.v.) or *roupignole* crowned with an argotic suffix. Others, however, believe the word to be Gothic in origin (the language of western Germany, spoken by the Visigoths): *raupa*, which signifies 'rags and things of little value'. [In Portuguese – and what is now Portugal was also colonized by the Visigoths – *roupa* (n.f.) also means clothes. *Translator*.] The skin of testicles being naturally wrinkly, if not gathered, you can easily understand the metaphoric allusion that compares them to little torn up rags.

> Live without his rags (*roupettes*), he would never have entertained the idea.
> **Roger Nimier (French novelist, 1925–1962)**

> Given my age, I have not yet worn my rags in female company.
> **San-Antonio, Si Queue d'Ane m'était conté ou La Vie Sexuelle de Bérurier**

Rantallion (English): an obscure word for a man whose scrotum is longer than his penis.

Revellers (French: *bambochardes* n.f.): a nickname for testicles, leaving one to suppose that their owner appreciates the joys of life in general, and sex in particular.

Rig (English): originally an improperly castrated animal (also riggald), now a reference to the whole collection.

Risers (French: *bandilles* n.f.): as a term for testicles *bandilles* derives from the verb *bander* which means to have an erection.

Rocks (English US): as in 'to get your rocks off.'

Rockingham china (English): a dated expression alluding to someone with well-filled trousers.

Rolls (French: *rouleaux* n.m.): a metaphor for testicles in use from the nineteenth century at least and perhaps merely transferring the meaning of a roll or something which is rolled. The word is nowadays used above all in the expression *le peau de mes rouleaux* (the skin of my balls), which means 'sweet FA', or 'bugger all'.

> One morning, Prince Mony Vibescu, stark naked and as handsome as the Apollo Belvedere, performed 69 with Cornaboeux. Both of them heartily sucked at their respective sticks of barley sugar and voluptuously fondled one another's rolls (*rouleaux*) which had no relation to those found in a phonograph.
>
> *Guillaume Apollinaire*, Les Onze Mille Verges

Rollocks (English): rhymes with bollocks and suggests a 'rollocking good time.' Tommy Rollocks is rhyming slang.

Roubignoli (Provençal: n.m.; French: *roubignoles* n.f.): the French word *roubignoles* emerged as a nickname for testicles in the second half of the nineteenth century (1862). It is taken straight from the Provençal *roubignoli* (testicles) which obtained that meaning by its reference to the Provençal sobriquet for a ram (*robin*), an animal well known for its attributes. These, of course, are eaten under the genteel disguise of *animelles*. It should be noted that *robin* also means testicles in the dialect of the province of Maine (this time the allusion is to the horned head the ram), and it is an infantile metaphor for the penis, although in this case it refers to its urinary role (from *robinet*, i.e. tap). By two different processes therefore, *robin* has spawned two complementary terms to denote both the penis and its acolytes. Finally, we should note that the game of *robignolle*, still called the game of *cocange* (which means nutshell – *coquille de noix* – the cups and balls game or shell game played by street con-artists) used to be played at fairs with the said nuts (another nickname for testicles) and that it is the ancestor of *le bonnetau* (three card trick). You will also find the spellings *roubignolles* and *robognoles*.

> And above all, at the moment when you arrest him, don't even think of leaving me to twiddle my *roubignoles* as you did last week when I missed

my recovery and found myself with all four paws in the air beneath your two hundred pounds as some form of poultice.

San-Antonio, Fais-moi des choses

Roubinches derives from *roubignoles*:

> You've got a red-hot poker in your trousers, an itchy dick, and rough waves in your *roubinches*!

San-Antonio, Princesse patte-en-l'air

Ribouis probabably derives via *verlan* (see above, p. 197) from *roubignoles*:

> You'll find Pinuche down in the dumps with his faithful Salami laying his muzzle on his *ribouis*.

San-Antonio, La Queue en trompette

Roustons (French: *roustons* n.m.; *roustagas* n.m.; *roustamponnes* n.f.; *roustimballes* n.f.): a French term for testicles that first appeared in 1836. It derives from the southern French Languedoc *roustoun* (also meaning testicles) which comes in turn from the Low Latin *rustum*. It had its hour of glory, notably in bawdy songs and detective novels.

> The goldsmiths, unhappy with that
> Climbed onto the rafters to bugger the cat.
> Cat, little cat, you're scratching me,
> You little rascal, you're scratching my bollocks (*roustons*).

Song, 'Les Trois Orfèvres' (The Three Goldsmiths).

> But the whore she was hot
> And put pitch on her cunt.
> *And purr she did ballurette*
> *And purr she did balluron*
> But the whore she was hot
> And put pitch on her cunt.
> But the whore she was hot
> And put pitch on her cunt.
> And in those pillared halls
> She was welded to his balls (*roustons*).
> *And purr she did ....*
> And in those pillared halls
> She was welded to his balls.
> Want them back, my handsome
> Must pay first the ransom.
> *And purr she did ....*
> Want them back, my handsome
> Must first pay the ransom.
> Want them back, my handsome

Must first pay the ransom.
Hundred crowns for your cock,
Same again for each bollock.
And purr she did ....
Hundred crowns for your cock,
Same again for each bollock.
And if you won't pay the bill,
We'll cut them off, we will.
And purr she did ....
And if you won't pay the bill
We'll cut them off, we will.
And if you won't pay the bill,
We'll cut them off, we will.
They'll serve as a sign, they will
O'er the door to a brothel
And purr she did ....
They'll serve as a sign, they will
O'er the door to a brothel
They'll serve as a sign, they will
O'er the door to a brothel
And everyone will grunt
They're the balls of a cunt.
And purr she did ballurette
And purr she did balluron.
                    Song, 'Le Gendarme de Redon' (The Policeman of Redon).

Let's go to Messina, fish for sardines;
Let's go to Lorient to fish for the herring.
The big prick said to the cunt, you be the boat,
I will be the mast, upward sticking.
My right bollock (*rouston*) will be the ship's captain.
Let's go to Messina, ...
My right bollock will be the ship's captain.
Let's go to Messina, ...
My right bollock will be the ship's captain.
My left bollock will be midshipman.
The hairs on my arse the mast will retain.
Let's go to Messina, ...
The hairs on my arse the mast will retain.
And platoons of lice will drive me insane.
Let's go to Messina, ...
And platoons of lice will drive me insane.
And the skin of my balls have the winds kept in
Let's go to Messina, ...

And the skin of my balls have the winds kept in
And the hole of my arse will give wind once again.
Let's go to Messina, fish for sardines;
Let's go to Lorient to fish for the herring.
Let's go to Lorient.

Folk song

Your hand gently tickles his bollocks (*roustons*)
While he balls you and fondles your titties.

Louis Protat (French writer of pornography, 1819–1881)

Even when you're not on heat
Your cock is still the stuff of sighs
It hangs, golden white between your thighs,
On your bollocks (*roustons*), a swarthy treat.

Paul Verlaine (French poet, 1844–1896)

Bite them gently, like a mare nibbles her foal. Certainly not too hungrily!
Once you nearly killed me, going at it as if it were a kidney with Madeira
sauce.

San-Antonio, Fais-moi des choses

There was a friend called Léonce Durand in my army days who got his
kicks in an idiosyncratic way, the lamb. He tied a long velvet ribbon
around his willy, tied it really tight, covering the whole thing from his
bollocks (*roustons*) to the glans. Then he tapped the stem with a knitting
needle: tap, tap, tap, just like that from the bottom to the top, until it all
came spurting out.

San-Antonio, Si Queue-d'Ane m'était conté ou La Vie sexuelle de Bérurier

Roustagas, roustamponnes and *roustimballes* all derive from *roustons*, the latter
seems to have come under the influence of *balles* and *balloches*.

Rummagers (French: *triquebilles* n.f.): in the plural, the French word *triquebilles*
means testicles, whereas in the singular it means the same as *trique*, i.e. penis.
It is formed from the root *trik* which means to stir or rummage. [I have taken
this very useful word, rummager, from the technology of whisky distilling. The
rummager is a sort of paddle that turns at the bottom of the still to stop the mash
from catching. *Translator.*] In my view, therefore, it is not a combination of penis
(*trique*) and balls (*billes*) which is the derivation one might presume.

Triquedondaines is also formed from *trik* meaning stir, together with *donder*,
which means much the same – stir, rummage – the word is therefore redundant.

Safety valves (French: *soupapes* n.f.): a metonymic metaphor:

He's waiting for his lover to pork her for the first time, once work's over, while his wife waits for him in the country. He needs a massive hard-on before he strikes up his band, and I presume his safety valves are swollen beyond measure....

San-Antonio, Bacchanale chez la mère Tatzi

Saints: *St Frusquin* can be a nickname for the penis and the expression *tout le saint-frusquin* (or Frusqui) may mean the entire paraphernalia, judge and jury. [In fact, this is relatively uncommon, and it should be stressed the expression has nothing to do with a real-life saint. More generally, it derives from the argot word for clothes, which was *frusques*. This is first recorded in 1628 (Robert). Nowadays, *saint-frusquin* means, 'everything that I stand up in' or all that I own. It is occasionally recorded as indicating the female sex organs.] There is a semantic slippage from denoting the covering to the covered (just as *sarouel* below).

La Sainte-Paire (The Holy Pair) is a pun on *Saint-Père* (Holy Father), and is one of the dialectical masterpieces of Frédéric Dard:

> You remain troubled by the religion of your birth, your hereditary faith. There is every reason to refuse to go along with it, you can deny the Holy Father – by calling him His Holy Bollocks (*Sa Sainte Paire*) – and his fancy palanquin and all that jazz – pomp, procession and benediction *rubis et orbite** (as Béru says) – but you are deeply marked.

San-Antonio, A prendre ou à lécher

*Allusion to the annual blessing *urbis et orbis* (the city and the world). Béru's version plays on testicles on the *rubis* (*ribouis*, see *roubignoli,* above) and penis in the *orbite* (*bite*). *Translator.*

The Holy Trinity (*la Sainte Trinité*) is an obvious reference to the sexual paraphernalia.

Samendrüse (German): the word means seed gland, ergo testicles.

Sandra Bullocks: rhyming slang. Other examples include Niagara Falls, orchestra stalls, Royal Albert Halls, Berlin Walls and coffee stalls.

Sarouel (Arabic): this is the Arabic for trousers and is used, by extension and metonymy, to refer to the sexual parts of the body that are found therein.

Scrote (English): a worthless person, from scrotum.

Scrotum (English and French): the cutaneous wrapping around the testicles but, just like 'purses', the word describes both the container and the contents. The word scrotum is sometimes used to denote testicles in the widest sense.

> We are taking part in a cute little session of 'go-on-we-are-going-to-reach-the-point' with the pink cheeks of confusion in evidence. In her own way,

Rita appears relatively honest. She stands to earn 20,000 francs from the generous donor, by some clever verbal twists and turns, some sensual exclamations, some manipulation of the scrotum, fingers up the arse, tweaking of the prick… proper craftsmanship, in other words.

San-Antonio, Béru et ses dames

Seminal lobes (French: *lobes séminaux* n.m.): in anatomy, lobes are the round, protruding bits of any sort of organ (ears, lungs, liver, foie gras). Seminal lobes are more specifically the testicles.

Servants (French: *servants* n.m.; *servantes* n.f.; *valets* n.m.): *servants* in French refers to the military: they are the soldiers employed in the service of an army and therefore responsible for provision or munitions (*servant de canon*, *servant d'artillerie*) with the the bawdy implications you can easily guess at.

Servantes (feminine) has another sense in that here we are dealing with the maid-servants of the seigneur, or the penis.

Valets emphasizes the serving role of the testicles to the penis. It is used in the expression *les deux valets*. It is similar to deputies or companions (qq.v.).

Sex (French: *sexe* n.m.): an evasive term to designate the genital regions of men and women, and by extension men (*le sexe fort*) and women (*le sexe faible* or *le beau sexe*) themselves. Use of the word in this general sense, without qualification, is no longer current English. It was widespread, however, in the eighteenth century, usually referring to the female sex: 'The sex of Venice are undoubtedly of a distinguished beauty' (Arthur Young).

Soualah (Arabic): means 'things' and is used for men as well as for animals, notably lambs.

Sperm banks/pots (French: *réservoirs à sperme* n.m.; *vases spermatiques* n.f.): a metonym for testicles. A container. See containers, above.

Sports tricycles: a neologism coined with his habitual wit by Detective San-Antonio to describe the panoply of male equipment:

Me? What do you want me to do? I take her in my arms, I give her a hug, I bring up her mouth and tickle her tonsils with the tip of my tongue, and my wanger goes up like Punch's truncheon. I put my hand up her skirt and between her legs to verify that she feels the same about me and greedily rip off her pants (easier said than done) unchain my sports tricycle and proceed to the introit after putting her in starting position. This I perform with increasing movements, equivalent in force to the displacement of the *Bratwurst*.

San-Antonio, Princesse patte-en-l'air

Stones (English): an old-fashioned term, used in the King James Bible, which goes back to Middle English. Variants include 'privy stones', 'precious stones' and 'stones of gendure.'

Stuffers (French: farceuses n.f.): a facetious epithet.

Sweets (French: *berlots* n.m.; *berlingots* n.m.; *bonbons* n.m.; *pruneaux* n.m.): in the singular, a *berlingot* [*berlingots* come from Carpentras or Nantes, they are hard cylinders of sugar flavoured with fruit essences] can mean a penis, a woman's vagina, a clitoris or her virginity, according to context. In the plural form, the word means testicles, thus a complement to the extended family of sweets to suck or lick. *Berlots,* for testicles, is probably a contraction of *berlingots*.

Bonbons (sweets) is another nickname. It is used in the expression *casser les bonbons,* like the American 'break my balls'.

'Chupa Chups' is a affectionate little epithet conferred by the French on testicles. It's a reference to the famous globular Spanish lollipops and the name is a pleonasm: *chupa* means suck in Spanish, and 'Chupa Chups' means something like 'sucker to suck', or 'suck-suck'; they therefore suggest strongly that they have a vocation...to be sucked. It should be noted that there are now Chupa Chups XXL. As regards Mega-Chupa (800 g), they are the stuff of dreams... Stop Press: Chupa Chups Fruit Chew have just been launched! They are brimming with fruit-flavoured sap...

Coucougnettes is a familiar term for testicles which has been popular for a couple of decades. The French television presenter Christophe Dechavanne largely contributed to its popularity in the 1980s. Just to fill you in: the artisan sweet and jam-maker Francis Miot of Pau created 'les coucougnettes du Vert galant' which were elected 'Best French Sweet' at the 45th International Salon of Sweets in 1999. *Coucougnettes* are hand-rolled with crushed almonds and cane sugar mixed with grilled almonds caramelized with a little ginger brandy and a dash of armagnac. The heart of the *coucougnette* is a whole sweet almond, grilled and covered with dark chocolate.

Dragées or sugared almonds is a gourmand epithet that comes in the subset of sucking sweets. And just like *pruneaux* or *dragées, pralines* (chocolates) can mean, in French slang, revolver bullets (after they have been fired) as well as (more affectionately) testicles. As with the other names of sweets, there is an implicit invitation to suck them.

See also the entries under fruit (plums) and under marshmallows.

> I nonchalantly slip my finger into my pocket and, with an imperious index, I make a hole in the bottom like a schoolboy who decides to play pocket billiards during a natural science lesson, and I slip the little thing in question (I'll tell you later what it was if you promise not to squash my prunes [*pruneaux*] for a while) into my arse.
>
> *San-Antonio,* Béru-Béru

I ended up by felling him with a massive truncheon blow in the prunes [*pruneaux*].

San-Antonio, Un éléphant, ça trompe, Paris 1975

Swingers (French: *ballottes* n. f.; *brandilloires* n.f.; *pendillantes* n.f.; *pendilloires* n.f.; *pendiloches* n.f.; *pendoires* n.f.): all these terms seem applied to balls to evoke their swinging. It is used above all in the expression *patiner les ballottes* (to polish or to fumble with the balls). *Ballottes* is an old argot word for balls.

Brandilloires are testicles, the word coming from the verb *brandiller* meaning to move gently, shake or frig (Pierre Guiraud, *Dictionnaire érotique*). It is close to the verb *bandouiller* which is a synonym for wank or masturbate.

Pendillantes (from the verb *pendiller*, to flap), *pendilloires* (ditto, and may also be a name that emphasizes their apple- or pear-shape and the fact they hang like a ripe fruit; there is of course the old breed of apple, the *Court pendu plat*), *pendiloches* (deriving from the verb *pendre*, to hang, with the argotizing suffix *-oche*) and *pendoires* are hangers or swingers (a *pendoir* is a butcher's hook).

He asked her if her husband had hangers (*pendillantes*) on the bottom of his belly.

Those things that flap (*pendilloires)* are not apples, rather they take the shape of plums.

And these are man's natural swingers (*pendiloches*).

Béroalde de Verville (French novelist and poet, 1566–1626)

Tackle (English): variants include 'wedding tackle'. Partridge (*Dictionary of Historical Slang*) dates its use thus to the late eighteenth century.

Tallywags (English): rhymes with scallywags, and seems clearly a term of endearment. Partridge (op. cit.) records its use in the singular as meaning penis, surviving in north-western dialect. The word in the plural refers specifically to the testicles and its use is recorded from the seventeenth century.

Teabags (French: *petits sachets de thé* n.m.): this is an expression of Coco, my paternal aunt. She uses it for cats' testicles, because they look like teabags once they have given up their infusion to the boiling water. This is a find I shall dedicate to my friend Gilles Brochard, one of France's greatest tea specialists.

Testicles (French: *testicules* n.f.; *testons* n.m.): do not forget that the word is not merely anatomical but has the full force of the Academy behind it (see Mythology, above).

Millard obeyed. His organ was not very stiff, but he slipped it into me with the help of his hands. Then I reached out my hands and stroked his testicles, keeping two fingers at the base of his organ which I pressed when he moved. This instantly excited him, and his penis hardened and he began to make love to me. Then he stopped!

Anaïs Nin, Venus erotica *(Delta of Venus, 1977)*

A diamond as big as a sheep's testicle sparkled in her ear.

San-Antonio, Dégustez, gourmandes

Scamp that he is, the hot bunny must have run off into the cathouse where he had a whale of a time emptying his testicles as if there were no tomorrow.

San-Antonio, A prendre ou à lécher

Antonio the Magnificent found himself halfway across a hall decorated in the worst, most vulgar taste, with his big black Samsonite in his hand. He looked evasive, his heart was tight as a result of some confused anguish, but he was handsome for all that, a mature beauty, with his eyes, nose, mouth, his two ears, and his testicles as hard as avocado stones.

San-Antonio, Fais-moi des choses

She finally paid particular attention to my sex, tapping the testicles, penis and the glans, which she had popped out and popped back with flower-scented water before spreading a cloud of talcum powder over it with a make-up brush, which finally managed to stifle its excitement.

Alina Reyes, Derrière la porte

Testons is made up of a combination of *testicules* and *roustons* (q.v.).

Thieves (French: *larrons* n.m.): here is another binary metaphor, referring this time to the two thieves in the Bible who were crucified alongside Christ: the good on his right side (the side of the elect, because he has repented) and the bad on his left. It would be difficult to maintain that the right ball is more respectable than the left. On the other hand it is clear that they are 'as thick as thieves'. As for the third thief, you can guess who that was like the nose in the middle of your face.

Them (French: *les* pronoun): a grand euphemism to denote testicles, as it uses a totally elliptic way of suggesting them in diverse locutions such as 'I'm freezing them off', 'you're breaking them', etc. It is obvious that balls are meant. The French singer and poet Georges Brassens' song *Les Casseuses* (Vandals) puts 'them' in the limelight slightly apologetically. It is in this respect a masterpiece of humour. Here is the refrain:

> When you forget to handle them
> It's tantamount to breaking them
> My loves, forget them if you can
> Let them repose
> When you don't give them some kind strokes

It's like you're bashing the poor blokes
My loves, forget them if you can
Let them repose, oh man
Let them repose.

Georges Brassens, Les Casseuses, 1976

You're breaking them – the gentleman's Oscar, and you'd be breaking mine too if I had any.

San-Antonio, Les Vacances de Bérurier ou La Croisière du 'Mer d'alors'

Things, thingies, thingumbobs, thingumabobs, thingamies, thingamijigs, thingumajiggers (French: *choses* n.f.): a classic euphemism denoting testicles (see Mythology, above).

Judging at last that their quarry
Had endured their deal of dolour,
These furies, for their last flurry
Returned to make them holler
These furies, for all the horror it brings
It is so lowly to admit
Would even have chopped off their things
Happily, they didn't do it!
Would even have chopped off their things
Happily, they didn't do it!

Georges Brassens, Hécatombe, 1952

So I pushed the door and I went in.
And I saw lovely, barbaric, baroque and giddy-making things. But first of all Bérurier's things, rough and spread out, and as dark as truffles prior to peeling.

San-Antonio, A Prendre ou à lécher

My friend Alain Dutournier [chef-proprietor of the Carré des Feuillants, Paris] calls them '*les choses de la vie*' (the things of life) which is both pretty and appropriate.

Three-piece suite (French: *service trois-pièces*): the testicles and penis.

Tom Jones: the whole set, an allusion to the Welsh singer in his youth, with his long nose, fat cheeks and frizzy hair.

Trinkets / baubles / ornaments / curios (French: *bibelot* n.m.; *breloques* n.f.; *pendeloques* n.f.; *pampilles* n.f.; *pastrailles* n.f.): *bibelots* (baubles) are the whole collection, penis and testicles, used especially in the expression to 'polish the baubles', *astiquer les bibelots*.

Breloques (trinkets or baubles) is one of those French terms which stresses the little real or supposed value of testicles (see Mythology, above) and the fact that they hang. *Breloques* are paste jewellery or the baubles on a chandelier. The term is used in the expression *manier les breloques* (finger the trinkets), or stroke the testicles.

> 'I did everything I could,' he told me. 'Luckily I had your pin. It wasn't big, but I stuck it in his baubles (*breloques*). I told myself that as they were going to cut them off, it was hardly worth the trouble, you understand?'
>
> San-Antonio, Bérurier au serail

> As only I could see: the bagpipers were naked under their kilts.
> Oh! What a wonderful parade of baubles (*breloques*), bagpipes, marvellous instruments, appeared before my eyes.
>
> Alina Reyes, Derrière la porte

Pendeloques is another metaphor for testicles. The word means precious stones cut in the form of pears, generally used as earrings. They are sometimes supercharged with fantastic adjectives, as in the case of Frédéric Dard, who uses 'Japanese bangles' in a reference to the famous prints.

> They say that a pretty little woman has come to see you, you lucky sod! For crying out loud. So don't bust our bangles (*pendeloques*) with your 'word of honour!' It's more the word of a copper's nark, isn't it?
>
> San-Antonio, Béru et ses dames

> Luck is like something out of Dante, if by any chance you try to make out the opposite, you cheeky little horrors! Look, I'm going to dash to save Pinaud, and the daughter of the cop who tortured him lives in Angers. I will take the little moll home and make her admire my Japanese bangles (*pendeloques japonaises*) and what's more she sleeps forty-two metres twenty-six centimetres from the night club I'm interested in.
>
> San-Antonio, Bravo docteur Béru

Pampilles are the baubles that hang on curtains or form pendants in jewellery; while *pastrailles* also evokes the pendentive nature of the testes as well as their quality of bauble to the main sexual organ.

Troïka (Russian: *troika*): the Russian means a set of three. In French it means the whole collection of male assets.

Trousers (Arabic: *sarhouel*): an Arab epithet for testicles.

Truffles (French: *truffes* n.f.): a metaphoric usage in French, occasionally used for testicles because of the rough skin that evokes wrinked gonads.

Still in a subterranean vein, tubers (*tubercules* n.f.) is another metaphor that surfaces from time to time.

Twiddle-diddles (English): epithet for testicles. Mark Steven Morton (*The Lover's Tongue: A Merry Romp Through the Language of Love and Sex*, Toronto 2004) suggests the origin might be bored fingers and pocket billiards.

Two (French: *mes deux*): the use of this expression in Frech conversation is to express doubt, in the vein of 'my eye / foot / arse etc.': '*professeur de mes deux!*' (Professor! My arse!), '*commissaire de mes deux!*' (Detective! My eye!)

Undercarriage (French: *aine* n.f.; *train d'atterrissage* n.m.): the French word *aine* denotes that part of the body between the top of the thigh and the lower abdomen, where the sexual organs are tucked away. It is not used to designate balls in the proper sense, but comes from the Latin *inguen, inguenis*, which Virgil uses to mean the same as *aine*, and Suetonius employs for the lower abdomen; meanwhile Horace and Ovid use it for the sexual parts and Lucilius deploys it when discussing a tumour of the lower abdomen. For Pliny it is the the place where a branch is attached to a tree trunk (Félix Gaffiot, *Dictionnaire illustré latin-français*, 1934).

The metaphor *train d'atterrissage* alludes to the undercarriage that emerges from the belly of a plane when it comes in to land, which might make one think of an enormous pair of testicles. The comparison is all the more impressive when it is made with a jumbo jet. So, one says of a well-endowed man that he is a 'heavy-lifter with a fine undercarriage.' The expression, however, is no longer in vogue.

Vas (Latin): in classical Latin, the word *vas* (deriving from *vasum,* a vase) meant both the penis and the testicles, making reference to the content and the container.

Vegetables (French: *choux de bruxelles* n.m.; *patates* n.f.): Brussels sprouts are a metaphor for testicles. *Patates* (slang in itself, for potatoes) is used above all in the expression *avoir des patates au fond du filet* (to have some spuds at the bottom of the bag) meaning: hanging and empty after the match! (quoted by Pierre Perret in *Le Nouveau Petit Perret illustré*, 1984).

Little onions (*petits onions*) is a familiar but now rare term for testicles.

Vergognas (Spanish n.f.): the male sexual organs in Spanish. It must be related to the old French word *vergognes* or *vergoignes* which meant the earthy bits. The word *dévergonder* (to be debauched) comes from the same root.

Vestibules (French: *vestibules* n.f.): yet another of Frédéric Dard's unbridled neologisms.

> He inspected the giants, the family of stone effigies that surrounded us. 'Perhaps in there,' he said, stroking the backside of a stout matron. Perhaps in here', he continued, tapping the *vestibules* of a youth with a square jaw and a muscular midriff.
>
> *San-Antonio,* Béru et ses dames

To help him fall, he gets a kick in the arse to knock the stuffing out of
him and make him green about the gills. Then a second in the vestibules.
He let out a terrifying scream.

San-Antonio, Tu vas trinquer San-Antonio *(You're Going to Cop it San-
Antonio, 1980)*

Vilia membra (Latin): this Latin expression refers to both men and women.
Literally, it means vile or shameful parts or bits. The male are *virilia* and the
female, *muliebria.*

Vitals (English): the trinity of sexual parts, although more generally it refers to
the vital organs (heart, liver and lungs, etc.) necessary to sustain life (*OED*).

Wanderers (French: *baladeuses* n.f.; *flâneuses* n.f.; *vagabondes* n.f.; *trébillons* n.f.):
four old-fashioned words used by the French to denote testicles, it is easy to see
why. *Baladeuse* means a wanderer or one who strolls about, although nowadays it
might refer to a trailer for a car or a handcart. *Flâneuses* is another term referring
to the testicular tendency to roam. In more normal life is describes an idler, a
dawdler. *Vagabondes* has a similar sense, stressing the libertine character of their
owner. *Trébillons* is probably formed from the verb *biller* which means 'going
here and there, wandering':

> That means removing his wanderers from between his legs.
>
> *Béroalde de Verville (French novelist and poet, 1566–1626)*

Weapons of war (Latin: *arma virilia* n.f.): in Latin, literally 'male arms', i.e. the
genital organs.

Wheels (French: *borgne à roulettes* n.m.): a French expression which literally
means 'the one-eyed man with little wheels'. The one-eyed man, of course, is the
penis and the little wheels are the testes.

> She's a skilled technician. When it comes to lubricants, she knows her
> stuff. She goes to work on Béru first, with studied slowness, from the
> bonnet to his little wheels.
>
> *San-Antonio,* Princess patte-en-l'air

Whirligigs (English): Similar to 'thingumies' but with more of a dance rhythm.

Witnesses (French: *témoins* n.m.; *témoins à décharge* n.m.; English: testimonials):
a nickname for testicles that reverts to the original derivation of the Latin from
the word *testis*, i.e. witness (see Mythology, above). *Témoins à décharge*, witnesses
to discharge, is self-evident.

Yecous (French slang, *verlan: yecous* n.m.): *verlan* [see the note under the entry 'Nuts'] consists in saying half the word back to front. This is therefore *couilles* or balls.

Yeuks (French slang, *verlan: yeuks* n.m.): another version of *couilles* or balls in *verlan*. Used in *j'm'en bats les yeuks* (I don't give a fig).

Yoks (French slang, *verlan: yoks* n.m.): yet another version of *couilles* or balls in *verlan*.

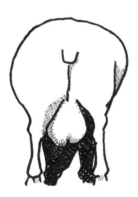